The Ethics of Writing

Culture and Education Series

Series Editors: Henry A. Giroux, Pennsylvania State University
Joe L. Kincheloe, Pennsylvania State University

The Ethics of Writing

Derrida, Deconstruction, and Pedagogy

Peter Pericles Trifonas

ROWMAN & LITTLEFIELD PUBLISHERS, INC.
Lanham • Boulder • New York • Oxford

ROWMAN & LITTLEFIELD PUBLISHERS, INC.

Published in the United States of America
by Rowman & Littlefield Publishers, Inc.
4720 Boston Way, Lanham, Maryland 20706
http://www.rowmanlittlefield.com

12 Hid's Copse Road
Cumnor Hill, Oxford OX2 9JJ, England

British Library Cataloguing in Publication Information Available

Library of Congress Cataloging-in-Publication Data
Trifonas, Peter Pericles, 1960-
 The ethics of writing : Derrida, deconstruction, and pedagogy / Peter Pericles
 Trifonas.
  p. cm. – (Culture and education series)
 Includes bibliographical references and index.
 ISBN 0-8476-9557-3 (alk. paper) – ISBN 0-8476-9558-1 (pbk. : alk. paper)
  1. Education—Philosophy. 2. Derrida, Jacques. 3. Postmodernism and
education. 4. Critical pedagogy. 5. Deconstruction. I. Title. II. Series.

LB14.7.T75 2000
370'.1—dc21

                                                    99-045589

Printed in the United States of America

∞™ The paper used in this publication meets the minimum requirements of American
National Standard for Information Sciences—Permanence of Paper for Printed Library
Materials, ANSI Z39.48–1992.

These words that will follow are dedicated with eternal love and boundless appreciation to *Elefteria*, whose selfless giving of the gifts of time and patience have made possible the chance for the fulfillment of what from its beginnings had always seemed an endless task of reading and writing. Thank you. I will forever be grateful.

Contents

Chapter Five

Chapter Six

Acknowledgments

I would like to acknowledge, first and foremost, my appreciation to John Willinsky for the endless reserves of patience and energy expended on reading versions of this text over the course of its inception and production. As well, I would like to thank Carl Leggo and Richard Cavell for the valuable comments each of them has offered along the way. There are others who also have to be thanked for their support: Bill Pinar, Nicholas Burbules, Denise Egéa-Kuehne, Peter McLaren, Michael Peters, Blane Déspres, Roger Simon, Dean Birkencamp, Rob Morgan, and Shirley Steinberg.

I am grateful to Professor Jacques Derrida for extending an open invitation to follow up with him (over a few continents) some of the traces of his work relating to "the educational problematic" of deconstruction that have found their way into this text.

Lastly, I extend my gratitude to Henry Giroux for reading my manuscript in the spirit it was intended—as an ethical writing about the right of education from a deconstructive point of view—and for making it possible to work with Jill Rothenberg, my editor and friend.

Chapter 2, "The Ends of Pedagogy: From the Dialectic of Memory to the Deconstruction of the Institution," has been published, albeit in a somewhat shortened version, in *Educational Theory* 46, no. 3 (Summer 1996): 303-333. The "Polemical Introduction," all but a paragraph or so, appears as part of the same article.

Polemical Introduction

A Pedagogical Prelude to Deconstruction
Jacques Derrida, Ethics, and the Scene of Teaching

> This, then, is not after all an undertaking of war or a discourse of belligerence. I should like it to be also like a headlong flight straight towards the end, a joyous self-contradiction, a disarmed desire, that is to say something very old and very cunning, but which also has just been born and which delights in being without defence.
>
> —Jacques Derrida, "The Time of a Thesis: Punctuations"[1]

The intra- and transnational sites of contestation that have emerged to engage the epistemological forcefulness of the *post*modern evolution of French thought spanning the ideology-based vicissitudes of continental philosophy over the past twenty-five years encompass the interdisciplinary junctures of a hermeneutic terrain permeated, more often than not, by a *critical radicality* defined in direct relation to deconstruction.[2] A philosophical endeavoring of a decisively non-dialectical fervor.[3] What the designation of this era as "poststructuralism" clearly attests to is the grand scale of its impact both *within* and *without* "the Academy": this deep breadth of its manifestations having served to underscore an unprecedented capacity to alter the reproducible stability of knowledge configurations. *Quand même,* because of this or perhaps, to a notable degree, in spite of it, the rapid rise of deconstruction to an enviable position of prominence at the "higher" echelons of the pedagogical institution has not been without controversy. Its unique provocations to the long-standing codes of the *Universitas* as a theoretical phenomenon transgressive of normative contingencies of value has fascinated, has engaged, and, in some cases, has even enraged intellectuals—either of the "left" or of the "right"[4]—reacting to the mutability of its many forms incurred among the "human sciences," including the disciplinary areas of educational studies.[5] In this right, the last stages of a transitional passage from the endings of a "modern age" pedagogy well versed in the cogitative techniques of *dialektike* expanded upon from early Greek thinking[6] to the beginnings of an "other age"—an age of the Other—are exemplified by the unique challenges the teachings of Jacques Derrida pose to the metaphysical pediments of Western philosophy and science. As the legacy of a pedagogical tradition preserved through the mode of argumentation constructing the logicality of Plato's dialogues and the contours of the path of *a thinking beyond,* the dialectic fervently guards the spirit of an ancient body of knowledge once believed to be wholly "educative," in every sense of the word, but most certainly experiencing successive phases of decline well into the latter half of the twentieth century.[7] Inevitably, it is the idealism of the *absolute reason* of the dialectic, as a teaching-learning strategy that carries the critical burden of an incalculable risk to the integrity of its truth, when the honor of its philosophical memory is violated by unforeseen transgressions into the uncharted territories of fundamental epistemic and pedagogical change.

The pedagogical path of deconstruction Derrida has initiated and has chosen to pursue both in France and abroad cannot, however, be arbitrarily reduced to the singular purpose of *simply* enabling a revolutionary defiance to the authority of the teachings of the dialectic of Western philosophy. Such an uninformed caricature is primarily the facile result of a distortion or ignorance of textual sources.[8] Tempting as this stereotypical "tract" might be for those like Jürgen Habermas, it places unmanageable limits upon the scope, if not the *intentionality (vouloir-dire),* of a "philosophical deconstruction" to fulfill nothing beyond a fatalistic rejection of the orthodox prophetics of modernity.[9] The charge of paving the way for advancing a pandemic nihilism—the discord of an apocalyptic tone[10]—usually accompanies the rationalization of this accusation when and where it has been leveled against the *leçons* of Derrida. And the demonstrated potential of deconstruction to address the discourse ethics of the self-reasoning institutions of teaching-learning subsequently inaugurated from the founding thought of the philosophy of the West is dismissed outright.[11] Rather, given the developmental course of *postmetaphysical thinking* since the first serious challenges Friedrich Nietzsche issued to the monography of Occidental reason, I would argue, it would be fairer and, indeed, considerably more accurate to view the "guiding role" for the *future of deconstruction* more or less imposed upon Derrida by those who read his texts or extol his thoughts, in quite another light. That is, as the inescapable summons to responsibility demanded of an intellectual undertaking thoroughly inscribed by and inscriptive of the conditional effects of a gradual, though steady, intensification of the ethico-political maturation of the states of theory.[12]

Derrida, for his part, has clearly acknowledged, "What we call deconstruction in its academic or in its editorial form is also a symptom of a deconstruction at work elsewhere in society and the world."[13] The importance of this "symptomatic" aspect of deconstruction is often overlooked. Its "case" of interceding to disrupt the calculability of the interchange between the subjective topographies of mind and body traversing discourse and life unquestionably complicates the idea of a *theory/praxis dualism.* A separation of the interiority of thought from the exteriority of action—inasmuch as it grounds the criteriological basis of consequences ostensibly in "the real"—only succeeds to close off the *socius* of the institutional sphere to the *ethicity* of implications accompanying any act of interpretation, whether formalized creatively through the pragmatic signs of language as "reading" or "writing." The following passage from "Mochlos; or, The Conflict of the Faculties" is worth quoting here at length to illustrate how the heteronomous situation of deconstruction "happens":[14]

> If, then, it lays claim to any consequence, what is hastily called deconstruction *as such* is never a technical set of discursive procedures, still less a new hermeneutic method operating on archives or utterances in the shelter of a given and stable institution; it is also, and at the least, the taking of a position, in work itself, toward the politico-institutional structures that constitute and regulate our practice, our competences, and our performances. Precisely because deconstruction has never been concerned with the contents alone of meaning, it must not be separable from this politico-institutional problematic, and has to require a new questioning about responsibility, an inquiry that should no longer necessarily rely on codes inherited from politics or ethics. Which is why, though too political in the eyes of some, deconstruction can seem demobilizing in the eyes of those who recognize the political only with the help of prewar road signs. Deconstruction is limited neither to a methodological reform that would reassure the given organization, nor, inversely, to a parade of irresponsible or irresponsibilizing destruction, whose surest effect would be to leave everything as is, consolidating the most immobile forces of the university.[15]

What today Derrida recognizes to be the richness of an unceasing profusion of *"deconstructions"* concedes the dehiscent multiplicity of conceptual dislocations readily achievable from the unpredictable flowering of the well-sown seeds of his own texts. Yet this *particularization of theoretical practice* that is required to address the contextual *aporias* of performing analytic gestures suitable to a critical task still comes to be motivated by the antinomic vocation of finding ways to extinguish the *paleonymic* mastery of the pedagogical icons of the ages before.[16] For Derrida, as is reaffirmed more and more by his recent writings, the situation of deconstruction *is, was,* and *should be* the consequential result of the conscious subjectification of a desire to enact "a positive response to an alterity,"[17] regardless of the mainstream of a *"good conscience"* of unreflective opinions or beliefs its working out may alienate along the way. Targeting the institutional ground that constructs the distinguishing of *pure difference* as the judgmental basis upon which to entrench a viable and tangible separation of *essentialized subjectivities*—e.g., "the Same" from "the Other"[18]—could lead, in its turning, to an eventual dissolution of the grounds of interpretative foundations for arbitrary real-world inclusions and exclusions. The *"pedagogy of deconstruction,"* in this sense, presupposes an affirmative answering of/to the call of the Other that, above all else, emphatically strives to hasten and improve the concrete possibilities of ushering forth a more equitable *new world picture*. The ethical-political aftermath of its aggressively interventive questioning of the limits of normativity allows for a qualitative expansion of the existential borders of selfhood (of the Being of beings) beyond the narrowly regulated structures of institutionalized authority framing the material horizons of the realities we inhabit and therefore shape.

Whether it be incorporated within "systematic" elements of the manifold guises of "post-Marxisms," "post-feminisms," "post-colonialisms," or any other "post-critical" discourses promoting the emancipatory need for protecting the agency of the subject against the ideological tamperings of cultural institutions, the groundbreaking work of Derrida has influenced recent theoretical re-evaluations of how to go about this common political and altruistic intent.[19] Deconstruction has breathed new life into a host of current modifications of stale methodological lenses through which to identify and to re-approach the ethical dilemma of social inequalities. In short, the thought of Derrida has availed "us" the opportunity for an original recasting of the complicitous grounds of our own academic responsibility.[20]

Given that the problem of the institutionalization of education is posed "at the [epistemological and performative] root of philosophy as teaching,"[21] the theorized status of the *applied site* of pedagogy has been of sustained interest for Derrida in this regard. And he has painstakingly reiterated this point many times before, for example, as in *"Où commence et comment finit un corps enseignant,"* to clarify the depth of its parameters for the sake of protecting the right to philosophy education: "Deconstruction—or at least that which I proposed under this name that is as good as *(qui en vaut bien)* another, but not more—has therefore always had bearing *(porté)* in principle on the apparatus and the function of teaching in general."[22] The initiative Derrida has taken to expose the umbrage in the decidable ethics of "right" and "wrong" active below the surface structures of the educational institution is counterpoised in accordance with the responsibility of a political obligation "to interrogate, to exhibit, to criticize [the conceptual cadre framing its characteristic features] systematically—with an eye toward transformation."[23] By unearthing the systemic indications of coercive elements in the actual "machinery-of-schooling" that have the potential to shape the trajectory of knowledge presentations or creations as the curricular products of a normative projection of a unified code of subjectivity, the concealed biases of pedagogical goals or aims are laid bare. It cannot be denied that in minimizing the gap or delay of a conceptual dichotomy separating theory from *praxis,* the "general principles" of Derridean deconstruction have sharpened the analytic wherewithal for the recrafting of "critical tools" with which to reveal the nature of covert interests that infuse the actual conditions of teaching and learning.[24] This focus alone can help and has—in some instances—helped educational theorists or critics of diverse ideological "bents" to politicize the *ethology* of the cultural situatedness of pedagogy once and for all with a view to the righting of wrongs. Deconstruction has heretofore set apart, among others, those who would scrutinize the power/knowledge nexus at work for the pedagogical canonization and thus the privileging of certain texts from those who would uphold the *sanctity* of a system of educational institutions engendered from the exclusionary heritage of their philosophical lessons. Born "of an other logic"[25] *parergonal*—outside but within the enclosure—of the conceptual oppositions of Western rationality, the intrepidity of its inferences has done that much to change the usually unexamined notions of polity assumed for the transmission of *given* or *common* understandings.

Despite the recurrent tendency of many proponents of educational reform associated with the aforementioned "movements" to overzealously appeal to, or even use, some of the Derridean tenets for the expressed purpose of "institutional inquiry" or "cultural critique" (e.g., difference, *différance,* trace, inversion-displacement, binarity, [phal]logocentrism, "metaphysics of presence," supplementarity, dissemination), the ethical and political efficacy of deconstruction continues to be vehemently questioned, argued, and vastly undertheorized or examined in this disciplinary area with some care for a certain "philosophical rigor."[26] In a cross-disciplinary and cross-cultural study of the reception of French and German theory by academia, Robert C. Holub correctly notes that the ongoing "attempt to politicize deconstruction [especially after the 'Yale school' brand of 'rhetorical poststructuralism'], of course, can more properly be considered a repoliticization of deconstruction for [North] American criticism, since the affinity with radical and marxist thought had existed in France from its very inception."[27] The matter-of-course underestimation or outright dismissal of the potential—if not the substantive value—of deconstruction for reconceptualizing the ethical questions of political issues such as those associated with pedagogy, essentially of interest for us within the field of education, is most curious. Nevertheless, it may be due to a lack of critical attention given (to) a considerable part of the corpus that is Derrida's writings: the texts deliberating the institutional plight of "Philosophy," the serious problem of maintaining the teaching-learning of its curriculum, indigenous to the ideological fluctuations of the educational climate in France.

Primacy having been allocated to the so-called philosophical or argumentative texts, the remaining writings have been unduly marginalized from the *oeuvre propre* on the basis of "rhetorical" or stylistic considerations.[28] A large proportion of what has been forged together at the periphery to form a significantly less recognized "subcanon" that has been short-shrifted, if addressed at all, is explicitly oriented to examining the politics of the institutionalization of *la Philosophie*; the pedagogical insolvency of its ethical underpinnings, as it were. The majority of these texts (essays, lectures, interviews, letters, etc.) were written in the seventies up to the early-to-mid eighties, at what was the height of Derrida's involvement with the GREPH (Groupe de Recherches sur l'Enseignement Philosophique*)*, a collective of *philosophes de profession,* teachers, students, and others devoted to protecting the discipline of philosophy against the educational mandates of a French state threatening its eradication. Considering the speed and the diligence with which Derrida's more recent writings have been translated, the fact that a good deal of these "secondarized" texts have not been available for the perusal of non-French-reading scholars reflects a certain downgrading of their critical weight and value.[29] And this glaring gap of omission concerning the most overtly ethical and political phases of his philosophical labor notwithstanding, there remains quite a healthy trend to *quasi-methodologize* well-known elements of the so-proclaimed canon by reappropriating their theoretical precepts under the all-too-generic label of an "applied deconstruction," supposedly modified and thus more amenable to facilitating the study of "real-world" phenomena than the *"authentic thing,"* whatever that may be.[30]

I will not endeavor to "go over" the minutiae of these well-worn contentions to support or to refute them *per se.* Yet, all the while, the sightlines of the succeeding chapters do more than merely map over the vast plane of what has been written *in* or *against* the name of *deconstruction.* Converging on that which pertains to educational theory and philosophy in the totality of the published work of Derrida to date while concentrating on the rereading of largely "unread" and "underread" texts and sources, the specificity of detail to be found in the analyses to follow seeks, *at the very least,* to fill some of the lacunae these recurrent phases of critical conjuncture have left open to date on the ethics and politics of deconstruction and, *at the most,* to facilitate the breaking of new ground for thinking about the practice of pedagogy at large. *Specifically, I will try to illustrate by example how the textuality-based machinations of the Derridean instance of deconstruction can offer a profound resistance to the instruments of domination embedded within the philosophico-institutional praxeology of teaching-learning. Furthermore, how it can provide an effective and efficient manner for undoing the ethical substrata reinforcing the politics of educational theory and practice that suffuse the discursive gradients of concepts such as "freedom," "truth," "reason," or "humanity" with ideological significance.*

In addressing the body of Derrida's texts to examine *this thematization of the ethico-political focus of deconstruction with respect to issues of educational theory and practice in general,* the "philosophico-methodological" approach I will take relies, more or less, on an *actively interpretative instance of the moment of reading as writing.* That is, the "formativity" of the textual production to be presented is attuned to the complexity of the *thinking-through* and *working-out, a thinking-working-through-out,* of the act of interpretation itself. Respecting what Derrida has called the "exigencies" of a classical protocol of reading, the modality of the writing I will use—its philosophical focus and style—integrates and establishes associative links to deconstruction to come to terms with an understanding of the significance of these texts for actualizing a positive transformation of the institution of pedagogy. It forces reflection on the objectifiable value of its own ground by enacting within the form of its structures an interpretative resistance to the decidability of meaning at the threshold of its own sense, in that, it compels "the reader"—as it does "the writer"—to push at the outer limits of subjective frames of knowledge and reference relative to conventions always already within the confinement of a normative parameter of reflexivity. The philosophico-stylistic results of the *working through* of the Derridean corpus must be articulated then as part of the "ec-centricities" of *reading as writing* wherein the ideas drawn from these texts are turned back upon themselves and *"worked over"* within the intertextual schematism of the ideo-logies, norms, frames, within which the interpretative psyche operates. In the complexity of such a context, what I shall seek to show through and by example is *how the radical polemics of deconstruction has value for analyzing the ethical and political implications of pedagogical contingencies of theory and practice.*

Notes

1. Jacques Derrida, "The Time of a Thesis: Punctuations," trans. Kathleen McLaughlin, in *Philosophy in France Today,* ed. Alan Montefiore (Cambridge: Cambridge University Press, 1983), 50.

2. For a most comprehensive discussion and documentation of this phenomenon of anti-Hegelianism, see Vincent Descombes, *Modern French Philosophy,* trans. L. Fox-Scott and J. Harding (Cambridge: Cambridge University Press, 1980).

3. See Michael Ryan, *Marxism and Deconstruction: A Critical Articulation* (Baltimore: Johns Hopkins University Press, 1982). Here Ryan develops a very thorough comparative analysis of deconstruction and speculative idealism while addressing the central question of his book: the potential of deconstruction for a rearticulation of orthodox marxism and dialectical materialism.

4. Jürgen Habermas, *The Philosophical Discourse of Modernity: Twelve Lectures,* trans. Frank Lawrence (Cambridge, Mass.: MIT Press, 1985) and Gerald Graff, *Literature Against Itself* (Chicago: University of Chicago Press, 1979) are examples of the rank and file of this "division" on opposite sides of the political fence of theory or criticism.

5. For example, Barbara Johnson, *The Wake of Deconstruction* (Oxford: Blackwell, 1994) and Jeffrey T. Nealon, *Double Reading: Postmodernism After Deconstruction* (Ithaca: Cornell University Press, 1993) are two recent books that present an "even-handed" outline of the trials and tribulations of the "splintering" of deconstruction in the North American academy.

6. See Roy Bhaskar, Plato Etc.: The Problems of Philosophy and Their Resolution (London: Verso, 1994).

7. In Gregory L. Ulmer, *Applied Grammatology: Post(e)-Pedagogy from Jacques Derrida to Joseph Beuys* (Baltimore: Johns Hopkins University Press, 1985), the metaphysical standards of a Hegelian pedagogy are outlined according to the demands of the dialectic and its protection of memorization for what is an "enlightened" learning.

8. See Jacques Derrida, "Afterword: Toward an Ethic of Discussion," in *Limited Inc.,* trans. Samuel Weber and Jeffrey Mehlman, ed. Gerald Graff (Evanston: Northwestern University Press, 1988). The retort to his critics Derrida provides here (in the form of written answers to the questions of Graff) does much to dispel the myth that deconstruction is apolitical and that its textualization of human experience does not take ethics into account. William B. Stanley in *Curriculum for Utopia: Social Reconstructionism and Critical Pedagogy in the Postmodern Era* (Albany: State University of New York Press, 1992) presents an excellent overview of the discussion along with some insight into the curricular implications of the ethics of deconstruction.

9. This is the basis of the critique of Derrida and deconstruction in Jürgen Habermas, *The Philosophical Discourse of Modernity.*

10. The (non)relation of deconstruction with apophatic thought (e.g., negative theology) is discussed in Jacques Derrida, "Of an Apocalyptic Tone Recently Adopted in Philosophy," trans. John P. Leavy Jr., *Oxford Literary Review* 6, no. 2 (1984): 3-37.

11. Such is the position taken by Thomas McCarthy (a translator of Jürgen Habermas) in "The Politics of the Ineffable: Derrida's Deconstructionism," *The Philosophical Forum* 21 (Fall-Winter 1989-90): 146-168 and by John M. Ellis in *Against Deconstruction* (Princeton: Princeton University Press, 1989). Cf. Gayatri Chakravorty Spivak, *Outside in the Teaching Machine* (New York: Routledge, 1993), Rodolphe Gasché, *Inventions of Difference: On Jacques Derrida* (Cambridge, Mass.: Harvard University Press, 1994), and Christopher Norris, *Derrida* (London: Fontana Press, 1987). See also Barbara Foley, "The Politics of Deconstruction," in *Rhetoric and Form: Deconstruction at Yale,* ed. Robert Con Davis and Ronald Schleifer (Norman: University of Oklahoma Press, 1985), 113-134 and Bill Readings, "The Deconstruction of Politics," in *Reading De Man Reading,* ed. Lindsay Waters and Wlad Godzich (Minneapolis: University of Minnesota Press, 1989), 223-243.

12. Even though many have hailed the most "politicized" statement of deconstruction to be Jacques Derrida, *Specters of Marx: The State of the Debt, the Work of Mourning, & the New International,* trans. Peggy Kamuf (New York: Routledge, 1994), the continuation of an elaboration on general themes taken up in this text around the problems of ethics, democracy, ideology, and history has been addressed before in the earliest of his texts. See also the more recent, for example, Jacques Derrida, "Force of Law: The 'Mystical Foundation of Authority,'" trans. Mary Quaintance, *Cordozo Law Review* 11, nos. 5-6 (1990): 919-1045; Jacques Derrida, *Du droit à la philosophie* (Paris: Galilée, 1990), a collection of previously published texts (from 1975 to 1990) on the ethico-juridical and socio-political sphere of the institution of philosophy education in France; and more recently, Jacques Derrida, *Politiques de l'amitié* (Paris: Galilée, 1994).

13. Jacques Derrida, "On Colleges and Philosophy," in *Postmodernism: ICA Documents,* ed. Lisa Appignanesi (London: Free Association Books, 1989), 22.

14. See the interview with Jacques Derrida entitled "Deconstruction and the Other," in *Dialogues with Contemporary Continental Thinkers,* ed. Richard Kearney (Manchester: Manchester University Press, 1984), 105-126, for a lucid explanation of this symptomatic appearance of deconstruction and its concern with the repressed Other of desire that demands recognition.

15. Jacques Derrida, "Mochlos; or The Conflict of the Faculties," trans. Richard Rand and Amy Wygant, in *Logomachia: The Conflict of the Faculties,* ed. Richard Rand (Lincoln: University of Nebraska Press, 1992), 22-23.

16. See Jacques Derrida, "Some Statements and Truisms about Neo-Logisms, Newisms, Postisms, Parasitisms, and other Small Seismisms," trans. Anne Tomiche, in *States of Theory: History, Art, and Critical Discourse,* ed. David Carrol (New York: Columbia University Press, 1990), 63-95, for Derrida's contribution to the polylogue and polyglot of "isms" currently bandied about in academic discourses and for a clarification of some of the ethical-political value that is "misread" out of deconstruction.

17. Derrida, "Deconstruction and the Other," 118.

18. This anti-phenomenological theme (e.g., the dissimulation of auto-affection) goes back to an early text, Jacques Derrida, *Speech and Phenomena: And Other Essays on Husserl's Theory of Signs,* trans. David B. Allison (Evanston: Northwestern University Press), in which the identity of representation and the trace of the Other are major preoccupations as regards reflection. See also Rodolph Gasché, *The Tain of the Mirror: Derrida and the Philosophy of Reflection* (Cambridge, Mass.: Harvard University Press, 1986).

19. For an example of incorporating deconstruction in post-marxist social theory, see Ernesto Laclau and Chantal Mouffe, *Hegemony and Socialist Strategy: Towards a Radical Democratic Politics* (London: Verso, 1986); for a feminist nod to deconstruction—albeit a reductive one since the point is to discuss postmodernism—as related to research and education, see Patti Lather, *Getting Smart: Feminist Research and Pedagogy with/in the Postmodern* (New York: Routledge, 1991); for smatterings of a postcolonial rendering of deconstruction, see Homi K. Bhabha, *The Location of Culture* (New York: Routledge, 1994). I will further pursue the question of the conception of difference in these discourses with respect to the principle of education equality and equity, and the value of deconstruction for reconceptualizing what is a very problematic articulation of the concept of difference therein, in future work.

20. See Denise Egéa-Kuehne, "Deconstruction Revisited and Derrida's Call for Academic Responsibility," *Educational Theory* 45, no. 3 (1995): 293-309.

21. Jacques Derrida, "Où commence et comment finit un corps enseignant," in *Du droit à la philosophie* (Paris: Galilée, 1990), 119. (All translations from this text are my own.).

22. Derrida, "Où commence et comment finit," 118-119.

23. Derrida, "Où commence et comment finit," 115.

24. Some representative examples include: Cleo Cherryholmes, *Power and Criticism: Poststructural Investigations in Education* (New York: Teachers College Press, 1988); William F. Pinar and William M. Reynolds, eds., *Understanding Curriculum as Phenomenological and Deconstructed Text* (New York: Teachers College Press, 1992); and Donald Morton and Mas'ud Zavarzadeh, eds., *The-*

ory/Pedagogy/Politics: Texts for Change (Urbana: University of Illinois Press, 1991).

25. Derrida, "Où commence et comment finit," 121.

26. See Paul Jay, "Bridging the Gap: The Position of Politics in Deconstuction," *Cultural Critique* 22 (Fall 1992): 47-73, Gregory S. Jay, *America the Scrivener: Deconstruction and the Subject of Literary History* (Ithaca: Cornell University Press, 1990), and John D. Caputo, *Against Ethics: Contributions to a Poetics of Obligation with Constant Reference to Deconstruction* (Bloomington: Indiana University Press, 1993).

27. Robert C. Holub, *Border Crossings: Reception Theory, Poststructuralism, Deconstruction* (Madison: University of Wisconsin Press, 1992), 112.

28. See Richard Rorty, "Is Derrida a Transcendental Philosopher?" in *Derrida: A Critical Reader*, ed. David Wood (Oxford: Blackwell, 1992), 235-246.

29. Many of these "institutional" or "pedagogical" texts are collected in Jacques Derrida, *Du droit à la philosophie* (Paris: Galilée, 1990). A voluminous book 663 pages in all) that is edited for a decidedly French audience, one that would assuredly be familiar with the institutional plight of philosophical pedagogies. All of the book's content seriously engages some fundamental educational problems at the "cutting edge" of debate today in many disciplines. Some of the "chapters" in the compenduim have been translated into English as separate texts (e.g., "Mochlos; or, the Conflict of the Faculties," "The Age of Hegel," "The Principle of Reason: The University in the Eyes of Its Pupils,"), but have been acknowledged by only a handful of critics referring primarily to poststructural/postmodern transformations of literary studies and even less by the more "radical" schools of educational theory that need to address the "real effects" of power/knowledge distributions in pedagogy directly. This neglect on behalf of both groups respectively, yet more conspicuously of the second, may account to some extent for the fact that the "ethics and politics of deconstruction" has remained in a constant state of questioning, even by those who, nevertheless, cite its proper name to derive an *avant-garde* or postmodern authority without applying its "general principles" to the search for various "methods" of cultural criticism. To illustrate, a recent book states (rather baldly, I might add): "In writing about Derrida and education we are faced with the problem that he appears to have *nothing directly to say about education* [my emphasis]." And if this were not enough of a gross error, the authors continue, "Thus to read Derrida from the standpoint of an educator, with an educational perspective and with a view to gaining educational 'payoffs' from one's reading, must inevitably force us beyond our immediate standpoint into foregrounding, sooner or later, the general question of how a writer is to be read, of how a writer 'speaks' to us." I submit that this is precisely the uninformed opinion that has passed for "expert commentary" on Derrida when the point is more to rehash a conservative reading of deconstruction without sufficient depth for the expedient purpose of convenient generalizations or harried cooptation. Both quotations were taken from Robin Usher and Richard Edwards, *Postmodernism and Education* (New York: Routledge, 1994), 119.

30. This is due to the now quite fashionable trend of appealing to/for a radical authority or poststructural respectability by attaching the label of "deconstruction" to a particular approach, to a critico-theoretical cause, or to a research project to sanc-

tion the semblance of such a *methodological* validity in terms of periodization or timeliness. This is the theoretical "double speak" of feigning an obedience to the aura of these so-called deconstructive precepts while adapting the core concepts of something else more methodologically stable or palatable for the purposes of passing it off as "new."

Chapter One

The Cultural Politics of the Sign
The Ethics of Writing and the Other

> To recognize writing in speech, that is to say *différance* and the absence of speech, is to begin to think the lure. There is no ethics without the presence *of the other* but also, and consequently, without absence, dissimulation, *différance,* writing. The arche-writing is the origin of morality as of immorality. The non-ethical opening of ethics.
>
> —Jacques Derrida, *Of Grammatology*[1]

Chapter 1 intervenes at the phenomeno-semiological core of the deconstruction of the institutional history of Western epistemology. It proceeds to show how the question of writing and a meditation of the ethicity of the teachings of metaphysics as "first philosophy" are inseparable, since the reduction of difference and exteriority by the sanguine fullness of presence constitutes a tradition of the exclusion of otherness. The chapter consists of two parts that take up the *cultural politics of the sign* and the deconstruction of the *legitimacy of the foundation of intersubjective violence* as Jacques Derrida articulates it in *Of Grammatology* and other texts of that time, most notably "Différance." Within this interpretative framework, the question of ethics, in the plenum of more than a "general formulizability," is addressed through an elucidation of the problems of negotiating the affectivity of Western epistemology in the pedagogical mode of *theory as praxis.* Specifically, the first part begins with an examination of Derrida's engagement with the philosophical history of the semiological underpinnings of the metaphysical model of cognition as it is developed in the seminal text of deconstruction, *Of Grammatology.* It is shown how the recognition of the ethnocentric prioritization of speech over writing is the product of understanding the "representationality" of language forms in terms of an *economy of signification.* The point is that deconstruction—and the radicality of its complication of the Occidental *fable of pure origins*—would not have been possible without the theoretical presuppositions of the teleological intimations of either semiological auto-affection or phenomenological transcendentalism. This focus is taken further in a rereading of Derrida's reading of Jean-Jacques Rousseau and the political utopianism of his pedagogical ideal of a "community of speech" that would inevitably resist the supplementation of the originary (meaning "innocent" or "unsullied") state of its human nature by the violence of "culture." The deconstruction of the ethics of the educational theory of the eighteenth-century philosopher is analyzed with respect to the question of the derivation of the subjectivity of "the child" and the implications of this inchoate mourning for the loss of the source of the Being of beings this romantic image of humankind portrays. In the second part of Chapter 1, the non-ethical aftermath of the sign is examined in relation to the characteristics of Saussurean semiology that enable Derrida to identify it as yet another example of the logocentrism of Western metaphysics. The epistemic value of a phonological theory of signification this type of "linguistic structuralism" posits is effectively questioned here by counter-posing its "linearist" premises predicated on the voice against the most crucial elements of the poststructural version of difference or the idea of the play of the sign of the writing of the Other. Thus are set the argumentative preconditions through which to gauge the "testing" of the theoretical matrix of deconstruction as it is brought to bear on the practical domain of the disciplinary areas of the application of structuralism within the "social" or "human sciences." The example we consider within this contextual site of *praxis* is Derrida's reading of "The Writing Lesson" to be found in Claude Lévi-Strauss's *Tristes Tropiques,* an ethnological master text representative of the "Age of Rousseau," the epoch of the founding of modern anthropology. By expanding upon the ethico-political dimensions of the deconstruction of the ethnocentrism of the representation of the Nambikwara given, the chapter here renders an interpretation of the intersubjective violence characterizing the cultural politics of the sign in light of the politology of a structuralist "educational" agenda dismissive of script. The second part ends with an elaboration of the ramifications of the "non-word," "non-concept" of *différance* Derrida details in the lecture of the same title, to offer it as the source of a grammatological reconstitution of semiology to resurrect the rethinking of writing. Drawing attention to the deferred traces of the difference of the Other within the history of philosophy facilitates the inquiry into how the post-structural, post-phenomenological infrastructurality of deconstruction contends for an ethics of alterity that is beyond the cognitive limits of the teleological trajectory of the subject of metaphysics.

The Writing of the Sign

Ontology and the *Logos*: A Pedagogy of the Voice

Derridean "grammatology" develops from the reversed displacement of the fundamental difference between writing and speech, deriving the originality of its formulation in reaction to, *on the one hand,* the classical doctrines of the sign (ancient, medieval, modern) and, *on the other hand,* linguistics and structuralism. The effectivity of this largely ignored semiological undercurrent upon deconstruction is fundamental to the articulation of its ethico-political potential for the examination of the sources of intersubjective violence as a "philosophy of the limit."[2] The tropology of the sign, in this respect, culls by prefiguring the radicalization of the phenomenological horizon of what is for Jacques Derrida the domain of the ethics of writing, *différance.* Only by noting this grounding premise "up front" can we begin to follow and appreciate the remarkable incursion *Of Grammatology* makes, along with other Derridean texts of the same period, toward the *deconstruction of the ethnocentrism and violence of metaphysics as the source for a body of paideia.* For it is within the philosophico-cultural scope of the history of semiology, following from the characterizing logic of Western thought that Derrida pinpoints the privileging of the voice, that *"presents itself* as the non-exterior, non-mundane, therefore non-empirical or non-contingent signifier,"[3] to be the cause for the reduction and confinement of writing "to a secondary and instrumental function."[4] The manifestation of speech being construed as relatively "pure," simple and "intentionalizing," and the concession to the mediacy of the *phone* links the elements of *self, signification,* and *cognition* to it. And here—under these auspices of the "inflation of the sign"[5]—Derrida reconstructs the idealism of the vision of the *lack of play* within the communicative constitution of the *pragmato-poiesis* of the spoken word that places writing in the fetishistic position of a "technics in the service of language":[6]

> It is as if the Western concept of language (in terms of what, beyond its plurivocity and beyond the strict and problematic opposition of speech [*parole*] and language [*langue*], attaches it *in general* to phonematic or glossematic production, to language, to voice, to hearing, to sound and breath, to speech) were revealed today as the guise or disguise of a "primary writing": more fundamental than that which, before this conversion passed for the simple "supplement to the spoken word" (Rousseau). Either writing was never a simple "supplement," or it is urgently necessary to construct a new logic of the "supplement."[7]

Leaving the question of the reconstruction of the supplement aside for the moment—for we will have cause to come to it soon enough—to gauge the restrictive effects of the non-supplementarity of the *logos* with respect to the auto-affective epigenetism and substantive immanence of the origin of the knowing Subject of the Self. The belief of "'hearing (understanding)-oneself-speak' through the phonic substance,"[8] in this sense of an interiorized monologue reflecting the *epideictic* non-neutrality of the sign of speech, permeates the Western ideology of world-origins and along with it the differentiations "between the worldly and the non-worldly, the outside and the inside, ideality and non-ideality, universal and non-universal, transcendental and empirical,"[9] cast around the centrality of presence upon which all metaphysics of "the book"—"a perfect totality"[10] of the form of meaning and of expression—is based. "Representation mingles with what it represents, to the point where one speaks as one writes, one thinks as if the represented were nothing more than the shadow or reflection of the representer."[11] Insofar as strict boundaries between the spoken and the written sign cannot be maintained without destroying the concept of the sign altogether, Derrida outlines the impossibility of elaborating from the artificiality of such a division the relation of discourse to text:

> [W]hat is a lineage in the order of discourse and text? If in a rather conventional way I call by the name of *discourse* the present, living, conscious *representation* of a *text* within the experience of the person who writes or reads it, and if the text constantly goes beyond this representation by the entire system of its resources and its laws, then the question of genealogy exceeds by far the possibilities that are at present given for its elaboration. We know that the metaphor that would describe the genealogy of a text correctly is still *forbidden*. In its syntax and its lexicon, in its spacing, by its punctuation, its lacunae, its margins, the historical appurtenance of a text is never a straight line. It is neither causality by contagion, nor the simple accumulation of layers. Nor even the pure juxtaposition of borrowed pieces. And if a text always gives itself a certain representation of its own roots, those roots live only by that representation, by never touching the soil, so to speak. Which undoubtedly destroys their *radical essence,* but not the necessity of their *racinating function.*[12]

Within the profuse entanglements of such an infinitizing dissemination of the twisting tendrils of the sign, *the grafting of writing to the eudaimonics of the sign-function of speech can only take place at the outer limits of the logocentric logicality of the history of metaphysics* "which as yet has no name."[13] Implicit in the Derridean description of the constitution of discourse and text is an overlooked bridging of values of conductivity between "the sensible" and "the intelligible" that confounds a classical reduction of the terms of signification to empirical contingency. Even though the prioritizing of "speech" over "script" reinforces a dominant conception of writing as the uncomplicated reproduction of the spoken word, "phonetic writing, the medium of the great metaphysical, scientific, technical, and economic adventure of the West, is limited in space and time and limits itself even as it is in the process of imposing its own laws upon the cultural areas that had escaped it."[14] Here the imperialism of the sign—the self-interested value of its *teleo-phono-graphism* Derrida describes as the sophistry of presence "immediately united to the voice and to breath"[15]—looks forward to an exporting or re-plantation of the pneumatic essence of itself within the reflective space of the temporality of the Being of the "wholly Other." But is the "route" of semiosis so progressively finite as to realize "in full" the capacity of language to self-sign, to carry meaning?

As the touchstone of the lesson of metaphysics, the voice stays close to the authority of the self-conscious Self—or Subject—to facilitate within itself the reappropriation of the presence of Being and to "buoy up" the certainty of the ground of meaning, the meaning of the certainty of the ground, as Derrida explains:

All the metaphysical determinations of truth, and even the one beyond metaphysical ontotheology that Heidegger reminds us of, are more or less immediately inseparable from the instance of the *logos,* or of a reason thought within the lineage of the *logos,* in whatever sense it is understood: in the pre-Socratic or the philosophical sense, in the sense of God's infinite understanding or the anthropological sense, in the pre-Hegelian or the post-Hegelian sense. Within the *logos* the original and essential link to the *phonè* has never been broken. . . . As has been more or less implicitly determined, the essence of the *phonè* would be immediately proximate to that which within "thought" as *logos* relates to "meaning," produces it, receives it, speaks it, "composes" it.[16]

From this perspective writing is hopelessly derivative, removed in its distanciation from the controlling sources of an expressive proclivity and conceivable only (akin to the basest of "nominalisms") as a sign of a sign, a signifier of a signifier, or a mark of a mark. This attitude of the "secondary" and "parasitic" (epiphenomenal, simulacral, *playful*) character of all versions of script, Derrida has shown, is illustrated in the *Phaedrus* of Plato with the opposition of "bad writing (writing in the 'literal' [*propre*] and ordinary sense, 'sensible' writing, 'in space')"[17] and "the ['good'] writing of the truth in the soul."[18] One (the former) is grammatological, "hieroglyphic," the other (the latter) pneumatological, "hieratic." The instability of the contrast of their properties—the cross-contamination of their valences—forms the *pharmakon* (both poison and cure) that Derrida differentiates as the ambivalence of the effects of *écriture.*[19] Or what is *a deceptive and self-forgetting play of the orders of simulacra springing from a semio-cognitive betrayal of the logocentric logic of the sign helpless before the sacrifice of the plenitude of presence.* It is an "outer limit" within the *field of writing* that itself opens outward to generate the metaphysical distinction between "good" and "bad" writing, the *histos* (up-righted-ness) of speech and the *bathos* of the *re*-mark, by leaving behind the speculum of an empty space—we might call it an ethical looking glass—reflecting in the difference of being, the *being-present of the absence of Being.* For Aristotle also, Derrida notes in this ultra-phonic vein of Greek philosophy, "spoken words *(ta en te phone)* are the symbols of mental experience *(pathemata tes psyches)* and written words are the symbols of spoken words . . . it is because the voice, producer of *the first symbols,* has a relationship of essential and immediate proximity with the mind."[20] Speech enables the production of the "first" signifier as the reflection of thought that "mirrors things by natural resemblance"[21] in the revealing of the *aletheia* of their presencing of self-presence, thus tying the representation of objects *(antikeimena)* with the process of thinking.

Modern semiology—for example, the linguistic proto-structuralism of Ferdinand de Saussure that we will address in the second half of Chapter 1—portrays the signifier and the signified "as two faces of one and the same leaf,"[22] whereas in classical theories of the sign there is a separation of *signans* and *signatum,* a strictly defined hierarchization of the sign-referent, signifier-signified relation. By acknowledging the strict ordering of the "elements" of signification on the expression and content planes of representation, Derrida easily draws the conclusion—as he will already have from the start—that *"logocentrism" is also a species of "phonocentrism."* This would be a tedious, or even almost a redundant observation, if it did not set the post-structural "ground rules" for further distinguishing between the difference of cognition and signification and signification and reception. Following the path of this theoretical move is essential for analyzing how the philosophical conditions for "deconstruction" come about in relation to the semiological basis of the cultural politics of the sign—the historicity of its Western heritage—as it is grounded on the "absolute proximity of voice and being, of voice and the meaning of being, of voice and the ideality of meaning"[23] through which the seduction of the auto-affective violence of the Reason of the selfsame can be said to impact on the representation of the subjectivity of the Other.

The term "deconstruction" makes its first appearance in the following quotation, from *Of Grammatology,* developing the historico-philosophical context of what Derrida considers to be a reaction to "the *ethnocentrism* which, everywhere and always, had controlled the concept of writing":[24]

> [A] writing thus enlarged and radicalized [referring here to grammatology as a "science of writing"], no longer ensues from a *logos.* Further, it inaugurates destruction, not demolition but the de-sedimentation, the de-construction, of all the significations, that have their source in that of the *logos.* Particularly the signification of *truth.*[25]

The necessity of a deconstructive call to (dis)order is premised on the *undoing of onto-theology* from the Heideggerian determination of the meaning of Being—due to the phonocentrism of its "metaphorology"—within the history of metaphysics, at least since Plato, as presence, *the non-play of difference.* The resolution of this philosophical tradition, the teleological self-groundedness of its intro-jective centering of subjectivity, in conjunction with the "hypothetical" history of language Derrida has forthrightly presented *on the way to deconstruction* to reveal a bias toward the exclusion of writing, cannot but lead to an incessant questioning of the self-reflexive act "by which, by virtue of hearing (understanding)-oneself-speak—an indissociable system—the subject affects itself and is related to itself in the element of ideality."[26] The "metaphysics of presence" identified as both the constitutive foundation and the semio-effect of the "'originary word' *('Urwort')*"[27] as arche-speech or as the "transcendental word"[28] that assures the experience of being and "the possibility of being-word to all other words"[29] to be thus "precomprehended in all language"[30] is pulled down by the very *sense* of its self-truth as the law of the *logos.* For "Language speaks,"[31] Martin Heidegger will say, and the logic of its reason SPEAKS US as the ground and the abyss of the Voice of Being. The conflux of logocentrism with the determination of *the Being of beings as presence,* however, does not keep Derrida captive to Heideggerian *Destruktion* or *Abbau.*[32] Contrary to what some critics would suggest,[33] deconstruction *does not* seek, in like fashion and by similar means, to recapture the essence of what is "proper" to the horizon of humanity outside of a *community of language* by obstreperously wanting a reclamation of the truth of the spirit of Being still very much alive and living within being, yet well lost, from the dawning of time. To do so would mean to be willingly imprisoned in the shadows of the "epoch of onto-theology, within the philosophy of presence"[34] that Heidegger was unable to escape from by, more or less, refusing to transgress a transcendentalizing phenomenology by moving to a plane of vision beyond the search for origins, to push outside of the framework of the enclosure of the concept of Being as presence, an inclination he ironically reinstates over and over again as the debilitating product of his own metaphysical enframing *(Gestell)* of the question of what it means *to ek-sist, to be.*[35] We must remember this, for it is often easily forgotten. But at the same time we have to recognize that Heidegger perhaps more than any other Western philosopher announced the end of the epoch of metaphysics. And with it, the end of "philosophy" and the beginning of thinking.

The repression of writing in "the epoch of the *logos*"[36] has meant the sustenance of its degradation into a merely visible aspect of the sign. Or so Derrida has argued. Rendered as a mediation of a mediation, the formativity of scripted expression symbolizes a stunted or negated power of indication—an empirical falling, outside of the expressive content of an absolute or ideal objectivity—that predicts the failure of representation in the destructive consequences of a total abstraction and abjection of reality. The pure exteriority of the sensible signifier disfigures the "intelligible face of the sign"[37] by turning it away from the inner voice of conscience, the "mental life" of the *logos,* "the word and the face of God."[38] Derrida refers to the "Platonic diagram"[39] of the catechisms of medieval semiology wherein the "sign and divinity have the same place of birth,"[40] to express the metaphysico-theological constitution of semiosis during, for example, the era of St. Thomas Aquinas,[41] but also to generally invoke the caustic virulence of those theories we are dealing with that attempt to "withdraw meaning, truth, presence, being, etc., from the [transcendental, 'phenomenological'] movement of signification"[42] beyond writing and interpretation. A mistrust of the teachings of "classical-based" semiotics was certainly not anything new to philosophy.[43] As Derrida correctly remarks, it had been going on "for about a century"[44] after which deconstruction would treat as suspect "the difference between signified and signifier, or the idea of the sign in general."[45] How is this to be understood? Derrida explains:

> Thus within this epoch, reading and writing, the production or interpretation of signs, the text in general as fabric of signs, allow themselves to be confined within secondariness. They are preceded by a truth, or a meaning already constituted by and within the element of the *logos.* Even when the thing, the "referent," is not immediately related to the *logos* of a creator God where it began by being the spoken/thought sense, the signified has at any rate an immediate relationship with the *logos* in general (finite or infinite), and a mediated one with the signifier, that is to say with the exteriority of writing. When it seems to go otherwise, it is because a metaphoric mediation has insinuated itself into the relationship and has simulated immediacy.[46]

The "metaphoricity" of the trace of language—the extra-semiological purport (variability) of the articulation of signification—will license Derrida to say that "there is no linguistic sign before writing"[47] and that "[a]rche-speech [in the causal formulation of its prescriptivity] is writing because it is a law. A natural law."[48] Arche-writing is thus born not as the "psychic imprint" of the *hyle* and *morphe* of sound, but from the *en-grammatic* spacing of the *graphie* of the mind, its ability to produce the differential mark of language, in tracing the origins of subjectivity as the voice of the self as another. The deconstruction of the main tenet of the classico-medieval tradition of semiology through the reversal of the relation of speech to script throws the most fundamental ethico-cognitive lessons of the phono-logocentric metaphysics of Western philosophy into a frenzy of confusion. And the rationale of the system of representation that upholds the *ethos* of a community of interpretation at large, more or less, begins to show cracks under the weight of the renewing of the question of the sign of writing. Let us examine some misunderstood aspects of the argument put forward against the logocentrism of semiology more closely.

It is true to say—and this is what is missed or not given adequate consideration by many commentators—that Derrida is not concerned with devaluing speech to "tear down" metaphysics, but carefully "sketches in [the] broad outlines [of] a theoretical matrix,"[49] the semio-deconstructive contentions of "grammatology," as the post-structural basis for a "theory of writing" that would grant philosophico-ideological status to the inscriptability or textuality of language. The aim is to produce "the problems of critical reading"[50] and not to demystify the cunning interactions of the Word in all of its manifestations. The presupposition is that "reading should free itself, at least in its axis, from the classical categories of history—not only from the history of ideas and the history of literature but also, and perhaps above all, from the categories of the history of philosophy,"[51] to actualize the demand for a means of analysis exhibiting much more "rigor," precision and depth, than a respectful "doubling commentary," while making oneself aware of the role of the vestigial remains of the effects of a theologico-cultural-epistemic memory—a long-term sub-mnemonics—latent within the hidden recesses of the encrypted *grammatico-logics* of the psyche. Or the paradigmatic relationality of the codic webbing of sign-functions—synchronic and diachronic—with the life-world *(Lebenswelt)* endowing the language of our interpretations with significance.[52] And this process of reflection on the "conditions" of interpretation, *reading and writing,* is crucial to the *working-out* and *working-through* of the ethico-political impetus of deconstruction. *The rethinking of thinking a thought thought-out promotes the cultivation of an informed grounding of action by tying it to the writing of strategy, a self-teaching of a teaching of learning, through which to approach the undecidability of the decision to sign. To leave the trace of the mark of the Self with and for the Other.* In this sense, what we could call a definitive non-typologizing of the play of "writing in the literal sense"[53] of the "sensible" and "finite" is for Derrida the freedom of a kind of writing not "thought on the side of culture, technique, and artifice"[54] within which we find the unmistakable markings of the ironical dictatoriality of the fallibility of "a human procedure, the ruse of a being accidentally incarnated or of a finite creature."[55] A chance to fight against the metaphysico-ontotheological Law of the non-ethics of the sign. The relegation of writing to an inferior position in the codicity or "semio-schematicism" of language as a metaphor of something ontologically "prior" or "originary" within a "system of a signified truth"[56] of predetermined and essentializing meanings is (or it can be) used to "put down" or to discredit the subjective or interpretative aspect of the signifying function of "the book." *For the difference of difference is the very thing the Empire of Metaphysics cannot bear.* Derrida calls this supposedly "lowered-form" of a "lowered-writing" that displays, as the main feature of its technical formativity within the subjectivism of a self-idealizing rationality, "a non-self-presence to be denounced,"[57] "a certain fallen writing."[58] Its identifying characteristic of supplementality we are told is represented by the problematic corpus of the figure of Jean-Jacques Rousseau, to whom we shall now turn.

The Logic of the Supplement: Educating a Nature of Divine Origins

Derrida approaches the double structure of the play of supplementarity by way of its appearance and disappearance within the essentialized differences of the "philosophical" and "autobiographical" texts of Rousseau. If, indeed, such a sharpened distinction can stand with the conflicting reasons for its fissuring after the genre-collapsing of deconstruction.[59] The intent of the focus on Rousseau—"the only one or the first one to make a theme or a system of the reduction of writing profoundly implied by the entire age"[60]—is both the result of choosing *one example among others* and providing, in the choice of example, the example *par excellence* for the exemplarity of the supplement of supplementarity itself:

> In certain respects, the theme of supplementarity is certainly no more than one theme among others. It is in a chain, carried by it. Perhaps one could substitute something else for it. *But it happens that this theme describes the chain itself, the being-chain of a textual chain, the structure of substitution, the articulation of desire and of language, the logic of all conceptual oppositions taken over by Rousseau,* and particularly the role and the function, in his system, of the concept of Nature. It tells us in a text what a text is, it tells us in writing what writing is . . . .[61]

Therefore, out of any *ordinary* respect, Rousseau comes to represent and symbolize the entire field of "conceptual oppositions" situated at the stabilizing center of the epochal structure of the signifying chain of metaphysics (e.g., nature/culture, speech/writing, subject/object, presence/absence) and the logic of the supplement becomes the general economy of the process by which the "propriety" of these "items" is made visible and invisible at one and the same time. Recalling the distinction made earlier between a "rootlessness" of "text" and a "rootedness" of "book," the example Derrida proffers as exemplary gains force as it moves outside the stigmatizing focus of itself as a singular point of reference to the exteriority of an orientation and deviation that may graft the irrepressible tensions of difference to the *sense* of its use in the first place. And so the idea of supplementarity here will begin to expand, gathering momentum, to culminate in the contradiction of a magnificent reversal:

> Rousseau inscribes textuality in the text [through the supplement]. It tricks with a gesture of effacement, and strategic relations like the relationships of force among the two movements [of presence and absence] form a complex design. This design seems to us to be represented in the handling of the concept of the supplement. Rousseau cannot utilize it at the same time in all virtualities of its meaning. The way in which he determines the concept and in so doing lets himself be determined by that very thing he excludes from it, the direction in which he bends, here as addition, there as substitution, now as the positivity and exteriority of evil, now as happy auxiliary, all this conveys neither a passivity nor an activity, neither an unconscious nor a lucidity on the part of the author. Reading should not abandon these categories of metaphysics—which are also the founding categories of metaphysics—but should produce the law of this relationship to the concept of the supplement.[62]

To perceive the inscription of textuality in a text may seem to be oxymoronic more than a philosophical *clin d'oeil* in the direction of the division of an "essence" of writing, properly speaking, from the appearance and disappearance of a transcendental signified that always already is and is not there to mediate for meaning creation. The semio-phenomenological "conjuring trick" Derrida sees in Rousseau, however, forms the texture of the complex design that is the contradictory skein of the pattern of supplementarity "harbor[ing] within itself two significations whose cohabitation is as strange as it is necessary":[63]

> The supplement adds itself, it is a surplus, a plenitude enriching another plenitude, the *fullest measure* of presence. It cumulates and accumulates presence. It is thus that art, *technè,* image, representation, convention, etc., come as supplements to nature and are rich with this entire cumulating function. This kind of supplementarity determines in a certain way all the conceptual oppositions within which Rousseau inscribes the notion of Nature to the extent that it *should* be self-sufficient.
>
> But the supplement supplements. It adds only to replace. It intervenes or insinuates itself *in-the-place-of*; if it fills, it is as if one fills a void. If it represents and makes an image, it is by the anterior default of a presence. Compensatory [*suppléant*] and vicarious, the supplement is an adjunct, a subaltern instance which *takes-(the)-place* [*tient-lieu*]. As substitute, it is not simply added to the positivity of presence, it produces no relief, its place is assigned in the structure by the mark of an emptiness. Somewhere, something can be filled up *of itself,* can accomplish itself, only by allowing itself to be filled through sign and proxy. The sign is always the supplement of the thing itself.[64]

The two movements of the supplement do not cancel each other out in a *stalemate of paralysis* or a *force field of negativity,* but magnify these tendencies to contextualize the impossibility of their full compatibility, a play of non-complementarity, that will translate for deconstruction to the inter-weaving of textuality. Thus, the "double b(l)ind" of the structure of this strange economy of signification, the simultaneity of presence and absence, is that "whether it adds or substitutes itself, the supplement is exterior, outside the positivity to which it is superadded."[65] The sign of writing is effaced within the difference of the presence of itself, as substituted for itself, by an addition that is only truly the tracing of its own inverse copy. The irony is the "superfluousness" of the origin, its center being perpetually in substitution, and announcing of the need of the institution of its own supplementarity or supplementation. And this play of presence and absence is what will make Derrida state that "from the moment we have meaning, we have nothing but signs."[66]

The noumenal—as I have alluded to above—is the "blind spot," the independent variable of performativity, that the system *cannot calculate or anticipate.* "The supplement is what neither Nature nor Reason can tolerate."[67] As Derrida shows, this was the case for Rousseau and the strong sentiment he often expressed against writing:

> Rousseau repeats the Platonic gesture by referring to another model of presence: self-presence in the senses, in the sensible *cogito,* which simultaneously carries in itself the inscription of divine law. On the one hand, *representative,* fallen, secondary, instituted writing, writing in the literal and strict sense, is condemned in *The Essay on the Origin of Languages* (it "enervates" speech; to "judge genius" from books is like "painting a man's portrait from his corpse," etc.). Writing in the common sense is the dead letter, it is the carrier of death. It exhausts life. On the other hand, on the other face of the same proposition, writing in the metaphoric sense, natural, divine, and living writing, is venerated; it is equal in dignity to the origin of value, to the voice of conscience as divine law, to the heart, to sentiment, and so forth.[68]

Rousseau embraces an "Ethic of Speech" and the spoken word that is linked to the political stance on community he adopted in *The Discourse on Inequality* and *The Social Contract* as the face-to-face reciprocity of a union between beings of different and varying abilities and talents. The vision of humanity is pure and organically tied to a state of perfectability within Nature. What Rousseau fears, according to Derrida, is the supplementarity of writing as the violent product of culture and the pursuit of progress that dislocates the presence of speech and leads the "noble" and "pure" heart of human being to the living of a lie, a life of self-perpetuated falsehood. A fictive referent of "the good" is thereby set up as a point of order in Nature, a gentle and benevolent utopia, where the supplements to it are seen as the source of *dénaturation, depravity, and evil.* This dominant theme in Rousseau is approached by Derrida by way of the *general question of education and the various themes related to it revolving around the problem of language.*

Much has been made of the deconstruction of the "masked" features of the "theory of writing" presented in *The Confessions,* but the pedagogical problems Rousseau situates at the center of his thought on the issue of the nature/culture conflict have been virtually eschewed. To quote Derrida: "Yet all education, the keystone of Rousseauist thought, will be described or presented as a system of substitution [*suppléance*] destined to reconstitute Nature's edifice in the most natural way possible."[69] The subject here is, of course, the first educational "guide book" Rousseau wrote, *Emile or On Education.* And Derrida hits upon the "duplicitous" supplementarity of the concept of Nature that is at work in the text as it refers to the evolving of human being. It is a contradiction Rousseau is blind to, because of his associated belief in the "violence done [by writing] to the natural destiny of language."[70] That is, the idea of nature as both full and lacking, a completeness requiring supplementarity. Derrida explains "the strange unity of these two gestures"[71] in the following manner related here around the theme of blindness—it is well worth quoting at length:

> Blindness thus produces that which is born at the same time as society; the languages, the regulated substitution of signs for things, the order of the supplement. One goes *from blindness to the supplement.* But the blind person cannot see, in its origin, the very thing he produces to supplement his sight. *Blindness to the supplement* is the law. And especially blindness to its concept. Moreover, it does not suffice to locate its functioning in order to *see* its meaning. The supplement has no sense and is given no intuition. We do not therefore make it emerge out of its strange pneumbra. We speak its reserve.
>
> Reason is incapable of thinking this double infringement upon Nature: that there is *lack* in Nature and that *because of that very fact* something *is added* to it. Yet one should not say that Reason is *powerless to think this*; it is constituted by that lack of power. It is the principle of identity. It is the thought of the self-identity of the natural being. It cannot even determine the supplement as its other, as the irrational and the non-natural, for the supplement comes *naturally* to put itself in Nature's place. The supplement is the image and the representation of Nature. The image is neither in nor out of Nature. The supplement is therefore equally dangerous for Reason, the natural health of Reason.
>
> Dangerous Supplement.[72]

Both versions of supplementarity mentioned earlier "operate within Rousseau's text"[73] to self-deconstruct the educational presuppositions that champion the retreat to the Reason of Nature—meaning also the essence of human nature itself, the presence of Being—as the source of purity and "the good." Exteriority supervenes the appeal to such innocence and is therefore evil, "[b]ut always by way of compensation [Derrida stresses] for [*sous l'espèce de la suppléance*] what *ought* to lack nothing at all in itself."[74] By wanting to supplement human nature with the "acculturative" (in this case "habit-forming") methods of education, Rousseau is basically admitting the insufficiency of the originary premises he supports about the completeness of human being, the self-sufficiency of its Reason. For if Nature is already full presence, how is it that Reason comes to supplement that fullness, to enrich it? Is not Reason in itself also the plenitude of presence not in need of supplementation? All these questions can be asked of Rousseau and his blindness to the reversibility of the truth he yearns for by creating the conditions for it himself in the state of Nature. The supplement plays and repeats as repeatability itself, but it is also *in-form-ing of itself,* in the shift from one principle of "pedagogical" action to another, from the order of Nature to that of Reason, culture, education, and so on, as Rousseau seeks to rediscover the beginnings of being, a Being before the fall, in an Edenic language of a unified community, within which its members are always within "earshot," one to the Other.

But Derrida allows a more moving subtlety to infiltrate this question of pedagogy by projecting upon it the ethical question of the practical needs of the subject: "Childhood is the first manifestation of the deficiency which in Nature calls for substitution [*suppléance*]. Pedagogy illuminates perhaps more crudely the paradoxes of the supplement. How is a natural weakness possible? How can Nature ask for forces that it does not furnish? How is a child possible in general?"[75] The ambition Rousseau has is to empower the child without subverting the "goodness" of human nature for culture, by *"holding back"* in the process of education to allow Nature—the good, "chthonic" mother of responsiblizing necessity—time to work before supplementing the talent of original virtues with the artifice of pedagogy. The "infamy" is, as Derrida tells us, "progress as the possibility of perversion, regression toward an evil that is not natural and that adheres to the power of substitution that permits us to absent ourselves and act by proxy, through representation, through the hands of others. Through the written [*par écrit*]. This substitution always has the form of the sign. The scandal is that the sign, the image, or the representer, become forces and make 'the world move.'"[76] The child—although inscribed at birth into the socio-cultural order of Reason by being named, a "propriety" of the proper—Derrida will claim, does not enter into the *order of the supplement* that mirrors the subtlety of the immediate relation to that of self with the problem of the Other until there is the sign of speech that can express the emotion "I hurt," to "no longer weep"[77] senselessly at the sensation of lack. The repression and the conversion of the "incommunicable," the meaninglessness of general feeling, is relinquished, as is powerlessness, in the instant of language. *"The child speaks before knowing how to speak."*[78] But that does not constitute absolute conscious reflectivity as much as the effect of intuitive reflex or just reaction, because "what is lacking in [the child's non-figural, pro-jective 'language'] is the power of *replacing itself,* of substituting one sign for another, one organ of expression for another."[79] Speech thus *entitles* childhood, saving it from its state of powerlessness to actively participate in the creation of its own fate, and yet for Rousseau the supplementation of Natural Reason as a moving away from "innocence" is the epitome of *catastrophe, the turning toward* "the origin of its perversion."[80] But what Derrida refers to is a "Nature" prior to good and evil, where the "incapacitations" of the child are made apparent and the Other comes to friendship, pity, and aid. That is why the "supplement will always be the moving of the tongue or acting through the hands of others. In it everything is brought together."[81] For meaning is the negotiation of presence and the irony that plays at its difference is the work of its reason, a question of the symbolic opening of community. The ethics of the supplement, the technical power of the substitution of the sign that allows for the construction of a society, also exposes it to the danger of its own destruction when the child—supplementarity itself—becomes a force of its own that is always already beyond good or evil. And there is a responsibility here concomitant with the value of freedom as a play of life and death. The supplement, by producing within itself the delimitations of its own excesses, so to speak, opens the space of truth and falsity, rhetoric and logic, speech and writing to a certain ethico-politicality of the sign that is culturally determined, in the metaphysics of the West at least, by the more than symbolic interaction of the simulacra of presence and absence.

Deconstruction insists upon a re-doubled economizing of an *other logic* that supervenes the Rousseauistic blindness of a *pedagogy of mimesis* put forward to fulfill the democratizing vision of a non-oppositional ("equal") relation between subjects, but within which the principle of identity developed is inscribed by the very violence of hierarchical replications it rejects. And here Derrida finds the "dangerous supplement" of Nature to be Nature itself, and the belief in the transparency of speech as presence:

> What are the two contradictory possibilities that Rousseau wishes to retain simultaneously? And how does he do it? He wishes on the one hand to *affirm,* by giving it a positive value, everything of which articulation is the principle or everything with which it constructs a system (passion, language, society, man, etc.). But he intends to affirm simultaneously all that is cancelled by articulation (accent, life, energy, passion yet again, and so on). The supplement being the articulated structure of these two possibilities. Rousseau can only decompose them and dissociate them into two simple units, logically contradictory yet allowing an intact purity to both the positive and the negative. And yet Rousseau, caught, like the logic of identity, *within* the graphic of supplementarity, says what he does not wish to say, describes what he does not wish to conclude; that the positive (is) the negative, life (is) death, presence (is) absence and that this repetitive supplementarity is not comprised in any dialectic, at least if that concept is governed, as it always has been, by a horizon of presence.[82]

The egality of the communitarianism Rousseau advocates, in fact, spurns difference as evil, a perversion of presence, to condone the reproducibility of the *Same.* The vision itself violates the possibility of a future by s(t)ealing time in the still-life of a vignette of the eternal perfection of being, untainted and at peace with the beauty of its true and pure Nature. That is why in the teaching of Rousseau's teaching, the "letter killeth," bringing with its concrete abstraction of supplementarity the terrible pain of a wound or hurt to the essence of the living soul of heaven on earth. *The mark of the ablation symbolizes the transgression of violence against the purity of presence and self-presence, of culture against spirit, and in this sense it wantonly mutilates the source of human dignity in language by subjecting it to the humiliation of having to face its own powerlessness, to acknowledge a lack of control over its very destiny to educate the self.*

But is not Rousseau repeating the ethnocentrism that relies on the biases of a philosophical anthropology with one utopic nucleus of reference, *a community free of writing*? The myth of the original innocence of an identity of speech—*a self-deceiving and self-denuding image of presence conquered*—uncontaminated by the violence of its Other, is what sets the metaphysical preconditions of a system for the ethico-political representation of being simply by identifying the statutoriness of norms of relation and behavior. Such an institution of laws, however, as deconstruction reminds us and illustrates through an ex-posing of the techniques of metaphysics, has within its structure *the violence of its own means of enforcement.* Or what is a reverie of pure auto-affection, unmediated self-presence and temporal continuity. A theme that we shall explore in the greater detail of its variations a little farther on, in the context of the deconstruction of the ethnological variation of Saussurean semiology in anthropological structuralism.

The Non-Ethical Aftermath of the Sign

Structure and Play: The Cultural Monumentality of the Sign Stratified

To return to the sign.

And so to the origins of the "ethnocentricity" of the mark of writing.

The modern example of sign theory that Derrida takes to be a primary instance of a "logocentric" or "ethnocentric" model of language is a "semiology of a Saussurean type":[83] both as it was constructed from the compilation of lecture notes that comprised the *Course in General Linguistics* of 1916 and as it emerged later in its most vigorous expression by taking the philosophico-scientific form of French Structuralism. The difference of these "newer" developments with the traditional archetypes of semiosis or signification had "an absolutely decisive critical role"[84] in "breaking up" the rule of the classico-medieval orthodoxy over semiosis by showing "that the signified is inseparable from the signifier, that the signified and signifier are the two sides of one and the same production."[85] The "two-sided unity"[86] of the formulation of the Saussurean sign establishes the differential (sensible) and the formal (intelligible) features of signification. At this point the concept of language has to be drastically rethought.[87] A quality of its "symbolicity" is indispensably effaced within an arbitrariness of sense that posits no "natural" or "inevitable" bond (e.g., no analogous, correlational, or motivational ties) of the sign to its referent, of signifier to signified (e.g., words to "things" or even linguistic expressions to concepts). The non-autonomy of instances of semiosis, but the differentiality of their inter-relation, therefore allows language to be construed as a signing system of differences of negative relation.

For Derrida, however, the tremendous potential of the new conception was not realized by Saussure to accentuate or to maximize the turning-back upon metaphysics the very concept of the sign borrowed from it. And thus this otherwise promising path of semiology remains tightly bound to the equivocal delimitation of hierarchizing effects rooted at the "'logocentric and ethnocentric limits'"[88] of the model itself "in systematic solidarity with stoic and medieval theology."[89] The problem Derrida isolates is that even though the "separation" between signifier and signified is innovatively managed to move toward the disintegration of the selfsameness of the metaphysical ideality of the word-concept, Saussure unfortunately also retains and conserves the mechanism of the sign-function, being unable to find any alternative to it:

> No more than any other, this concept [of the sign] cannot be employed in both an absolutely novel and conventional way. One necessarily assumes, in a non-critical way, at least some of its implications inscribed in its system. There is at least one moment at which Saussure must renounce drawing all the conclusions from the critical work he has undertaken, and that is the not fortuitous moment when he resigns himself to using the word "sign," lacking anything better.[90]

The sign assumes a "transcendental signified" that is an ending point in a series of significations, "which in and of itself, would exceed the chain of signs, and would no longer itself function as a signifier"[91] to supercede the concatenated elements comprising a given syntagm or "super-syntagm." The signified is, Derrida will counter, *"always already in the position of the signifier."*[92] The attempt to return to the false utopia of a "transcendental signified"—as it "leaves open the possibility of thinking a *concept signified in and of itself,* a concept simply present for thought, independent of a relationship to language, that is of a relationship to a system of signifiers"[93]—would posit an origin before the sign without any mediation or feasible connection to anything else. According to Derrida, the dream of this quasi-messianic hope of the truth of signification expressed in Saussurean semiology, the desire of a decidability fore-sworn, is "not being imposed [upon it] from without by something like 'philosophy,'"[94] but is a consequence of "everything that links our language, our culture, our 'system of thought' to the history and system of metaphysics."[95]

The concession to logocentrism can be seen elsewhere in Saussure's lectures on the "science of linguistics" in the privileging of speech over writing, the "phonic substance"[96] of the breath of voice tying the sign to the aspiration of the *phone* as "the regulatory model, the 'pattern,' for a general semiology of which it was to be, by all rights and theoretically, only a part."[97] "The thematics of the arbitrary, thus, is turned away from its most fruitful paths (formulation) toward a hierarchizing teleology."[98] For by emphasizing the unity of signifier and signified in speech, the voice is collapsed into consciousness only to blur the existence of the sign, sublimating it, through the illusion of the glossematic transparency of the immediate presence of sound. The focus, Derrida believes, should have been on the new found capability that presented itself to invent "a system of distinct signs"[99]—much like deconstruction has done—that could generate "the possibility of the code and of articulation, independent of any substance, for example, phonic substance,"[100] and not the modular construction of spoken language. The tendency again is to reduce the exteriority of the signifier, to stifle, in this sense, the opening of a channel to the *gift of writing.*

Similarly, in the "modern" conception of "structure" and "structurality" Derrida astutely perceived radically equivocal components of a theoretical function that could "simultaneously confirm and shake logocentric and ethnocentric assuredness."[101] Deconstruction, with no fixed system or hyper-logical architectonics to speak of, "but rather [as] a sort of strategic device, opening onto its own abyss,"[102] could and would use the "double-sidedness" of these elements to trouble the steadfastness of the foundation of metaphysics. For, as with the concept of the sign, the idea of structure "is as old as the *episteme*—that is to say, as old as Western science and Western philosophy."[103] And it is variously translated within the older phases of the metaphysical tradition as the expression of "unity," "connectivity," "order," "system," and so on. The *structurality of structure* has heretofore "always been neutralized or reduced,"[104] Derrida remarks, by the method of "giving it a center or of referring it to a point of presence, a fixed origin"[105] outside of the logic of itself, and not in total unison with an ideality of the vision of a *pure structurality of structure*. The following example is a concise expression of this judgment:

> The function of this center was not only to orient, balance, and organize the structure—one cannot in fact conceive of an unorganized structure—but above all to make sure that the organizing principle of the structure would limit what we might call the *play* of the structure. By orienting and organizing the coherence of the system, the center of the structure permits the play of its elements inside the total form. And even today the notion of a structure lacking any center represents the unthinkable.[106]

The moment of contradiction Derrida exposes is the reason for the self-violating violence of the "breach" of the metaphysical tradition that spawned nothing but antagonism to a deviation from the monolith of a typical cultural monomythism. This self-debilitating weakness manifests itself as the cruel invitation of an opening to the undermining of the hollow ground of its own epistemological premises. It presupposes and is presupposed by the potential disruption of the center that sets the parameters to the play of elements within a system to which it belongs, yet at the same time is separate from, being both "inside" and "outside" the formation of the structure it necessarily defines. The metaphysical "concept of the centered structure"[107] is incoherent to deconstruction if conceived in any other way than through "the concept of a play [of tensions, positions, effects, etc.] based on a fundamental ground, a play constituted on the basis of a fundamental immobility and a reassuring certitude, which in itself is beyond the reach of play."[108] *The center is there to hold what it cannot possibly fathom or foresee arising out of the logicality of itself.* For Derrida, the contradiction of this coherence, representing "coherence itself, the condition of episteme as philosophy or science,"[109] asseverates "the force of a desire"[110] to mitigate the difference of discipline and disciplinarity because it relieves the anxiety of freedom, that is, of the possibility of error, in the starkness of individuality: "And on the basis of this certitude anxiety can be mastered, for anxiety is invariably the result of a certain mode of being implicated in the game, of being caught by the game, of being as it were at stake in the game from the outset."[111]

The classical concept of structure or structurality, as such, is a system of "repetitions, substitutions, transformations, and permutations"[112] implicated in a historicity of meaning where the centricity of presence consummates the spirit of the first and last truth of being, and the re-educating of being. From its archeology to its eschatology, a value beyond the pleasure of play. To Derrida, and for deconstruction, the tradition of Western philosophy and science—and this is a vital aspect that has been disregarded—needs to be, indeed, "must be thought as a series of substitutions of center for center, as a linked chain of determinations of the center,"[113] within which the structurality of the general structure is kept under control by the reproductive resources of a metastatic nomenclature of *the Same*. In short, the *archia* of a language capable of reducing the whole to a part of its evolving yet quiescent self. "The history of metaphysics, like the history of the West, is the history of these metaphors and metonymies."[114] Now the *point d'appui* of its "matrix" (Derrida's word) is predicated on "the determination of Being as *presence* in all senses of the word. It could be shown that all the names related to fundamentals, to principles, or to the center have always designated an invariable presence—*eidos, arche, telos, energeia, ousia* (essence, existence, substance, subject) *aletheia*, transcendentality, consciousness, God, man, and so forth."[115] After the writings of Nietzsche and Heidegger, Sigmund Freud also, the "transcendental signified"—the absolute ideality of a center of meaning—hovering around the capacity of humanity to guide itself via a pedagogy (training and discipline) of the body, mind, and spirit is turned in toward the symptomaticity of itself as a function inside the structure it itself governs, proving to be nothing more nor less than one sign among other signs. An imaginary point of no real reference. With this realization—"that there was no center, that the center could not be thought in the form of a present-being [a being-present], that the center had no natural site, that it was not a fixed locus but a function, a sort of non-locus in which an infinite number of sign-substitutions came into play"[116]—everything is infinitely changed from the ground of metaphysics, and beneath it, upwards. Derrida perceives a similar breaking-through of the thought of the structurality of structure in the disciplinary context of Saussure's semiology that we have been addressing up to this point, as it informs the "human sciences" and particularly the structural ethnology of Claude Lévi-Strauss. However, in the case of the second, the ethico-political dimension is perhaps more outrightly emphasized.

Indeed, on the pragmatological plane of philosophico-scientific immanence, the scope of the structural ethnology of Lévi-Strauss is of keen interest to Derrida, and its deconstruction is essential to our own focus on the cultural politics of the sign. That is, for examining how the education of cognition through the fixing of values of representation and responsivity controls the interpretability of the Other. Especially, in this sense of the hypostatization of beings, as deconstruction relates to the problem of the ethics of writing and the ethnocentrism of interdictions against the play of the explanatory status of the sign of "humanity." It is an "affinity or filiation that binds Lévi-Strauss to Rousseau"[117] and exposes the modern re-hashing of the nature/culture dichotomy in the attempt made by an ethnologist to write about a particular group of individuals without suspending the value of general categories of ethical distinction. And this may be a harsh and even shocking indictment given the right of entitlement Lévi-Strauss has claimed and tried to secure for modern "Anthropology" as a discipline studying the relative breadth of "cultural difference" in every possible area of its manifestation.[118] Can we, however, resist the idea that ethnology would accept into its discourse the "premises of ethnocentrism,"[119] to lay, even if inadvertently, the troubling foundations for the hermeneutical violence of prejudice and racism? This is what Derrida more or less asks of Lévi-Strauss, and with good reason, due to the fact that appearances may have suggested otherwise with the "time-honored" reflectivity of the ethnographic text:

> In fact, one can assume that ethnology could have been born as a science only at the moment when a decentering had come about; at the moment when European culture—and, in consequence, the history of metaphysics and of its concepts—had been *dislocated,* driven from its locus, and forced to stop considering itself as the culture of reference. This moment is not first and foremost a moment of philosophical or scientific discourse. It is also a moment which is political, economic, technical, and so forth. One can say with total security that there is not anything fortuitous about the fact that the critique of ethnocentrism—the very condition for ethnology—should be systematically and historically contemporaneous with the destruction of the history of metaphysics. Both belong to one and the same era. Now ethnology—like any science—comes about within the element of discourse. And it is primarily a European science employing traditional concepts, however much it may struggle against them.[120]

The sign of the culture of reference specified—as it is complicit with and relies on logocentric metaphysics in the concrete form of a vested privileging of concepts through which to order reality—grants science the power to *arrest the play of difference by closing off the field of interpretation to the reason of the Other. What is defined from this sense of a limited and distorted perspectivism of the correlational valuation of the Being of beings is an ethnocentric reconciliation of specificity with generality through which "humanity" acquires and retains, at least on the surface, the mark of ambiguity.* Here, as much as anywhere else for Derrida, the potential "rehabilitation" of the sign of writing and its relation to violence is the central issue. One that no rereading of the ethico-political implications of deconstruction could ignore.

"What links writing to violence?"[121] A certain *materiality* or *exteriority* of the sign, as we have said. In its expansion or reduction, writing is the stuff of violence itself. Not a physical duress, as such, but a coercion of some "immeasurable" force or oppressive proportionality that brings a subject under the control of an active and dominating power, since language in all of its forms (discursive or textual, spoken or written) is an oriented structuring of a principal manifestation of hierarchization. It ranks, classifies, groups, and separates according to a system of differences or polarities by the subjective placing of value to objectify entities. The general strategy of the ethico-axiology of its oppositional schematics as transliterated from metaphysics to the sign is a deconstructive metaphor for violence. With Lévi-Strauss and Rousseau, Derrida here makes the same judgment, but in another direction, "radicalizing this theme, no longer considering this violence as *derivative* with respect to a naturally innocent speech, one reverses the entire sense of a proposition—the unity of violence and writing—which one must therefore be careful not to abstract and isolate."[122] That the *"ethno-poietical"* determination of language—the translation of its "figurativity" to a mythomorphic typologizing of the supplementary expression of cultural value—creates hierarchies perpetuating forms of social inequality or reinforcing situations of domination is considered true;[123] however, there is neither a militating against interpretative differences nor a castigation of writing as either the cause of human slavery (the Marxism of Lévi-Strauss) or the source of falsehood (the utopianism of Rousseau). For better or for worse, the means of the system of representation makes the attempt at community and communication imaginable because there is an intersubjective element to the ordering of "the space of its possibility, the violence of the arche-writing, the violence of difference, of classification, and of the system of appellations."[124] Derrida explores the validity of the moral judgment accompanying the inscription of the letter by a rereading of "A Writing Lesson," a seemingly insignificant chapter in Lévi-Strauss's ethnological travel-logue *Tristes Tropiques,* "which is at the same time *The Confessions* and a sort of supplement to the *Supplément au voyage de Bougainville* [by Denis Diderot],"[125] a cross between "autobiography" and "ethnography."[126]

The "experience" that is retold here for the benefit of Western eyes and ears "marks an episode of what may be called the anthropological war, the essential confrontation that opens communication between peoples and cultures, even when that communication is not practiced under the banner of colonial or missionary impression"[127] and is "recounted in tones of violence repressed or deferred"[128] to the "private" moments of the writer's guilty reflection "accusing and humiliating oneself"[129] as a "friendly intruder," one self-placed, without right or rights, among his cultural others, the Nambikwara. They are a people who "could not write," Lévi-Strauss tells us, emphasizing its obviousness "goes without saying."[130] The presupposition being, of course, it is *only what we could expect to expect.* The violent insurgence of the ethnologist's "penetration" (Derrida's word) into the life-world of the nomadic band is looked upon, in these terms during the narrative, as a giant step back in history, a descent into a "lost world" before time where humanity had once been eons before. Most importantly for Lévi-Strauss and the academic "prestige" of his fieldwork, the Nambikwara represent the survivors of an *epoch with no writing,* symbolizing all that is existentially projected backwards within the living frame of "'the childhood of our race.'"[131] Derrida begins to query the depiction presented of this indigenous people on the grounds of its Rousseauistic romanticism by bringing out salient points from the detail of the ethnologist's own notes that contradict the image of a "peaceful innocence." The ethnological portrait being, in this case, a doxographic exoticization of cultural otherness celebrating the non-violence of the un-educated, the un-taught. The likeness of the Nambikwara Lévi-Strauss will unveil is ethnocentric in the nostalgia of its yearning to return human being to a "primitivism" of orgins lost, the non-supplemental eco-logy of the Rousseauian "noble savage" free from writing, culture, and violence. And Derrida exposes this aspect of the representation of the "wholly Other" in the stratagem of such an imagism:

If writing is no longer understood in the narrow sense of linear and phonetic notation, it should be possible to say that all societies capable of
producing, that is to say of obliterating, their proper names, and of bringing classificatory difference into play, practice writing in general. No reality or concept would therefore correspond to the expression "society without writing." This expression is dependent on ethnocentric oneirism, upon
the vulgar, that is to say ethnocentric, misconception of writing. The
scorn for writing, let us note in passing, accords quite happily with this
ethnocentrism. The paradox is only apparent, one of those contradictions
where a perfectly coherent desire is uttered and accomplished. By one and
the same gesture, (alphabetic) writing, servile instrument of a speech
dreaming of its plenitude and its self-presence, is scorned and the dignity
of writing is refused to non-alphabetic signs.[132]

Derrida objects to the use of the Western concept of writing to order peoples
along a scale of "sophistication" according to the degree of their possession of
the *graphein*. The ethnocentrism permeating Lévi-Strauss's description of the
Nambikwara is revealed by the qualifying basis of this system of classification
ranging between the poles of "primitivism" and "modernism" configured "within
an ethico-political order, as an innocence and a non-violence interrupted by the
forced entry of the West and the 'Writing Lesson.'"[133] For Derrida, the peoples
said to be "without writing" lack only a certain type of writing: "[t]he genealogical relation and social classification are the stitched seam of arche-writing, condition of the (so-called oral) language, and of writing in the colloquial sense."[134]
And in ignoring the prohibition of the Nambikwara against the utterance of the
proper name as a protection against its "misuse" by exposing its double, a
bearer, to attacks of enemies, Lévi-Strauss is said to be naive to the "horizon of
intersubjective violence,"[135] the play of language and aggression, instituting the
laws of the ethics and politics of representation within the society of this culture
as an interdiction against behavior contrary to the standard of carefully circumscribed norms:

There was in fact a first violence to be named. To name, to give names that
it will on occasion be forbidden to pronounce, such is the originary violence of language which consists in inscribing within a difference, in clas-
sifying, in suspending the vocative absolute. To think the unique *within* the
system, to inscribe it there, such is the gesture of the arche-writing: arche-
violence, the loss of the proper, of absolute proximity, of self-presence, in
truth the loss of what has never taken place, of a self-presence which has
never been given but only dreamed of and always already split, repeated, in-
capable of appearing to itself except in its own disappearance. Out of this
arche-violence, forbidden and therefore confirmed by a second violence that
is reparatory, protective, instituting the "moral," prescribing the conceal-
ment of writing and the effacement and obliteration of the so-called proper
name which was already dividing the proper, a third violence can *possibly*
emerge or not (an empirical possibility) within what is commonly called
evil, war, indiscretion, rape; which consists of revealing by effraction the
so-called proper name, the originary violence which has severed the proper
from its property and its self-sameness [*proprété*]. We could name a third

violence of reflection, which denudes the native non-identity, classification
as denaturation of the proper, and identity as the abstract moment of the
concept. It is on this tertiary level, that of the empirical consciousness,
that the common concept of violence (the system of moral law and of transgression) whose possibility remains yet unthought, should no doubt be
situated. The scene of the proper names is written on this level; as will be
later the writing lesson.[136]

The proper name upholds the route to the possibility of a "pre-ethical violence"[137] preceding even the presence of the subject. It will allow for the discovery of the institution of the violence of writing at an ontologically prior stage in
"arche-writing." And here Derrida emphasizes a non-spatial exteriority that, nevertheless, is still the general difference of the "in-scription" of the sign. "To refuse the name of writing to this or that technique of consignment is the 'ethnocentrism that best defines the prescientific vision of [hu]man[ity].'"[138]

The instance of the episode of "The Writing Lesson"—and we will explain
the significance of the title momentarily—is a putting to practice of Rousseau's
ideas by Lévi-Strauss, who is most assuredly a committed and proud disciple of
the romanticism of the "anthropological" trend begun in the eighteenth century
toward facilitating the restoration of human being to Nature. Derrida describes
the utopianism of its modern outcome in structural ethnology as the peculiar
result of a busy time of colonial expansionism: "Non-European peoples were not
only studied as the index to a hidden good Nature, as a native soil recovered, of a
'zero degree' with reference to which one could outline the structure, the growth,
and above all the degradation of our society and culture. As always, this archeology is also a teleology and an eschatology; the dream of a full and immediate
presence closing history, the transparence and indivision of *parousia,* the suppression of contradiction and difference."[139] Wanting to gauge or test the Marxist
hypothesis of the debilitating effects of "writing," Lévi-Strauss introduces its
general principle of the inscribability of thought into the midst of the "primal
scene" of the Nambikwara when pencils and paper are distributed to them. The
leader of the band immediately allies himself with the "new" technology, "recognizing that writing could increase his authority, thus grasping the basis of the
institution without knowing how to use it."[140] According to Lévi-Strauss, the
result was predictable in the differences of status it reinforced as the dangerous
culmination of the cultural politics of the sign, a fact further solidified on these
grounds of the abuse of a system of symbolic exchange when the impending
threat of real violence to the ethnologist's entourage spontaneously arises and
must be squelched. Later on, the Chief himself was deposed and exiled for the
combination of the following actions:

> And now, no sooner was everyone assembled than he drew forth from a bas-
> ket a piece of paper covered with scribbled lines and pretended to read from
> it. With a show of hesitation he looked up and down his "list" for the ob-
> jects to be given in exchange for his people's presents. To so and so a bow
> and arrows, a machete! and another a string of beads! for his necklaces—and
> so on for two solid hours. What was he hoping for? To deceive himself, per-
> haps: but, even more, to amaze his companions and persuade them that *his*

intermediacy was responsible for the exchanges, that he had allied himself with the white man, and that he could now share his secrets. We were in a hurry to get away, since there would obviously be a moment of real danger at which all the marvels I had brought would have been handed over.[141]

The importation of writing into what Lévi-Strauss believed was "a micro-society of non-violence and freedom, all the members of which can by rights remain within range of an immediate and transparent, a 'crystalline' address, fully self-present in its living speech"[142] is blamed as the cause for the clumsy attempt made at the "exploitation" of the others by the chosen overseer. On the one hand, the lesson that the ethnologist teaches to the Nambikwara chief is a knowledge of how to capitalize upon the power of the "profoundly enslaving function"[143] of the letter, "here accessory, of communication, signification, of the [Western] tradition of a signified."[144] On the other hand, the violence of the *gesture of writing* as it is thought by Lévi-Strauss to repeat the general conditions toward a "proletarization" of society—an arbitrary lowering of the stature of some of its members for the benefit or advancement of others—concretizes the source of suffering in the materiality of a commodification of the sign and a system for the exchange of its value within an economy governing the means and modes of its production. Derrida comments on some of the unexamined presuppositions permeating these ethico-political aspects of the semiology-based "pedagogical" theoretics of "The Writing Lesson":

It [Saussurean phonocentrism upon which structural ethnology derives its philosophico-scientific credibility] is, however, an ethnocentrism *thinking itself* as anti-ethnocentrism, an ethnocentrism in the consciousness of a liberating progressivism. By radically separating language from writing, by placing the latter below and outside, believing at least that it is possible to do so, by giving oneself the illusion of liberating linguistics from all involvement with written evidence, one thinks in fact to restore the status of authentic language, human and fully signifying language, to all languages practiced by *peoples whom one nevertheless continues to describe as "without writing."* It is not fortuitous that the same ambiguity affects Lévi-Strauss' intentions.[145]

The concept of the exclusion of writing Lévi-Strauss supports ultimately "allows him to consider the passage from speech to writing as a *leap,* as the instantaneous crossing of a line of discontinuity,"[146] that is "epigenetist"[147] through its apportionment of a signifying pureness to the totality of the sense of the spoken word imbuing everything with a plenitude of meaning. Anti-ethnocentrism is equated with the spirit of Rousseau by the courting of a "semiological authenticity" of expression steeped in the recitative "memory and oral tradition of generations"[148] of supposedly "pre-literate" peoples.

For Derrida, the scene at question is not the example of the origin of writing among the Nambikwara, but "only that of the *imitation* of writing,"[149] a borrowing with no invention, transmission, or institutive effusion with the chance of repeatability. The demonstrativity of the event Lévi-Strauss orchestrates thus

displays the excesses of action *without knowing,* a playing on the cultural politics of signification, its objectifying of a value system or a system of values,
that essentially works against its pretender and does not hone a theory of the sign
or signing that could be used for the communication of ideas rather than for the
ruse perpetuating the "bad faith" of self-conscious misdirection. Within the space
of this parable of "sociological purposes" (a question of intersubjective function)
and "intellectual ends" (a question of cognitive goal-orientation) *"outside of
speech,"* the ethnologist begins to "think writing,"[150] as Derrida explains, the
"split between the factual certainty and its interpretative reconsideration"[151] being
of special interest to distinguish between the reporting of an "extraordinary inci-
dent" and philosophical reflection. The difference of the "close-up" involvement
of the description of the experience given and the introspective indulgence of the
analytical "viewing-of-the-incident-from-afar" that follows certainly brings together the antinomy of reflections Lévi-Strauss has on the corruption of knowledge and power by moving between the anthropological need for "identification"
(participation) and the scientific requirement of "distanciation" (objectivation) to
effectively "trademark" the interpretation of the negative effects of the rise of
literacy through an ideological confounding of the dictates of law and the persua-
siveness of authority to criticize the violence of the letter. Writing is hailed as a
late cultural arrival "not at all pertinent to the appreciation of historical rhythms
and types."[152] An assertion that by extension denies the "specificity [conceded] to
the scientific project and to the value of truth in general"[153] in terms of the unstable fluctuations of a quantitative advancement of knowledge. But there are
problems with the logic of this perspective that Derrida will take careful note of
to break down the cultural unilinearity of universal standards of progress Lévi-
Strauss establishes by "exoticizing" the otherness of the Other in the ethnocentric mirage of a stereotypical "primitivism" to deny the Nambikwara writing as a
community of "innocent and unoppressive speech":[154]

> Is not the notion of the quantity of knowledge suspect? What is a quantity of
> knowledge? How is it modified? Without speaking of the science of the or-
> der or of quality, we may wonder what the quantity of the science of pure
> quantity signifies. How can it be evaluated in quantity? Such questions can
> only be answered in the style of pure empiricity. Unless one attempts to re-
> spect the very complex laws of the capitalization of learning, something
> that cannot be done without considering writing more attentively. One can
> say the opposite of what Lévi-Strauss says and it would be neither truer nor
> more false. One can say that during such and such a half-century, even before
> "modern science," and today every minute, the accretion of knowledge has
> gone infinitely beyond what it was for millennia. So much for accretion. As
> for the notion of fluctuation, it presents itelf as perfectly empirical. In any
> case, propositions of essence can never be made to fit a scale.[155]

As Derrida finds it, because many types of "script" preceded the alphabet, the
institution of the "deep structures [social, economic, technical, political, and so
on] upon which we still live"[156] are the result of a "theoretically infinite transmissibility"[157] of knowledge only thinkable with a "methodicity" for the archiv-

ing of information. That writing—in this extended discretion of the *arche-trace of the mark of the sign*—is the "indispensable condition" of the possibility of the fruition and advancement of knowledge, "that there is no science without writing,"[158] is the issue Lévi-Strauss cannot avoid, and "his entire argument founders on or is contaminated by the gross mark of empirical approximation"[159] legitimating in itself the ethnocentrism of the Western prejudice for a model of pure speech at the very moment when "writing as the criterion of historicity or cultural value is not taken into account."[160]

The description of the "historical facticity" of the evolution of the organic conditions of "civilization" is in total conformation with the political ideology of a Marxian vision of the institution of "capitalist society." And here, in what is more than an observational exposition of evidence or proof to support this thesis, a startling conclusion is stated by Lévi-Strauss: "If my hypothesis is correct, the primary function of writing as a means of communication is to facilitate the enslavement of other human beings."[161] However extreme the judgment may seem to be, it is also an example of the metaphysical recuperation of a "cognitive materialism" valorizing the "vocative" or "dative" dimension of language as the *living presence of speech* to be the performative equivalent of the communicative enunciation of the truth of meaning.[162] Derrida reacts by confirming the thesis with some essential modifications at the ethical level of its "politology":

> It has long been known that the power of writing in the hands of a small number, caste, or class, is always contemporaneous with hierarchization, let us say with political *différance*; it is at the same time distinction into groups, classes, and levels of economico-politico-technical power, and delegation of authority, power deferred and abandoned to an organ of capitalization. This phenomenon is produced from the very onset of sedentarization; with the constitution of stocks at the origin of agricultural societies. Here things are so patent that the empirical illustration that Lévi-Strauss sketches could be infinitely enriched. This entire structure appears as soon as a society begins to live as a society, that is to say from the origin of life in general, when, at very heterogeneous levels of organization and complexity, it is possible to *defer presence,* that is to say *expense* or consumption, and to organize production, that is to say *reserve* in general. This is produced well before the appearance of writing in the narrow sense, but it is true, and one cannot ignore it, that the appearance of certain systems of writing three or four thousand years ago was an extraordinary leap in the history of life. All the more extraordinary because a prodigious expansion of the power of *différance* was not accompanied, at least during these millennia, by a notable transformation of the organism. It is precisely the property of the power of *différance* to modify life less and less as it spreads out more and more. If it should grow *infinite*—and its essence excludes this *a priori*—life itself would be made into an impassive, intangible, and eternal presence: infinite *différance,* God or death.[163]

Lévi-Strauss creates an absolute identification between culture and violence or between writing and violence that exhibits as self-evident the real-world impossibility of the liberation of humanity by the unjustly wielded power of a textualized code of undiscriminating law. The combination of the drive to eradicate illiteracy through compulsory schooling, combined with military service, the stratification of society, and the policing of the enforcement of adherence to a particular order of executive power in the legislation of rules of behavior is considered evidence of the intent of this oppression. The "happy co-incidence" of these duties and responsibilities mandating the diminishment of the freedom of the citizen by the State exists so, as Lévi-Strauss asserts it, "authority can decree that 'ignorance of the law is no defence'"[164] to the transgression of a specific "generality of [ethical] and political interest"[165] upheld thanks to the hegemonism of a ruling minority. Derrida does not simply oppose a classical system of the critique of writing. On one level, as we have explained above, he acknowledges it as having some merit. However, the idea of an "enslaving violence [being] assigned to a total literacy"[166] is rejected because it cannot be "rigorously deduced from these premises"[167] that liberty is the result of "illiteracy and the absence of compulsory military service, public instruction or law in general."[168] The "libertarian ideology"[169] Lévi-Strauss assumes to protect the "anti-colonialist and anti-ethnocentric hue"[170] of his text—its being "misread" or "wrongly interpreted"—is paradoxical to the Rousseauistic imperative for an intersubjective negotiation of social contract and the communal consent of a self-fulfilling vision of the non-violent association of beings. Driven as the ethnologist is by the "phono-logo-centrism" of a "metaphysics of presence," the adoption of a univocal conception of Law and State, freedom and equality that substitutes the illusion of the idyllic harmony described among the Nambikwara with the revolutionary call for an anarchical resistance to the violence of writing is somewhat unusual, contradictory even. And yet it is because of an ethical edge to the *bricolage* of structural anthropology that Lévi-Strauss confesses the desire to achieve a reconciliation of the difference of culture with a hypothetical sameness to be found amid an innocent nature so as to reduce or eradicate the degradation of the unity of community by the insurmountability of intersubjective violence. For Derrida, the "accidental finitude"[171] of such an attitude and the objectivization of its metaphysical valuations of the voice produces results paralleling the negative effects of the "demagogic harangue"[172] of the State and the "unneighborliness" of "modern" society objected to in the first place:

> Finally, the value of "social authenticity" is one of the two indispensable poles of the structure of morality in general. The ethic of the living word would be perfectly respectable, completely utopian and a-topic [*utopique et atopique*] as it is (unconnected to *spacing* and to difference as writing), it would be as respectable as respect itself if it did not live on a delusion and a non-respect for its own condition of origin, if it did not dream in speech a presence denied to writing, denied by writing. The ethic of speech is the *delusion* of presence mastered.[173]

By construing the exclusion of writing to be the criterion for the "social authenticity" of the Nambikwara, "the image of a community immediately present to itself, without difference,"[174] Lévi-Strauss "uses this dream [of 'transparent proximity in the face-to-face of countenance and the immediate range of the voice']¹⁷⁵ as one weapon or instrument among others,"¹⁷⁶ in a celebration of the Other that manages to deny the difference and *différance* of otherness due to the metaphysical idealism of the representation of alterity as the logocentric paralogism of a "good" versus "evil" structure of identity. The desire to escape violence and repression by rejecting the manifestations of culture and writing is to endeavor to think the unthinkable, for what comes before the "already-there-ness" of institutionalized values and the exteriority of a form of language once the effect of origins are objectified in an inaugurating logic of the selfsame is "always already" unreachable. And does this serious dilemma not descry "the question of the relations between belonging and opening, the question of the closure"¹⁷⁷ that opposes and supports the totality and the infinity of the call to the Other? Within this muted expressivity of a positive and negative proximity is the subject "drawn out" from its own isolation or inwardness to a state of transcendence beyond the confines of the egological essence of its own being. The idea of phonologocentrism Derrida examines in the context of ethnology identifies the cognitive dimension of thought itself with the creation of hierarchies, oppositions, and structures of exclusion. It is a hermeneutical violence Lévi-Strauss repeats as an ethnocentrism replicated in the name of anti-ethnocentrism by a discharging of what is the only ethical possibility; that is, the *différance* of the writing of the Other.

The Subject of *Différance*: Re-writing the Ethicity of the Sign

For Derrida, Lévi-Strauss, like Saussure, Plato, Aristotle, and Rousseau, among others, excluded writing "as a phenomenon of exterior representation, both useless and dangerous."¹⁷⁸ This, of course, was a metaphysical judgment safeguarding the reduction of the exteriority of the sign for the sake of the voice. For Saussure, for example, the logocentric favoring of the seeming presence of one over the absence of the other must have been justified by the model of "phonetic-alphabetic"¹⁷⁹ script used to delimit language, a "type" sustaining the impression of *presenting speech* while simultaneously erasing "itself before speech."¹⁸⁰ Conversely, Derrida has tried to show "there is no purely phonetic writing, and that phonologism is less a consequence of the practice of the alphabet in a given culture than a certain ethical or axiological *experience* of this practice."¹⁸¹ Within this practicability of metaphysics, the implication is clearly as follows:

> Writing should erase itself before the plenitude of living speech, perfectly represented in the transparency of its notation, immediately present for the subject who speaks it, and for the subject who receives its meaning, content, value.¹⁸²

The most significant point for Derrida is "not only not to privilege one substance—here the phonic, so-called temporal, substance—while excluding another—for example, the graphic, so-called spatial, substance—but even to consider every process of signification as a formal play of differences."¹⁸³ The enigmatic modification deconstituting and dislocating the "linear expressivity" of the sign reinforces the need to ask the question, How can "grammatology" be introduced, and with it "writing" and "text" or "textuality" in the deconstructive sense of the articulation of an "non-disciplinary" object, when there seems to have been a neutralization of "every substance, be it phonic, graphic, or otherwise?"[184] We may possibly receive the following answer from Derrida: "Of course it is not a question of resorting to the same concept of writing and of simply inverting the dissymmetry that now has become problematical."[185] And, to be more specific, the broader and more radical re-defining of the concept of writing that is proposed to encompass every kind of expression, communication, and coding (phonic, graphic, artistic) "can be called *gram* or *différance*."[186] The distinguishing characteristic of this semio-scriptology would be the "play of differences" involving the interweaving of syntheses and references, but not to the extent that a "simple element" of its significo-psychic generation would be "present in and of itself, referring only to itself"[187] as the auto-affective arbiter of complete, unmitigating and unrelenting, sense.

As such, the "text" and "textuality" of this writing is a *chaining of signs,* not simply sign-functions standing in for a (cultural) center of mediated meaning, but "only, everywhere, differences and traces of traces,"[188] within which the "gram" would come to be *the most general sign and semiology would be therefore reconstituted as grammatology.* This is the clarification of the outline Derrida presents for the *"science of a new writing."* Since the gram "is a structure and a movement no longer conceivable on the basis of the opposition presence/absence"[189] and flourishes within the codic play of differences, it is as *différance* that the grammatological conversion of semiology takes place via deconstruction. There are some crucial sticking points, however, that we must address. On the basis of the above function, *différance* is incompatible "with the static, synchronic, taxonomic, ahistorical motifs in the concept of structure"[190] and yet, contrastingly, it is *not* "astructural." Derrida insists on this because the "systematic and regulated transformations"[191] in the specificity of its general workings are able to develop, in certain cases, "the most legitimate principled exigencies of 'structuralism.'"[192] That would be, for example, in the extended concatenation of sytagmatic units of expression whose traces are *deferred* and *multiplied* to some degree within the *differential* or *fragmented* proportionality of discursive or narrative structures. And here we come to the crux of the matter we must next follow, as Derrida defines it. It cannot be said from this vantage that some "present and in-*different* being"[193] in any shape or form "precedes *différance* or spacing,"[194] for example, a subject "who would be the agent, author, and master of *différance,*"[195] or upon whom *différance* would impose itself. Why? Because, to Derrida, "Subjectivity—like objectivity—is an effect of *différance,* an effect inscribed within a system of *différance.*"[196] We will now begin to evaluate the implications of this claim—the effectivity of why and how it is made—for the phenomenality of the writing of Being, the being written, all that relates deconstruction and the institution of pedagogy in the cultural politics of the sign. It would seem, at least for the moment, that the ethico-axiological agency of the "being-present" of the sign, *its being as presence,* is forever undercut as such, and with it is summarily extinguished the metaphysical light of both the educational edifice of a valuation of truth and the psychological comfort of a sense of origin.

The most affable text for gauging the complexity of these ramifications is "Différance," the lecture Derrida addressed to the *Société Française de la Philosophie* on January 27, 1968.[197] As is noted in the preamble to the discourse "proper," the French verb *différer,* like the Latin *differre,* suggests two meanings of association, "to differentiate" and "to delay," thus relating the idea of difference in two dissimilar ways:

> On the one hand, it indicates difference as distinction, inequality, or discernability; on the other, it expresses the interposition of delay, the interval of a spacing and temporalizing that puts off until "later" what is presently denied, the possible that is presently impossible. Sometimes the *different* and sometimes the *deferred* correspond [in French] to the verb "to differ." This correlation, however, is not simply one between act and object, cause and effect, or primordial and derived.
>
> In the one case "to differ" signifies non-identity; in the other case it signifies the order of the *same.* Yet there must be a common, although entirely *différante,* root within the sphere that relates the two movements of differing to one another. We provisionally give the name *différance* to this *sameness* which is not *identical.*[198]

Using the letter "a" from the present participle of the verb *différer,* e.g., "*différante,*" Derrida constructs the noun *différance,* a new word, a "non-word" that is, in his estimation, a "non-concept"—profoundly ametaphysical—precisely because it cannot be either "narrowed down" or "fixed" to a single part of both of its meanings. It is perhaps the penultimate of deconstructive terms, if that were possible in this *post-structural* sense, given that the difference of *différance* is only perceptible *in writing,* since the change of spelling is inaudible—the "e" for which the "a" is substituted is silent to the (French) ear. Thus, the "semanteme" that is "neither a *word* nor a *concept*"[199] expresses both meanings of differentiation as spatio-temporality and as the movement that structures each kind of dissociation in the "middle voice" between passivity and activity like the penumbra of an irreducible origin of production. It is perhaps the offspring of the monstrosity Derrida predicts at the end of his famous lecture at Yale University, "Structure, Sign, and Play in the Discourse of the Human Sciences" (1966), deconstruction already having given form in itself to a *species of non-species marking the un-namable in the alterity of a philosophical subject metaphysics cannot stomach or mouth.* And here it would be tempting—yes it is—to consider *différance* an operating principle, to criticize it as the ambi-valent counterpart to a philosophy of origin upon which the Other must rely or fall. But this would also be to mis-understand, not to do justice to the interpretative formativity of a "doubling commentary" Derrida has said is possible at some minimal parameters of signification,[200] by representing *différance* as external to identity instead of it being always already within the non-indicative self-relation of the being written of Being, modifying the *here* and *now* "at the zero-point of the subjective origin."[201] What it is that it does to the sign—for our purposes *the trace of the writing of the Self as Other*—is evident in the semiological prospectus of signification: the structural necessity of its repeatability, or re-iteration, beyond a single, unitary point of expression. If we acknowledge, as we should, that a "sign" can signify *only through the force of repetition,* the consequences of *différance* render the sign relational rather than identical (e.g., not the self-same, or "iconic," possessing the properties of its "referent"), thus bringing indication into line with expression to undo the Husserlian idea of a "pre-expressive intentionality" of pure consciousness. This line of argument de-centers the subject, brings it out of the shell of the Cartesian *cogito* that shelters its attempt at realizing the security of a self-discourse with itself—what Derrida shows to be an instance of non-communication, because in the equating of self-hood with self-presence, the Other is effaced to the point where an inner-monologue with one's "Self" is not really an instance of transmissibility at all, but the self-deceptive verification of the desire for auto-affection. Or an attempt at the reduction of *différance.* In order to ascertain the existence of itself, a subject must refer outside of itself to the *world of the signs of the Other* using the resources of what does not begin "within" itself, therefore striving to refrain from obliterating itself just as it seems to have authenticated its existence. It is this relational aspect that Derrida makes us aware of about the ethical grounding of *différance* by referring to the constitutive function of the *sign-trace* of the Other; the deferring difference between presence and repetition, self and non-self, reveals itself as undecidability at the proliferative core of identity.

Returning, once again, to the text of the lecture, Derrida suggests that *différance* is or can stand for "the juncture—rather than the summation—of what has been most decisively inscribed in the thought of what is conveniently called our 'epoch.'"[202] An age of the irreducible play of the sign summarized as the delimitation of onto-theo-logy, of the metaphysics of presence (logocentrism) and the possibility of an ethical opening of the subject toward the difference of the Other. The following are given as examples of the reason of the proto-typical thinkers leading to *différance*: "the difference of forces in Nietzsche, Saussure's principle of semiological difference, differing as the possibility of [neurone] facilitation, impression and delayed effect in Freud, difference as the irreducibility of the trace of the other in Levinas, and the ontic-ontological difference in Heidegger."[203] All of these individuals have no doubt figured greatly in the elaboration of Derrida's *working of deconstruction,* but more importantly the list displays the "discoveries" or "inventions" of varying fields from the history of philosophy to theology and psychoanalysis that have changed or altered perceptions of the ethics of Western metaphysics in their refusal to be subdued or dominated by the dizzying substitutions of master signs within its self-enclosed system of truth and meaning. The exposition of the breadth of the contributions to the theory of *différance* makes a previous point quite clear: *différance* is not only "irreducible to every ontological or theological—onto-theological—reappropriation, but it opens up the very space in which onto-theology—philosophy—produces its system and its history. It thus encompasses and irrevocably surpasses onto-theology and philosophy."[204] The alogicality of its structure also prevents an aforeplanned linearity within the reading of the writing of signs, for example, the ordering of a "reason" of strategy or of finality of purpose, a tacticality toward teleology, "philosophical-logical discourse"[205] and its symmetrical opposite "logico-empirical speech."[206] The alternative to these more or less traditional discourses of epistemological fortitude and forbearance is a "semiotics" of the play of difference as *différance,* a subject Derrida favors and has little difficulty in handling regarding elements of the teachings of Nietzsche, Freud, Saussure, Heidegger, and Levinas.

With respect to Nietzsche and Freud, both are excellent examples within the context of the lecture because they "often in a very similar way, questioned the self-certitude of consciousness"[207] and showed up the traumatizing elisions of the substantive Self of metaphysics that wrought the pragmatological center of a pedagogical en-framing *(Ge-Stell)* of being. The main point for Derrida is that this was done "by starting out with the theme of *différance.*"[208] An accurate, but nevertheless, audacious claim. Concerning Nietzsche, the understanding of *différance* is evident to Derrida in his argument that "'the important main activity is unconscious'"[209] and that "consciousness is the effect of forces whose essence, ways, and modalities are not particular to it."[210] The force determining consciousness, as we have said earlier, being *never present as presence to itself,* but rather, "only [as] a play of differences and quantities."[211] The "postulating" of *différance* in Nietzsche correlates to a "symptomatology" diagnostic of the "adiaphoristic repression"[212] and indifference of a philosophy dedicated to the Same at the expense of the Other, *a pedagogy of the one and only Reason.* The postmetaphysical interpretation, however, does qualify *différance,* not as "the disclosure of truth as a presentation of the thing itself in its presence,"[213] but as "an incessant deciphering,"[214] an on-running hermeneutics of *ressentiment* based on a "cipher without truth, or at least a system of ciphers that is not dominated by truth value."[215] And the struggle to demythologize the objectification of the meaning of a Will to the Power forming an *economy of interests weighed against interests* according to the profit of function is consequently "understood, inscribed, and circumscribed"[216] within the history of episteme and philosophy. Nietzsche, Derrida will say, thought "this active (in movement) discord of the different forces and of the differences between forces"[217] in direct opposition "to a system of metaphysical grammar, wherever that system controls culture, philosophy, and science."[218]

With Freud—leaving Saussure to the side, for we will have dealt with him earlier—another "diaphoristics," this time a questioning of "the primacy of presence *qua* consciousness"[219] is transformed to a psychoanalytic questioning of the authority of consciousness. The two meanings of *différance* as differentiation and deferral are inextricably fused in Freud's thought, especially in the concepts of the trace *(Spur),* facilitation *(Bahnung),* memory *(Erinnerung),* inscription *(Niederschrift),* and the repressive reserve *(Vorrat)* of delay *(Nachträglichkeit).* Derrida emphasizes the play of this structure of psychic *retardement,* developed in *Beyond the Pleasure Principle,* that suggests the ego's drive toward self-preservation motivates the temporary displacement of the pleasure principle by the reality principle, but without surrendering the drive to an ultimate increase in pleasure, thereby requiring the temporary suspension of gratification through the willful tolerance of displeasure. Within the vision and certitude of the prevalent system of thinking we have called after deconstruction, "metaphysical," that requires the objectification of the value of its "content" as "form" in the act of teaching *(enseignement)*, the exteriority of language inscribes the interiority of consciousness from the production of the intersubjective violence of a welcomed *socius*. In this sense of the transitive apportionment of the Self to the *infinity of the secret of the Other*, the thought of Emmanuel Levinas is anything but psychoanalytic. And so Derrida confirms by maintaining that the Heideggerian "forgetting of Being" acknowledges the radicality assigned to *ethics as first philosophy*, an assertion already expressed in Edmund Husserl's conception of phenomenology. In *Speech and Phenomena*, Derrida will have come to deconstructive terms with, *on the one hand*, the intuition of essence analogous to perception adequating the act of cognition with "the thing" of its object and, *on the other*, the possibility that the apodicticity of evidence requires no adequation of the phenomenality of its apperception beyond the retensions and protensions of experience, a consciousness of a past and future ego. Or a consciousness of *"other selves,"* a presupposition of the recognition of materiality—the body of the Other, physical presence, etc.—for the exteriority of "a thing" outside "the Self" is not reducible to the presentation of the language of its re-presentation. Derrida accepts this as a justification for the infinite transcendence of the Other, a positive infinitude of the ego involved in the inability to actualize a totality of experience, but paralleling by "analogical appresentation" the Self's relation to the Other as the Other's ego to one's own. This is a "peaceful" resolution of the rendering of the "sense" of subjectivity. The result is the approximation of experience that solidifies the alterity of the Other, the being of the Self depending on the being of another ego, and this transcendental economy of Hussurlean phenomenology does not do violence to the Other Derrida has claimed against Levinas, because it respects the difference of being: "Levinas *in fact* speaks of the infinitely other, but by refusing to acknowledge an intentional modification of the ego—which would be a violent and totalitarian act for him—he deprives himself of the very foundation and the possibility of his own language."[220] It is not a question of transcendental phenomenology as "metaphysical idealism" or "metaphysical realism" because in the suspension of empirical and metaphysical "factuality" there is at least some semblance of "non-neutrality" garnered through the intentional quality of the ego as the basis for language and subjectivity that shows up in the equating of exteriority as an openness to the Other. Is this a paradox or an incoherence with respect to fundamental ontology? Derrida comments:

> It is true that Ethics in Levinas' sense, is an Ethics without law and without concept, which maintains its non-violent purity only before being determined as concepts and laws. This is not an objection; let us not forget that Levinas does not seek to propose laws or moral rules, does not seek to determine *a* morality, but rather the essence of the ethical relation in general. But as this determination does not offer itself as a *theory* of Ethics, in question, then is an Ethics of Ethics. In this case, it is perhaps serious that this

Ethics of Ethics can occasion neither a determined ethics nor determined laws without negating and forgetting itself. Moreover, is this Ethics of Ethics beyond all laws? Is it not the Law of laws? A coherence which breaks down the coherence of the discourse against coherence—the infinite concept, hidden within the protest against the concept.[221]

What sort of discourse can be beyond the scope of the law as external to the phenomenological closure of the frame of the logic of reference? There is difficulty in responding to or philosophizing about what is *otherwise than being.* Especially, for Levinas whose discourse, Derrida reminds us, seems to be all about the ethics of discourse itself, the engagement and aversion of intersubjective violence in the face-to-face relation with the Other. But the concept of "the trace and the enigma [that is also an opening] of absolute alterity, that is, the Other [*autrui*]"[222] certainly parallels the give-and-take of psychic (dis)indications that led to the inscription of the Freudian rebus of the unconscious, a "mystic writing-pad" of the mind, dis-covered by dis-arming the pedagogical value of the "teaching-being" and the "being-taught" of a face-to-face exchange of hidden memory with the self. Yet, to go further in another direction, Nietzsche occupies a more prominent position in the lecture itself and is "held up" in conjunction with the significance of Heidegger for deconstruction, in all probability the intellectual figure to whom Derrida is most closely tied, yet also the furthest from. *On the one hand,* it must be said that "in a particular and strange way, *différance* [is] 'older' than the ontological difference or the truth of Being,"[223] because in its horizon is born and bound the play of the deferral of traces demarcating the living-depth of existence. *On the other hand,* Heidegger pioneered the "epochality" of textuality and language, the insight making a rethinking of the Being of beings possible, but not "actual." Derrida believes that we "must stay within the difficulty of this passage [of ontological difference, recognizing the necessity for it as a *point of reference among others*]; we must repeat this passage in a rigorous reading of metaphysics, wherever metaphysics serves as the norm of Western speech, and not only in the texts of 'the history of philosophy.'"[224] This two-sided "tack" is in itself the responsibility of an ethic of *différance,* of difference and deferral, the non-end of a keeping within to move beyond the present to the future.

Derrida will ask, here as elsewhere, a more fundamental question intriguingly posed, after Heidegger and the unfolding of the language of BEING SPEAKING, exterior to the "in-stallment" of signification: "How do we conceive of the outside of a text?"[225] We could reply to this unanswerable question with another: How do we conceive of the inside of a text? And to some extent we have been broaching an answer to the radical opening of the ethics of both of these impossible *aporias* all along.

For Loose Ends:
At the Proximity of a Teaching of the Other

Deconstruction integrates semiological difference within the radical irreducibility of the infrastructurality of *différance* marking the *arche-trace of the Other* to expose how the telepathy of the *logos* is deferred by the self-effacement, erosion, *phthora,* of the plenitude of the *eidos* of presence. Derrida—complicating the "archive fever"[226] of Western epistemology at the base of its desire to exclude the "im-proper," that which does not belong to the *"place of consignment,"*[227] by re-introducing the idea of an outside to the eco-nomy of the *arkheion*—begins to address the relative specificity of the larger question *"of pedagogy"* around a re-thinking of the classical thematizations of the nature/culture opposition of meta-physics, its main pragmatico-logical focus. The engagement of deconstruction with what it means *to think, to learn, to teach, to know* takes shape in the "early" texts comprising the biblio-blitz of the collection of "writings" appearing alongside *Of Grammatology* as a resituating of the intelligibility of the institu-tionalization of knowledge at the level of the historicity of the sign. Or, what are the socio-theo-philosophical sources of a *non-natural ethics before and after the letter of writing.* Deconstruction convenes post-structural interventions into topical variations of the educational problematic (origins, mimesis, nature, "primitivism," childhood, reason, etc.) around the issue of the paradoxical stric-ture of supplementarity, the middle-ground between the *fullness* of presence and the *lack* of absence, to show that there is no neutral or apolitical safe haven of language or representivity, an unmediated, "un-policed" point of decidable exteri-ority, from which to approach the horizon of intersubjective violence, the line-arist techniques of the repetition of impressionability. The ethico-theoretical hierarchy of the cultural politics of the sign privileging an edifying speech can-not persevere, as such, after the dis-position of an ideal of objectivity as dis-continuous with the reality of an ethnocentric deflation of the grapheme exacted at the expense of the heterogeneity of the writing of the Other. That is, the graft-ing of subjective originarity from within the play of the interiority of con-sciousness and the exteriority of the pro-jection of being. What counter-acts the irresponsibilizing drive of metaphysics to secure a teleological trajectory of the subject for its "just completion" along the lines of a teaching of a normative ethics, a normative ethics of teaching, is the deconstructive obligation to grant a vertiginous plurivocity to the re-tracing of semiological difference as the deferral of the self-presence of the sign, the law of an open-ended justice always already set beyond the divisibility of nature and culture in the order of *différance* and the impossibility of gaining access to a single and determinate Truth.

Notes

1. Jacques Derrida, *Of Grammatology,* trans. Gayatri Chakravorty Spivak (Bal-timore: Johns Hopkins University Press, 1974), 139-140. (Translation has been modified.)

2. This is the alternate name—a *"re-name"*—Drucilla Cornell gives deconstruc-tion for its ability to push the boundaries of ethics, law, logic, and so on in a book by the same title, *The Philosophy of the Limit* (New York: Routledge, 1992). See also on the question of the deconstructive economy of limits, boundaries, margins, and so on as addressed through a variety of themes, Herman Rapaport, *Heidegger & Derrida: Reflections on Time and Language* (Lincoln: University of Nebraska Press, 1989); Irene Harvey, *Derrida and the Economy of Différance* (Bloomington: Indiana

University Press, 1986); Bill Martin, *Matrix and Line: Derrida and the Possibilities of a Postmodern Social Theory* (Albany: State University of New York Press, 1992); and Arkady Plotnitsky, *In the Shadow of Hegel: Complementarity, History, and the Unconscious* (Gainesville: University of Florida Press, 1993).

3. Derrida, *Of Grammatology,* 7-8.

4. Derrida, *Of Grammatology,* 8.

5. Derrida, *Of Grammatology,* 6.

6. Derrida, *Of Grammatology,* 8.

7. Derrida, *Of Grammatology,* 7.

8. Derrida, *Of Grammatology,* 8.

9. Derrida, *Of Grammatology,* 8. (Translation modified.)

10. Jacques Derrida, *Positions,* trans. Alan Bass (Chicago: University of Chicago Press, 1981), 3.

11. Derrida, *Of Grammatology,* 36.

12. Derrida, *Of Grammatology,* 101.

13. Derrida, *Of Grammatology,* 102.

14. Derrida, *Of Grammatology,* 10.

15. Derrida, *Of Grammatology,* 17.

16. Derrida, *Of Grammatology,* 10-11. (Translation modified.)

17. Derrida, *Of Grammatology,* 15.

18. Derrida, *Of Grammatology,* 15.

19. See Jacques Derrida, *Dissemination,* trans. Barbara Johnson (Chicago: University of Chicago Press, 1981) for an extended discussion of the Platonic theory of writing as it is related to and through the idea of the *pharmakon* capacitated by the mythopoieic rendition of the appearance of the letter presented in the *Phaedrus* and the *Philebus.*

20. Derrida, *Of Grammatology,* 11. (Translation modified.)

21. Derrida, *Of Grammatology,* 11.

22. Derrida, *Of Grammatology,* 11.

23. Derrida, *Of Grammatology,* 12.

24. Derrida, *Of Grammatology,* 3.

25. Derrida, *Of Grammatology,* 10. (Translation modified.)

26. Derrida, *Of Grammatology,* 12.

27. Derrida, *Of Grammatology,* 20.

28. Derrida, *Of Grammatology,* 20.

29. Derrida, *Of Grammatology,* 20.

30. Derrida, *Of Grammatology,* 20.

31. Martin Heidegger, *Poetry, Language, Thought,* trans. Albert Hofstadter (New York: Harper & Row Publishers, 1971), 191.

32. Derrida goes over the history of "deconstruction" and its relation to Heidegger's "destruction" in "Letter to a Japanese Friend," trans. David Wood and Andrew Benjamin, in *Derrida and Différance,* ed. David Wood and Robert Bernasconi (Evanston: Northwestern University Press, 1988), 1-11.

33. In Luc Ferry and Alain Renault, *French Philosophy of the Sixties: An Essay on Antihumanism,* trans. Mary H. S. Cattani (Amherst: University of Massachusetts Press, 1990), it is suggested that Derridean deconstruction is a rehashing of Hedeggerianism in the worst sense of a repeating of Heidegger with Derrida's style. But the fundamental differences between the philosophers are ignored on grounds bearing little relation to the specificity of the philosophies of either. It is more a matter, Ferry and Renault claim, of French Heideggerianism not being able to pull itself free from the theme of ontological difference in a facile repetition where nothing is lost

and nothing is gained. The more recent work of Derrida—that in fact comes out of the early texts—is itself an answer to this charge of repeatability. For example, "*Geschlecht,*" "Philopolemology: Heidegger's Ear," "*Geschlecht* II: Heidegger's Hand," *Of Spirit: Heidegger and the Question.*

34. Derrida, *Of Grammatology,* 12.

35. See Martin Heidegger, *Being and Time,* trans. John Macquarrie and Edward Robinson (New York: Harper & Row Publishers, 1962).

36. Derrida, *Of Grammatology,* 12. (Translation modified.)

37. Derrida, *Of Grammatology,* 13.

38. Derrida, *Of Grammatology,* 13.

39. Derrida, *Of Grammatology,* 18.

40. Derrida, *Of Grammatology,* 14.

41. See the dissertation of Umberto Eco (1954) published as *The Aesthetics of Thomas Aquinas* (Cambridge, Mass.: Harvard University Press, 1988).

42. Derrida, *Of Grammatology,* 14.

43. Charles Sanders Peirce and Friedrich Nietzsche were two philosophers who had begun to question the *reason of the sign.* Peirce engaged the problem on pragmatic grounds and Nietzsche on the basis of the genealogy of Western morality.

44. Derrida, *Of Grammatology,* 14.

45. Derrida, *Of Grammatology,* 14.

46. Derrida, *Of Grammatology,* 14-15. (Translation modified.)

47. Derrida, *Of Grammatology,* 14.

48. Derrida, *Of Grammatology,* 17.

49. Derrida, *Of Grammatology,* lxxxix.

50. Derrida, *Of Grammatology,* lxxxix.

51. Derrida, *Of Grammatology,* lxxxix.

52. See Jacques Derrida, "Freud and the Scene of Writing," trans. Alan Bass, i n *Writing and Difference* (Chicago: University of Chicago Press, 1978), 196-231.

53. Derrida, *Of Grammatology,* 15.

54. Derrida, *Of Grammatology,* 15.

55. Derrida, *Of Grammatology,* 15.

56. Derrida, *Of Grammatology,* 15.

57. Derrida, *Of Grammatology,* 17.

58. Derrida, *Of Grammatology,* 15.

59. This is the theme of Jacques Derrida, "Before the Law," trans. Avital Ronell and Christine Roulston, in *Acts of Literature,* ed. Derek Attridge (New York: Routledge, 1991), 181-220; and Jacques Derrida, "The Law of Genre," trans. Avital Ronell, *Glyph* 7 (1980): 176-232.

60. Derrida, *Of Grammatology,* 98.

61. Derrida, *Of Grammatology,* 163.

62. Derrida, *Of Grammatology,* 163.

63. Derrida, *Of Grammatology,* 144.

64. Derrida, *Of Grammatology,* 144-145.

65. Derrida, *Of Grammatology,* 145.

66. Derrida, *Of Grammatology,* 150.

67. Derrida, *Of Grammatology,* 148.

68. Derrida, *Of Grammatology,* 17. (Translation modified.)

69. Derrida, *Of Grammatology,* 145.

70. Derrida, *Of Grammatology,* 144.

71. Derrida, *Of Grammatology,* 144.

72. Derrida, *Of Grammatology,* 149.

73. Derrida, *Of Grammatology*, 145.
74. Derrida, *Of Grammatology*, 145.
75. Derrida, *Of Grammatology*, 146.
76. Derrida, *Of Grammatology*, 147.
77. Derrida, *Of Grammatology*, 248.
78. Derrida, *Of Grammatology*, 247.
79. Derrida, *Of Grammatology*, 247.
80. Derrida, *Of Grammatology*, 147.
81. Derrida, *Of Grammatology*, 147.
82. Derrida, *Of Grammatology*, 245-246.
83. Derrida, *Positions,* 18.
84. Derrida, *Positions*, 18.
85. Derrida, *Positions*, 18.
86. Derrida, *Positions*, 18.
87. See Umberto Eco, *A Theory of Semiotics* (Bloomington: Indiana University Press, 1976) and Algirdas Julien Greimas, *Structural Semantics: An Attempt at a Method,* trans. Daniele McDowell, Ronald Schleifer, and Alan Velie (Lincoln: University of Nebraska Press, 1983).
88. Derrida, *Positions,* 17.
89. Derrida, *Positions*, 17.
90. Derrida, *Positions*, 19.
91. Derrida, *Positions*, 19-20.
92. Derrida, *Of Grammatology,* 73.
93. Derrida, *Positions,* 19.
94. Derrida, *Positions*, 20.
95. Derrida, *Positions*, 20.
96. Derrida, *Positions*, 21.
97. Derrida, *Positions*, 21.
98. Derrida, *Positions*, 21.
99. Derrida, *Positions*, 21.
100. Derrida, *Positions*, 21.
101. Derrida, *Positions*, 21.
102. Jacques Derrida, "The Time of a Thesis: Punctuations," trans. Kathleen McLaughlin, in *Philosophy in France Today,* ed. Alan Montefiore (Cambridge: Cambridge University Press, 1983), 40.
103. Jacques Derrida, "Structure, Sign, and Play in the Discourse of the Human Sciences," trans. Alan Bass, in *Writing and Difference,* 278.
104. Derrida, "Structure, Sign, and Play," 278.
105. Derrida, "Structure, Sign, and Play," 278.
106. Derrida, "Structure, Sign, and Play," 278-279.
107. Derrida, "Structure, Sign, and Play," 279.
108. Derrida, "Structure, Sign, and Play," 279.
109. Derrida, "Structure, Sign, and Play," 279.
110. Derrida, "Structure, Sign, and Play," 279.
111. Derrida, "Structure, Sign, and Play," 279.
112. Derrida, "Structure, Sign, and Play," 279.
113. Derrida, "Structure, Sign, and Play," 279.
114. Derrida, "Structure, Sign, and Play," 279.
115. Derrida, "Structure, Sign, and Play," 279-280.
116. Derrida, "Structure, Sign, and Play," 280.
117. Derrida, *Of Grammatology,* 101.

118. For a detailed reading of the "contradictory allegiances" of the structural ethnology of Claude Lévi-Strauss, especially relating to humanism and "cultural relativism," see Tzvetan Todorov, *On Human Diversity: Nationalism, Racism, and Exoticism in French Thought*, trans. Catherine Porter (Cambridge, Mass.: Harvard University Press, 1993).

119. Derrida, "Structure, Sign, and Play," 282.

120. Derrida, "Structure, Sign, and Play," 282.

121. Derrida, *Of Grammatology*, 101.

122. Derrida, *Of Grammatology*, 106.

123. See Jacques Derrida, "Structure, Sign, and Play."

124. Derrida, "Structure, Sign, and Play," 110.

125. Derrida, "Structure, Sign, and Play," 107.

126. See Clifford Geertz, *Works and Lives: The Anthropologist as Author* (Stanford: Stanford University Press, 1988). Especially the chapters entitled "The World in a Text: How to Read *Tristes Tropiques*" and "Being There: Anthropology and the Scene of Writing."

127. Derrida, *Of Grammatology*, 107.

128. Derrida, *Of Grammatology*, 107.

129. Derrida, *Of Grammatology*, 114.

130. Cited in Derrida, *Of Grammatology*, 110.

131. Cited in Derrida, *Of Grammatology*, 108.

132. Derrida, *Of Grammatology*, 109-110.

133. Derrida, *Of Grammatology*, 110.

134. Derrida, *Of Grammatology*, 125.

135. Derrida, *Of Grammatology*, 127.

136. Derrida, *Of Grammatology*, 112.

137. Derrida, *Of Grammatology*, 125.

138. Derrida, *Of Grammatology*, 83.

139. Derrida, *Of Grammatology*, 114-115.

140. Claude Lévi-Strauss, *Tristes Tropiques*, trans. John Weightman and Doreen Weightman (New York: Pocket Books, 1977), 339.

141. Cited in Derrida, *Of Grammatology*, 125-126.

142. Derrida, *Of Grammatology*, 119.

143. Derrida, *Of Grammatology*, 122.

144. Derrida, *Of Grammatology*, 122.

145. Derrida, *Of Grammatology*, 120.

146. Derrida, *Of Grammatology*, 120.

147. Derrida, *Of Grammatology*, 120.

148. Derrida, *Of Grammatology*, 124.

149. Derrida, *Of Grammatology*, 127.

150. Derrida, *Of Grammatology*, 127.

151. Derrida, *Of Grammatology*, 126.

152. Derrida, *Of Grammatology*, 128.

153. Derrida, *Of Grammatology*, 128-129.

154. Derrida, *Of Grammatology*, 121.

155. Derrida, *Of Grammatology*, 129.

156. Derrida, *Of Grammatology*, 129.

157. Derrida, *Of Grammatology*, 128.

158. Derrida, *Of Grammatology*, 130.

159. Derrida, *Of Grammatology*, 130.

160. Derrida, *Of Grammatology*, 121.

161. Cited in Derrida, *Of Grammatology,* 130.

162. See the interview of Jacques Derrida conducted by Jean-Louis Houdebine and Guy Scarpetta in *Positions* for reasons why deconstruction had up to that time not engaged Marxism.

163. Derrida, *Of Grammatology,* 130-131.

164. Cited in Derrida, *Of Grammatology,* 132.

165. Derrida, *Of Grammatology,* 132.

166. Derrida, *Of Grammatology,* 132.

167. Derrida, *Of Grammatology,* 132.

168. Derrida, *Of Grammatology,* 132.

169. Derrida, *Of Grammatology,* 132.

170. Derrida, *Of Grammatology,* 132

171. Derrida, *Of Grammatology,* 139

172. Derrida, *Of Grammatology,* 137.

173. Derrida, *Of Grammatology,* 139.

174. Derrida, *Of Grammatology,* 136.

175. Derrida, *Of Grammatology,* 138.

176. Derrida, *Of Grammatology,* 138.

177. Jacques Derrida, "Violence and Metaphysics: An Essay on the Thought of Emmanuel Levinas," trans. Alan Bass, in *Writing and Difference,* 110.

178. Derrida, *Positions,* 25.

179. Derrida, *Positions,* 25.

180. Derrida, *Positions,* 25.

181. Derrida, *Positions,* 25.

182. Derrida, *Positions,* 25.

183. Derrida, *Positions,* 26.

184. Derrida, *Positions,* 26.

185. Derrida, *Positions,* 26.

186. Derrida, *Positions,* 26.

187. Derrida, *Positions,* 26.

188. Derrida, *Positions,* 26.

189. Derrida, *Positions,* 27.

190. Derrida, *Positions,* 27.

191. Derrida, *Positions,* 28.

192. Derrida, *Positions,* 28.

193. Derrida, *Positions,* 28.

194. Derrida, *Positions,* 28.

195. Derrida, *Positions,* 28.

196. Derrida, *Positions,* 28.

197. Although the text of this discourse has appeared in many different places, the version of "Différance" I will be using is found in Jacques Derrida, *Speech and Phenomena: And Other Essays on Husserl's Theory of Signs,* trans. David B. Allison (Evanston: Northwestern University Press, 1973), 129-160. (Translations have been modified unless otherwise indicated.)

198. Derrida, "Différance," 129.

199. Derrida, "Différance," 130.

200. See Jacques Derrida, *Limited Inc.,* trans. Samuel Weber and Jeffrey Mehlman, ed. Gerald Graff (Evanston: Northwestern University Press, 1988). The chapter entitled "Afterword: Toward an Ethic of Discussion" is most clear about the misrepresentation of Derridean undecidability and the play of the sign.

201. Derrida, *Speech and Phenomena,* 94.

202. Derrida, "Différance," 130.
203. Derrida, "Différance," 130.
204. Derrida, "Différance," 135.
205. Derrida, "Différance," 135.
206. Derrida, "Différance," 135.
207. Derrida, "Différance," 148.
208. Derrida, "Différance," 148.
209. Derrida, "Différance," 148.
210. Derrida, "Différance," 148.
211. Derrida, "Différance," 148.
212. Derrida, "Différance," 148.
213. Derrida, "Différance," 149.
214. Derrida, "Différance," 149.
215. Derrida, "Différance," 149.
216. Derrida, "Différance," 149.
217. Derrida, "Différance," 149.
218. Derrida, "Différance," 149.
219. Derrida, "Différance," 149.
220. Derrida, "Violence and Metaphysics," 125.
221. Derrida, "Violence and Metaphysics," 111.
222. Derrida, "Différance," 152.
223. Derrida, "Différance," 154.
224. Derrida, "Différance," 154.
225. Derrida, "Différance," 158.
226. See Jacques Derrida, *Archive Fever: A Freudian Impression,* trans. Eric Prenowitz (Chicago: University of Chicago Press, 1996).
227. Derrida, *Archive Fever,* 11.

Chapter Two

The Ends of Pedagogy

From the Dialectic of Memory
to the Deconstruction of the Institution

A typical movement of the Hegelian text: speculative dialectics sets on its course a sometimes quite precise piece of historical information, but without precautions. A certain number of very determined effects result from this, and in the very form of that which Hegel elsewhere criticizes: the juxtaposition of an empirical content with a henceforth abstract form, an exterior form superimposed on that which it should organize. This is manifest particularly in unnoticed contradictions, contradictions without concepts and not reducible to the speculative movement of contradiction.
—Jacques Derrida, "The Pit and the Pyramid:
Introduction to Hegel's Semiology"[1]

Chapter 2 follows the educational force of the "cross-over" in the *translation (Über-setzen)* of the ethnocentric historicity of the sign of the *logos,* the phonetic writing of speech, to the *relève* of the auto-bio-graphy of memory as the motivation for the post-structural re-tracing of the semiological difference of *différance* beyond the dialectical absolutism of the teaching of the speculative Idea. To do this, I offer a reading of a marginalized text of Jacques Derrida, "The Age of Hegel," a deconstructive rereading of a "special report" about the ethico-cultural predicament of philosophical pedagogy within the structure of the Prussian system of "general education" during the early nineteenth century. An "officious" document useful for the political purposes of the State that Hegel was requested to carefully prepare and submit to the Ministry of Public Instruction, the year being 1822. The chapter is divided into three parts. The first part commences by reinvoking the ethical and political circumstances of the text-context relation Derrida elucidates to situate the report Hegel signs within the specificity of the conditions of its necessity and the fate of its reception. With constant reference to deconstruction, the analysis explores how the state of affairs that spawned the "ideology" of the report for the political purpose of actualizing educational policy can be reread through a gauging of the speculative presuppositions of the pedagogical memory of childhood Hegel reveals, as is found in the exposition of the dialectical laws of the philosopher's own texts (e.g., the *Philosophy of Right* and the *Phenomenology of Spirit*). It is followed by a technical analysis of the *auto-bio-graphical* moment of the philosophical age of Hegel. Or what is the reflexive instant of ideality—when the subjective identity of being is concretized through a self-referential writing posed against the reality of itself as an auto-affective recapitulation of the thought of memory thinking itself as stemming from the Hegelian rejuvenation of a Platonistic rewriting of anamnesis *without* the creative intuition of signs. The question at hand here is: How does the signature of the proper name as a life-writing of the Self stabilize the pedagogical "truth" of a childhood memory from the past to sanction the institutionalization of a speculative modality for the teaching and learning of philosophy in the future? The last part moves the deconstructive protocol of reading away from the contradictions of the representation of the empiricity of subjective identity that penetrate the ideology of the report Hegel signs into the actual ethics and politics of the *scene of teaching* to continue to open up to scrutiny the accepted codes or institutional codability of a "dialectical schooling." It ends with a discussion of some of the recommendations Derrida makes to the GREPH for achieving a rewarding critique of the pedagogical institution of philosophy and expands upon their implications.

The Text-Context/Context-Text *Dialangue*

Breaking Down the Philosophical Barriers between Subject, State, and the Educational Institution

> [A]nd if I may be permitted to evoke my own experience . . . I remember having learned, in my twelfth year—destined as I was to enter the theological seminary of my country—Wolf[f]'s definitions of the so-called idea clara and that, in my fourteenth year, I had assimilated all the figures and rules of syllogism. And I still know them.
> —Hegel, *Letter to Altenstein, 16 April 1822*[2]

To begin with then, a rememoration of, and for, a curriculum.

The *auto-bio-graphical* portrayal of a pedagogical moment from childhood is ascribable to the experience of the German philosopher identified by the proper name of Hegel (Georg Wilhelm Friedrich), for his signature sanctions its reiteration *a posteriori* the labor of its extraction, from the nadir of an other time and space that is memory, into writing. Citation to the pastness of this event evokes the historicity of the selfsame subjectivity marked from the auto-appellative force of the signature of the proper name operating as a closing salutation to an "official correspondence." In actuality, the anecdote is not part of a letter at all, but of an "official study" commissioned from Hegel, Derrida reminds us, "by a [Prussian] State bureaucracy in the process of organizing the nationalization of the structures of philosophical education by extracting it, based on historical compromise, from clerical jurisdiction."[3] This *seemingly* wandering digression of subjective thought re-thinking itself in the spontaneous flashing of an interiorizing reflection—the example of a memory of adolescence that interrupts the illustrative contents of the report for *argument's sake*—is anything other than accidental *retors*, a slip of the pen.

What "happens" within the textual confines of this report follows closely on the enforcement of mandatory schooling during the reformation of the pedagogical institution in early nineteenth-century Germany, having been "recently adopted for academic freedom, and the defence of the university against feudal powers."[4] Altenstein, Minister of Public Instruction since 1817—and Hegel's benefactor—proves to be a devoted advocate of the State cause of seeing through the initiation of a *public schooling*.[5] The position he occupies as a career bureaucrat in the dawning of the "age of European civil service"[6] is "sensitive, precarious, vulnerable";[7] it is soon evident to the parties concerned that the struggle against the more resolute among the proponents of feudalism must be waged with "suppleness, negotiation, and compromise"[8] to ensure a complete victory. Hegel—the apologist for the *rationality* of the State (expounded in the three revisions of the *Philosophy of Right* [1822][9] that had, in his own words, "thoroughly scandalized the demagogues")[10]—is desperately needed to assist the "budding bureaucracy"[11] with the major task of enacting the cultural instauration of educational policy. Expediently summoned to Berlin by Altenstein himself, he is unceremoniously offered Johann Gottlieb Fichte's chair and appointed to the university's faculty as Professor of Philosophy.

For Hegel, the intricate subtleties of "networking" to secure faithful alliances of patronage from within the bureaucratic ranks of the state's government is at the personal jeopardy of losing non-political liaisons. That is the cost to be paid, for the stakes, both private and professional, are high, the risks to be taken, immense. An unstable, albeit promising, locality of fortuitous transpositions that creates this sudden opening, it leaves Hegel "caught between the 'feudalists' and the 'demagogues,' giving signs of allegiance to the 'right' when the situation or the relation of forces seems to require that he do so, [while] secretly protecting his persecuted friends on the 'left,'"[12] as Derrida has cause to note of the philosopher's *double bind.* The bureaucratic desire to quell the irrepressible tensions enveloping the contextual field of intersecting though "discrete" interests is all-pervasive (e.g., "this skein where 'private interests' and the interests of historical reason, special interests and the interests of the State, the interests of the particular state and the universal historical rationality of the State are so conveniently intertwined").[13] And the growing urgency of the situation, now being ripe for intervention, underwrites the axiology of the ethico-political premises required to secure the countersigning of *yet-unspoken-of* contracts enjoining philosopher and State in the hard-to-be-fought mission of pedagogical restoration. The institutional and monetary terms of reciprocation—those tangible advantages Hegel explicitly wants and most assuredly will receive after the fierce lobbying of "the same ministerial sponsor"[14] fighting for the privilege of genius—are to be exchanged by the bureaucratic fraternity Altenstein speaks for, in return for the philosopher's unwavering public support of the State's educational policy mandates. The details of the agreement are scrupulously stipulated in the Hegel-Altenstein correspondences prior to as well as after the appearance of the report.[15]

The "pact," once made in principle, is contingent on the immanent eminence of the *proper* name of 'Hegel': a value measurable by the extent of its ability to exert influence on the discourse or the actions of others for the benefit of the State technocracy. Altenstein requires the veneration inspired by the straightforward utterance or re-writing of the sign of 'Hegel' to empower the visionary spirit of his project of educational reform. The legitimating authority of the proper name is adjudicated as the "metalinguistic" expansion of its potential to affect reality by superseding the semiological restrictions of representational forms available for signifying identity. For Derrida, the *laws of proper name* operating here to the obvious advantage of both parties are commensurable with a logocentric aspiration to bridge the pneumatic abyss between writing and difference.[16] Altenstein counts heavily on the symbolic propriety to be derived from the *deictic* stimulus of *onomasia* that the signature of Hegel must consistently and irrefutably validate in spite of the mediacy of language. This totalizing movement from ideality to identity hopes to preserve the continuity of subjectivity and world through the erasure of the absence of the subject in writing. I will return to this again. For now, let us concentrate on analyzing how the "ideological" pretext of the anecdote abides with the stringent pressures the situation places Hegel under to act without haste. How, in Derrida's judgment, a remembrance of childhood as the memory of memory itself "is intended to carry a conviction and pave the way for political decisions"[17] by lending the credibility of intellectual support to a thesis referring to the *"proper age"* for philosophy education.

The strategic reserve of this "techno-bureaucratic region of Hegelian confiding"[18] permeates the unsolicited memory of childhood that the signature of the philosopher ratifies. It works, most conveniently, to counterbalance, *on the one hand,* the politico-economic site of its engendering with, *on the other,* the philosophico-ethical reasons of the arbitration for the attainment of pedagogical ends. Derrida elucidates the extent to which the *implicit* goals of the philosopher and the *explicit* objectives of the State are aligned for the eventual attainment of a speculative knowledge on which to ground the development of learning:

> By addressing his report to Altenstein, he [Hegel] is not simply acting as a "realistic" philosopher, compelled to reason with the powers that be, with the contradictions inherent in these powers, and with his interlocutor's strategy within these contradictions. It is not the powers-that-be *(Le pouvoir)*—considered as a monolithic whole—which are compelled to reckon with the Hegelian system; and indeed, Hegel will say nothing in his pedagogical-philosophical propositions that is not in keeping with this system, a system which, admittedly, can fold and turn in on itself without breaking. Only a *fraction* of the forces in power is represented in the summons to Hegel. At any rate, the space for the intricate negotiations between

the forces in power (however contradictory they may be and however determined may be a particular stasis of contradiction) and Hegel's philosophical strategy must be open, possible, already practicable. Without this, no compromise, no implicit contract would even have been sketched. This space, like the topic upon which it depends, can construe itself neither within Hegel's *oeuvre*—as if something of the sort existed in a pure state—nor in what we could regard as the non-philosophical realm exterior to it. Neither the "internal necessities of the system" alone nor the generally accepted opposition between "system" and "method" can account for the complexity of these contracts or compromises.[19]

Altenstein reinforces "the locus of the exchange and of the contract, the insurance of the one and the assurance of the other"[20] by defending the decision to honor the request Hegel makes (to him) for extra dispensations in consideration for the loyalty of previous services freely rendered unto the State. The minister brings to the attention of the bureaucratic elite not only the scholarly solidity of speculative idealism—the deftness of its demonstrated capacity to repulse the "pernicious infiltration of a philosophy without depth"[21]—but also the admirable skillfulness with which its philosopher "has dashed the presumptions of young minds."[22] Derrida does not fail to tell us how in the report surrendered to Altenstein, Hegel admits he is acutely aware of the State resolve: to prevent "philosophical teaching in the Gymnasium [high school] from losing itself in a babble of hollow formulas *(sich in ein holhes Formelwesen verliere)* or from transgressing the limits of school-teaching."[23] And that there must be the "figment" of a negative educational correlate to speculative philosophy, one whose postulates are supposedly relentless in their unmitigating hostility to the future attainment of a correctively prescriptive *Reason* within the *populus* of the State citizenry.

This refined logic of communitarian universalism is the philosophical bedrock for the State's purpose of working toward the re-inscription of the same through the education of the subject. It solicits the motivational basis entreated to sustain the minister's claim for arbitrarily securing the implementation of one curriculum at the expense of another. The political urgency of implementing "new" educational policy is ideologically structured as the impetus of a perceived need that both philosopher and State commend: first and foremost, to censor the distractions *lesser* philosophical discourse imposes on the indiscriminate tastes of young (and rebellious) minds. Realizing political support to bolster the forcefulness of this educational policy decision that Altenstein urges his collegues to make necessitates the citational authority of the formal recommendations for a propaedeutic Hegel had elaborated in the letter to the Prussian Ministry of Education only months before. Its attainment involves the minister's predicting the answers to the following kinds of questions Derrida would ask about the latent ideology of the presuppositions the philosopher carefully put forward in the concrete form of a "teachable curriculum": "What is the hollowness of formulas? What is babble? Who is to define it? From what point of view? According to what philosophy and whose politics? Does not every new or subversive discourse always constitute itself through rhetorical effects that are necessarily identified as gaps in the prevailing discourse, with the inevitable phenomena of discursive degradation, mechanisms, mimetisms, etc.?"[24] So, for the essential purpose of politically justifying the ethics of the curricular choice Altenstein is seen to have given way to—the "higher reasons" to exclude metaphysics proper from the Gymnasium—Hegel cannot avoid presenting a precise content and methodology of philosophy instruction. One that, he believes, "does not exceed the intellectual capacities *(Fassungskraft)* of Gymnasium students"[25] and would therefore be remediating in its response to the undisciplined transitoriness of juvenile memory.

The apparent complicity of the pedagogical proposal the philosopher endorses with the expressed urgency of the ministerial request can be of no great surprise to Derrida: "[I]n this case [it is] the dialectic of speculative idealism—as a general criteriology that distinguishes between empty and full language in education. And which also determines the limit between schoolteaching and that which lies outside its domain."[26] As we have seen, Hegel's most difficult decisions very naturally display the tendency to predicate the "agendas" of the major actants—those subjects in power—driving the crucial outcomes of this complex situation. Derrida's rhetorical questions punctuate the sharp irony of the alliance when he pointedly asks, "Can we not say that the basis of the negotiation with the ministerial request was extraordinarily narrow? Does this not explain why the Altenstein-Hegel episode was without issue *(sans lendemain)*?"[27]

To return (momentarily) to the autobiographical anecdote of the report.

Taking the stylistic form of an aside, almost an afterthought or a "flashback" of memory, the portrait of childhood self that Hegel puts forward supplies the minister with the *good reasons* for navigating the fine line drawn between the competing discourses of oppositional forces in the political arena. An ethics of commitment to the educational priorities of these *"good reasons"* is above the need to be explained or even broached, modeled as it is after the philosophical conviction of a *naturally progressive* capacity for conceiving the system of the Absolute Idea in the university after the formative years of early schooling. The image of quiet genius Hegel discreetly lays out "justifies itself, thereby effacing its anecdotal singularity by invoking an older common experience *(die algemeine ältere Erfahrung)*."[28] The ideology of its design is intended to bolster political support for a non-speculative propaedeutic the philosopher seeks to promote by a restructuring of core areas of the existing philosophy curriculum around the faculty of *Gedächtnis* (flatly translatable as "memory," but a more apt meaning here due to the pedagogical thrust of expediating the *natural gifts* of the faculty is the classical routine of "rote memorization" or "learning by heart"). The faint aura of a semi-detached humility consolidating the appeal of the representation licenses the implementation of a philosophical curriculum of unproductive memorization. Derrida very succinctly underlines the theoretical importance of a developmental theory of mnemonics to speculative idealism to evoke the well-known recitations of Hegelian philosophy:

> For Hegel, memory was both a beginning and an end; he remembers (his twelfth year) and remembers that he began by remembering that which he first learned by heart. But at the same time, this homology of the system (the dialectical concept of *Gedächtnis*) and of the autobiographical situation that gave Hegel the inducement and freedom to think, this homology is to

be enriched again by its pedagogical version: by beginning with teaching the content of knowledge, before even thinking it, we are assured of a highly determined prephilosophical inculcation which paves the way for good philosophy *(la bonne philosophie).*[29]

The curricular system outlined in the report to Altenstein is most remarkable. It sketches out a method for how the teaching-learning of philosophy should be initiated at an early age beginning with the administering of a highly formalized method of instruction that is intended to facilitate for the *conscientious* transference of ideas, from teacher to student, from writing to mind, etc., via the memorization of preselected "kernels" of knowledge. Insofar as Hegel attempts to react *favorably* to the professional requirements of the episode in its singularity, there is a betrayal of the logic of non-contradiction between his thought and actions that Derrida draws attention to:

> this capacity, to which the little, eleven-year-old Hegel bears witness, i s *not yet* a philosophical capacity as such (that is a speculative capacity, but rather, a memory of certain lifeless contents, contents of understanding *(entendement),* contents that are forms (definitions, rules, and figures of syllogisms). And this not-yet propagates its effects throughout the letter, permeates the entire pedagogical machinery that Hegel proposes to the Minister. This *not-yet* of the *already . . .* interdicts precisely that which it would seem to promote, namely, the teaching of philosophy in the Gymnasium.
>
> When Hegel says that he still remembers the *idea clara* and the syllogistics, we note a mixture of coyness (refinement and play, the put-on puerility of the great mathematician who feigns astonishment that he still remembers his multiplication tables), a certain affected tenderness for the remnants of the child in himself; most of all, a portion of irony in his challenge to pedagogic modernity, "a challenge directed at current prejudices against autonomous thought, productive activity." And what is more current (even today, for the age of Hegel will have lasted that long) than the monotonous pedagogic modernity that takes issue with mechanical memorization, mnemotechnics, in the name of *productive* spontaneity, of initiative; of independent, *living* self-discovery, etc.? But Hegel's irony is double: He knows that he has, elsewhere, objected to mnemotechnic formalism and learning "by heart." We cannot, therefore, suspect him, of being simply and *generally* a partisan of such techniques. It is a question, precisely of age, of the order and teleology of acquisition, of *progress.*[30]

With the appearance of the *Philosophische Propädeutik* in 1808, a good deal before the problematic occlusion of the anecdote related to Altenstein, these public resolutions on the subject of philosophical pedagogy are well documented.[31] Hegel, in fact, had resisted the nostalgia of recapitulating the connivance of teaching matter without meaning by speaking derisively at this time of the dangers of a memorization devoid of "materiality," of a de-accented learning without the "in-signing" of images *(bildlos).*

Textuality, History, Institution

Deconstructing the "Ideology" of Educational Policy Reform: Memories of a Philosophical Child of State Reason

To query the validity of this recollection of childhood that reinforces a pedagogy of memory, Derrida problematizes the generalizability of what is foregrounded in the textual staging of this personal retrospection outlined in the report the philosopher freely signs for "to render apparent the essence of a [curricular] possibility: every normal healthy child could be Hegel. At the moment when the old Hegel remembers the child Hegel, but also thinks him and conceives him in his truth, this child Hegel plays, no doubt, like all children, but plays here the role of a figure or of a moment in the pedagogy of the mind."[32] The "double reading" of the memory episode attended to in "The Age of Hegel" tests the value of its certainty by clarifying the intertext of philosophical arguments germane to working toward a fuller understanding of the *ideology* of the report "proper," e.g., the desire of what is left unsaid, held in reserve, or closely in check as insufficient explanation. It does so by locating the authority of the signature of the life-writing of Hegel at the ethico-political parameters of a discursivized field enframing the tensions of competing socio-economic and epistemological-historical forces vying for sovereignty over the pedagogical institution. And it allows for the allusion to what might be called a *vulgar chronology* evident in the memory Hegel signs for to be played off homonymically against itself, in light of the dialectical precepts of speculative philosophy, by a more eclectic recourse to:

> the basic interpretation of the philosophical "age" as *epochality* (that is, a Heideggerian interpretation that designates the Cartesian event as one of certitude, as a reassuring foundation of subjectivity that becomes the basis of all post-Cartesian metaphysics until and including Hegel). This *epochal* interpretation, with all its machinery, could be connected (either as proof or as derivation) to the Hegelian, onto-teleological interpretation of the philosophical "age" as moment, form, or figure, totality or *pars totalis,* in the history of reason. We could then pose the question whether, in this form or in ancillary ones, such a debate could dominate, indeed could shed light on, the problematic of the structures of teaching . . . —whether that which we first recognize in terms of its regional determinants—psycho-physiological, technical, political, ideological, (etc.)—could be rendered comprehensible by such a debate, or whether it would, instead, force us to revise our premises.[33]

The confluence of this replacement of the epistemic contents of the report the signature of the philosopher valorizes, within the juridical scope of the issues apropos the pedagogical institution and philosophy education, illustrates the importance of the ethical obligation to solve the dilemma that brings together the State and Hegel. This "tactic" enables Derrida to undertake an interpretative modulation in the reading of the "letter" temporarily away from the problem of memory to stress the central question of developmental "age." Or more precisely, the nebulousness of this question of the "age" (both as epochality and as chronology) to be most suitable for the teaching-learning of philosophy.

The warring factors bringing the issue of pedagogy to a climax in the early years of nineteenth-century Prussia are, Derrida contends, "neither simply *within* nor simply *external* to philosophy."[34] Their cumulative effects span the breadth of socio-cultural and ethico-political forces lurking beneath an irreducible aggregate of discourses that imbue the spectrum of ideologies specific to the historical site of the struggle for control over the institution of education, but also reach far beyond the immediate distance of its horizons. Even though conflicting perspectives about outcomes proliferating from the rich signifying frame of such a heterogeneous textuality are often irreconcilable in the end, Derrida lists primary sources to which an interpretation of the "age of Hegel" must refer "for a minimal intelligibility of the Letter":[35]

> Hegel's place [in the context of the situation and the role of the "letter" in the complexity of it] can really not be determined without the simultaneous and structural cognizance of an entire general textuality, consisting (at least) of: (1) his "great" philosophical works, the most obvious being the entire *Philosophy of Right,* which is to say . . . the "three" philosophies of right; (2) his other writings, that is, *at least* all his letters, even the secret ones, those which he hid from the police as an act of solidarity with certain victims of persecution; (3) his actual practice in all the complexity that has always been more or less evident, but which, as we know, cannot be reduced (far from it) during the Berlin period to that of an official and respectful (indeed, obsequious) philosopher of the State.[36]

The hermeneutic stance suggested does not harbor aspirations of accessing *complete understandings* of past actions or events that coordinate the educational problematic of the *age* of Hegel. "Certain of the sharper features of this episode [that is isolated] indeed remain without issue,"[37] the contextualization of the curricular battle revolving around the principal efforts made to resolve "a situation whose political interpretation is immediately and necessarily relevant to the fundamental stakes of all the political struggles in Europe during the 19th and 20th centuries."[38] Derrida goes on to explain:

> rather than constituting a philosophical, political, or pedagogical revolution, it developed (like Hegelian philosophy) and accumulated a past; and to a large extent it has survived. . . . Which is neither to allege that Hegel responded so admirably and in such detail (art or chance?) to a demand formulated *elsewhere,* in the empirical field of historical politics; nor vice versa. But a possibility had been opened to this common language, to all its secondary variations (for Hegel was not the only philosopher to propose his pedagogy, and the entire systematic range of these variations remains to be studied), to its *translatability*. This common possibility is legible *and* transformable neither simply within the philosophical system [of Hegel], if such a thing existed in a pure state, nor in a domain foreign to any sort of philosophy.
>
> Taken in its greatest singularity, the Altenstein-Hegel endeavor was undoubtedly a failure; but the general structure that opened it and that Hegel tried to keep open is where we find ourselves today, and it does not cease to modify its modalities. This what [sic] I call the age of Hegel.[39]

The interpretative thrust of the *retranslation* of philosophy to pedagogy, of text to context impels the deconstructive *rereading* and hence *rewriting* of the archive situating Hegel's age, the contextuality adumbrating the nuances of the report. The re-transcription of the operative expansiveness of this "deceleration of a great philosopher"[40] and "his great philosophemes in their most forceful internal arrangement"[41] expunges the reductionist predilection of arbitrarily historicizing the intellect. Moving diacritically across the rebus of "the past" from the textual demesne of ideas and philosophy to the "actual world" of pedagogy and politics then back again abates the dangers of arbitrarily externalizing the expressivist complexions of the human mind by merely contextualizing thought vis-à-vis the cultural materiality of writing. To assess the magnitude of this erstwhile *minorized* text of Hegel's, it becomes unavoidable for Derrida to furnish an account of, and to account for, a deconstructive tract that would interpolate by finding meaning for the dynamism of a life-work matrix enjoining reality and thought, being and consciousness, history and language.[42] But, again, the interpretative purport is not aimed *locus in quo* at reconstituting the *Zeitgeist* of a metaphysical *logos* that can be attributed *ex post facto* to the textualized products of culture: to render their contents immanently legible as the self-directed projections of a "truthfulness of spirit" symbolic of the times.[43] The "original" or "intentional" meanings of a writing are not concretizable from the *de-reading* of an opaque textuality readily poised to confess the obtainable conditions of its inception within a transparent history reflecting and inhering the facticity of its discursive and narrative structures.

An exegesis of the significance of context to the "production" and "consumption" of the report Hegel writes for Altenstein entails that the axiomatics of the interpretative focus be induced from the culpability of reading the interstices or interspaces of text-context relations. Entering into a cross-textual dialogue pitting the diachrony of textuality and culture against the synchrony of writing and subjectivity, the rereading of the "letter" Derrida presents summarily converges on the discursive ruptures in the conceptual structuring of the argument the philosopher weaves, the framework of an interlocking core of concepts (philosophy, justice, rationality, teaching, etc.) that inscribe the operating space of ideology in the unifying logic of the ideas about education.[44] Analyzing the *thematism* permeating the premises of Hegel's report—e.g., those controlling concepts of speculative dialectics that function in the ideational structuring of the argument to help guide Altenstein and the State in defending the actualization of such specifically reproductive pedagogical or curricular practices—is tied to penetrating the interactions between a symbol system governing stylistic considerations of morphology for encoding the representation of ideas in the form of signs and a social system facilitating a semantic code for the goal of decoding the signs to make them meaningful at some " level" of abstraction beyond sheer referential analogy. What this *"semio-deconstructive"* approach to reading the ideology of the report incurs in "The Age of Hegel" is the obligation of supplying the historiographic means for exploring the *cultural politics of textuality*. Or the critical liability for a surveying of the *rational* bases of sign referent/signifier-signified associations punctuating the conjunctions and disjunctions of the conceptual veneer of language as an interpolation of "reality."

While referring to the curricular pragmatics of teaching-learning that Hegel's report condones, Derrida augurs precisely such an analytic shifting of emphasis to a semiotico-textuality of communication "to move beyond a prestatist problematics of education and of philosophical education."[45] A linking of the semantic consequences of signification to the socio-political and historico-cultural dimensions constituting the discursive field of "Sense" automatically problematizes the articulation and dissemination of meaning as it relates to the controversy over the issue of schooling. The "ideology" of the textuality spun round the concept of "philosophy education" comes to be defined from the uncovering of residual excrescences of value stemming from the exhibited (self-)interest of the parties involved. In "The Age of Hegel," Derrida shows how the ineffable of language belies what are believed to be the *natural* correspondences of sign-referent/signifier-signified relations within the variable structures of this text-context *dialangue*. Instead of the truth of the signs of writing or of discourse, what deconstruction teaches us to read literally *of* the report is the *meaning of its meaning*; or, more generally, how the affectivity of what is negotiated through the retranslation of concepts, turns of mind, progression of thought, values and ideals of individuals, groups, or societies embodied in various textualized forms across the cultural milieus of a historical epoch comes to be enunciated as the *sayable* and the *unsayable*.[46] A semiotic rethinking of text-context distinctions—that Derrida identifies in "The Age of Hegel" with "the original irreducible configuration in which our questions [about education] are asked"[47]—makes it feasible to disrupt the *relative autonomy* once granted ideology to ensure the total reproducibility of meaning-constructions in the subject as the order of the conceptual sense of signification propagated through the media of an inflected discourse. The "linguistic turn" of a deconstructive reading of the report can then illustrate how the written text itself contains self-rationalizing aspects working to normalize the "matter" of a conceptual content while reinforcing the prefigured meanings of a collection of ideas indicative of "Truth." By keeping the semantic network *in tune* with the ideological alterations of the interpretation, the ethical-political idiomatic of the discourse Hegel unfolds seeks "to pass itself off as universal or absolute"[48] in an effort to expedite (in the future) the institutionalization of speculative idealism as a State pedagogy in the age of the concept.

Derrida confronts the problem of the ideological in "The Age of Hegel" by superimposing an array of epistemology-oriented questions on the historico-cultural scene of the "letter" to connect the content of the text with its intraphilosophical context relative to the political conditions that produced the discourse on the role of the State in public education:

> Interpreting the age of Hegel involves keeping in mind this boundless textuality, in an effort to determine the specific configuration that interests us here: the moment at which systematic philosophy—in the process of becoming philosophy of the State, of Reason as the State—begins to entail, more or less obviously, but essentially, indispensably, a pedagogical systematics governed by the necessity of entrusting the teaching of philoso-

phy to state structures and civil servants. The business most certainly began
before Hegel. . . . But can we not date from the age of Hegel the most power-
ful discursive machine of this problematic? Is this not indicated by the fact
that the Marxist, Nietzschean, and Nietzscheo-Heideggerian problematics
that now dominate all questions concerning the relations of education and
the State must still come to grips with Hegelian discourse?[49]

The discourse of a radical resistance to the institution—reflective of an unfettered
will-to-action à la Nietzsche, Marx, or Heidegger—is elided with a transformational re-reading of the metaphysical infrastructure supporting the political use of
ideology prevalent in Hegelian pedagogical architectonics, remediated as it is by
the ethical theory of the State. For Derrida, this "slipping" of Hegelianism or
speculative dialectics into a fusion of philosophy and history in the form of non-
universalizable rules for educational praxis implodes the usual text-context distinctions. As Michael Ryan has correctly observed of demystifying the "applied
ethics" of hegemonies after deconstruction, "Ideology is the political use of
metaphysics in the domain of practice."[50] Derrida, from this perspective, is left
to push the socio-cultural exigencies of this post-Hegelian, post-speculative
ground even further to dissolve the epistemological possibility of an "extradis-
cursive" or linguistically unmediated point of departure from which to study the
report without neglecting the philosophical intricacies of the *concept of age* or
the politicization of what now are well-known reconfigurations of pedagogical
issues surrounding the ethical problem(s) of the state of education and the education of the State that are rehearsed in the "letter" (e.g., What content should be
taught? Who should define it? How should it be defined? How should it be
taught? How should it be implemented in the curriculm?). The text-context rap-
prochement on which to query the ideological basis of the philosophical
propaedeutic Hegel outlines in the report to Altenstein is the space identified by
Derrida to be "between the Idea of the State defined in the third part of *The Philosophy of Right* (reality as an act of substantial will, as a goal in itself, absolute, immobile, knowing what it wants in its universality, etc.) and personal
subjectivity or particularity, whose most extreme forms the modern State has the
power to perfect."[51]

Hegel's *Philosophy of Right*: The Right of Hegel's Philosophy

Hegel did indeed anticipate (philosophically, if not practicably) in *The Philosophy of Right*—the theoretically overdetermined idea or concept of the modern State central to his political thought and on which his conception of education interdepends—the fundamental decree of his commitment, that is, "making
teaching—particularly philosophical teaching—into a structure of the State."[52]
For Hegel, the education *(Bildung)* of subjectivity constitutes the subordination
of individual freedom(s) to an overarching principle of undeniable universality or
"Reason" apprehended from within the Spirit or Mind *(Geist)* and actualized
through its progressive becoming as the essence of Being. The mediacy of a
willful determination of human consciousness culminates vicariously in the
formation of the State: a "hieroglyph of reason"[53] supplying the uncontestable

grounds for existence relative to the socio-political and juridico-ethical constructions of an autotelic nomothetic order (e.g., institutions of civil society, state bureaucracies, military apparatus) constituted from the indissoluble linkage of inner and outer senses of "reality" moving toward the attainment of absolute knowledge.[54] Filling up the void of immanence in its passing to transcendence, this self-determinateness of being as the logic of Being signals the emergence of Objective Spirit from Subjective Spirit and finally a synthetic ascension to Absolute Spirit takes the shape of a tripartite dialectical division encompassing the totality of thought or the finitude of Mind, understanding *(Verstehen)*:

I. Logic: the science of the Idea in and for itself.

II. Philosophy of Nature: the science of the Idea in its otherness.

III. Philosophy of Spirit: the science of the Idea come back to itself out of that otherness.[55]

Affective influences on the distillation of individual identity outside of the rational technologies of self are not discounted *tout court,* but placed in auxiliary importance to the intersubjective nature of a communal development that codifies the nexus of Being from the symbolic products of a shared "cultural capital" or from the results of conscious *energeia* for engendering the *aletheia* (literally the "non-forgetting")[56] of the Spirit (or Mind) and of its reasoned development throughout the enactment of "history." What is crucial to the Hegelian systematic exposition of categories—as an infinitesimal extension of the Kantian imperative toward the apprehension of reality in Spirit (or Mind)—is the continuity of memory *(Gedächtnis)* and the anamnesic interiorization *(Erinnerung)* of empirical knowledge for the procreative unfolding of human self-consciousness. Following the dialectical metaphysics of the speculative stratagem to its "logical" closure, there is a limitation to thought *(Gedanke)* that is bound to the certainty of sensory sources of empirical reality, the perceptual fulfillment of which springs forth a transcendentalized meaning tempered from the *apocalypsis* of Spirit (or Mind) as a "self-producing, self-justifying and self-correcting system, an eternal activity of self-alienation, self-discovery and self-union."[57] Spirit (or Mind) therefore reveals itself in the pronounced ideality of its own "structures" and is verified in the passing through of subjective and objective states of consciousness to "absolute knowing." It bears out its "right" from the detailed logic of a systematic grammar of the conditions of thought, the knowledge that we already possess: for what is not interiorized and subjected to the living memory of itself cannot be known in totality. But what of the valuation of memory in this pedagogical quest for pinpointing the age of philosophical identity Hegel pursues in the report?

Limits of Signing and the Dialectic of Pedagogical Identity: Undecidability, Anamnesis, and the *Life-Writing-of-the-Self*

The idealization of memory in the example of impressionable youth Hegel evinces is permitted by an *a priori* notion of subjectivity. The unitariness of an auto-reflexive reconciliation of consciousness to self-consciousness unwaveringly succors the decidability of the mnemotechnically engineered pedagogical identity that is demarcated to moderate for the truth of a memory of unphilosophical "age." Hegel can attest to the efficacy of this educational methodology as a surviving "model" of the discernable ends of a schooling nearly identical to what is described in the "letter" written to Altenstein. The apologaic form of the example adjudicates the start of subjective identity, the life-writing of which is authorized by the indelibility of the signature functioning as the mark of the truth of memory to the self. "The Age of Hegel" asks (among other things) whether what Hegel is doing with (and to) the anecdote in the report by staking the claim of being able to determine with undaunted precision and absolute singularity the major source of pedagogical influence on the realization of "philosophical selfhood" is even plausible; or whether the story of origins, itself suspect, is a clever invention for the institutional sake of speculative philosophy; "if he plays with the example the way, elsewhere [in the *Phenomenology of Spirit*], he teaches the *Beispiel* [example]."[58]

Paralleling the Nietzschean preoccupation for exploring 'how one becomes what one is,' Derrida interrogates the auto-bio-graphical limits constitutive of subjective identity through a *life-writing-of-the-self* to undermine the sense-certainty of the unsolicited retrospection Hegel freely gives testimony to by ever-so-humbly signing for it. There is a strong deconstructive rationale for sustaining the auto-bio-graphical reading of the report that concentrates, more or less, on the signing of memory veiled under the guiles of the proper name, while addressing the ethical-political aspects of key curricular questions regarding the institutionalization of philosophical pedagogies of ages past and present: the contradiction or "incompatibility between the teaching and the signature, a schoolmaster and a signifier . . . even when they let themselves be thought and signed, these two operations cannot overlap each other *(se recouper).*"[59] The pedagogical ramifications of this *double metaphorical writing* of the signature of the proper name of Hegel as a sign of the truth of the philosophical memory of speculative dialectics have been dealt with extensively by Derrida:

> Hegel presents himself as a philosopher or a thinker, someone who constantly tells you that his empirical signature—the signature of the individual named Hegel—is secondary. His signature, that is, pales in the face of the truth, which speaks through his mouth, which is produced in his text, which constructs the system it constructs. This system is the teleological outcome of all Western experience, so that in the end Hegel, the individual, is nothing but an empirical shell which can fall away without subtracting from the truth or from the history of meaning. As a philosopher and as a teacher, he seems to be saying that not only is it possible for his signature and his proper name to disappear without a loss, to fall outside of the system, but that this is even necessary in his own system because it will prove the truth and autonomy of that system. . . . It appears, then, that Hegel did not sign. . . . Yet, in fact, Hegel signs. . . . One could show, as I have tried elsewhere,[60] in what way it was difficult to dispose with the name of Hegel

in his work, to withhold its inscription—call it personal or biographical
from his work. It implies a reelaboration of the whole biographical within
philosophy.[61]

The idea that one can write-the-self from the *arche-text* of memory, and by so
doing, extract from the terms of representation an intersubjective code of meaning-making pregnant in its pedagogical implications for the Other, is linked to a
dialectics of the signature, or the *sign-function* of identity, as recuperative of the
built-in differentiality of subjectivity. By reconceptualizing subjectivity and its
exteriorizable corollary of identity as consolidated in the guises of the signature
of the proper name, Derrida can deconstruct the pedagogical formulations of the
report to reveal what is concealed in the ideological subtext of the speculative
logic informing the ethics and politics of the life-writing of the memory.

The empirical act of signing Hegel performs is a cathexis of the example.
Moving beyond the form of representation to "real-life," it names and appropriates for the disunity of subjectivity in the very materiality of its significatory
content. It replaces and supplements the semblances of an originary difference of
self-identity that this instance of life-writing from memory would otherwise unveil in the transl(iter)ation from sign to *eidos,* from text to context, from writing
to life itself: "Memory and truth cannot be separated. The movement of *aletheia*
is a deployment of *mnèmè* through and through. A deployment of living memory, of memory as psychic life in its self-presentation to itself."[62] Endorsing the
pedagogical "authenticity" of such an attempt at utter and unmitigated self-
representation are the borders of a negative space stipulating the affirmation of
selfhood or identity to be delineated from the conscious ascription of difference to
an Other. The signature of Hegel itself "notarizes" the autonomy of this inwardly
projecting totalization of subjectivity by containing the implicature of a consolidation of origins, wherein the nominative capacity of the form of the proper
name that is excerpted in writing is granted the right to "self-sign" or to "sign-
self" from the continuity of the living-memory trace.[63] The signature comes to
personify the visible difference of identity: a conflating of the subject Hegel with
the sign of the proper name of "Hegel." From the arbitrariness of a self-
referential sign-grouping, the heterogeneity of subjectivity is expunged under the
dominant modes of graphematic articulation available for the concatenation of
the proper name.

Hegel signs for the memory of childhood. And the signing of the proper
name that Hegel reenacts to justify the curricular schema is (and also must be)
the synoptic periphrasis of a *surfeit of textuality* concentrated within the lexematic structures of the signature; it maintains the illusion of not exceeding the
strictures of its formal features, but does just so, given the teleological sys-
tematicity of the epistemological presuppositions on which it rests. Because the
signature is a politico-juridical fetishization of writing gathered under what Martin Jay calls the normative ethics of a *phallogocularcentric*[64] non-
supplementarity of the graphical form, it substitutes the resemblance of the *sign*
of identity for the *"truth"* of identity. That is so the sign of 'Hegel' can be made
to stand in ideal or un(equ)ivocal relation to the non-arbitrariness of itself as a
semaphorical retypification testifying to the "truthfulness" of its referent, the

philosopher Hegel. More importantly for Altenstein's political purposes, what the inscription of the empirical signature of Hegel at the conclusion of the "letter" ensues is: the availability of a *mechanismos* for a retransposition of the "real-world" estimation (societal, economic, cultural, academic, etc.) deemed the human signified that the signutatum refers to, to the content of thought the philosopher espouses in the text about philosophical education on behalf of the State. The signature discharges unto the subject-philosopher Hegel what is the equivalent of an undiminishing and *after-the-fact* responsibility for the pronouncements of memory and for the memory of self expounded in the report. The act of signing carries over to join the anteriority of the past to the posterity of the future. Its effects are perceived much later. This juridical-ethical power of the signature Hegel appends to this "letter" is duly conferred by the oath Hegel took as a citizen of the State to uphold a bureaucratic code of decorum that decrees the officiousness of bearing witness to the truth of signing one's own name. The proper name of the philosopher countersigns the legalistic jurisdiction of its own symbolic authority to intercede in the intense politics of the debate over education: to attempt to affect those conditions by a defense of speculative idealism and of the State, for the rights of which Hegel has signed before and often enough, throughout the corpus of his philosophical texts, lectures, correspondences, and so on. Derrida "do[es] no more than name, with a proper name as one of the guiding threads, the necessity of a deconstruction"[65] of the memory of the sign of self.

Déjà-Pas-Encore: The *Already-Not-Yet* of a Post-Cartesian Subjectivity

The exemplar of "unschooled" youth that Hegel imparts is a reminiscence depicting the quality of a *not-as-yet* philosophical subjectivity, or what was, once upon a time, the childhood experience of his own developing pedagogical identity. An attempt to reify a past subjective identity from the life-writing of an ideal reflexivity—to make the "truth" of memory speak the self-consciousness of itself, as it were—entails the eradication of the undecidability always already immanent to the personal conception of what one is. There is too much interfering with the ego's reception of perceptual sense-data coloring the way it sees itself as subject that Hegel chooses to disregard or to explain away. The signing of the life-writing of memory in this "retrograde vision" revolves around the recognizable presence of a self-presence that is present to itself and signs for the Being of itself as being. It is a projection of an autogenetic subjectivity, or an effortless reflexivity amalgamating the diversity of the realms of consciousness combining the simultaneity of Self, as both same and Other, in its returning to itself through the "spectacle" of introspection.[66] The teleologicality of the reminiscence is adducible only by positing prior to the instance of the ego's self-remembering a timeless state of Being charged fully as the enunciation of unchanging presence.[67] The continual suppression of the absence of presence that hypostatizes (fixes, enframes, parodies) subjectivity makes it capturable in the still-of-life and perpetuates the idealistic premises igniting the memory of non-philosophical identity Hegel puts forward. Pretending to look back in time and space at the "source" of the "present-day" self through the inverted lens reflecting a mirrorlike past, Hegel has immediately interceded to predict for any retranslation of the pedagogical significance of the living memory trace the episode highlights. And by defining the terms of a subjective writing of identity from the consistency of a negatively defined logics designed to fulfill the speculative ends of dialectical philosophy, the "teleological gesture of return inquiry"[68] establishes an ideal frame of reference crucial to the engendering of the ego's "absolute knowledge" of itself. The subjective vision could then be generalized (by Altenstein or Hegel) to serve as the fountainhead of universalizable curricular or pedagogical truths.

The "entire 'system' of speculative dialectics organizes this childhood anamnesis to suit the ministerial project"[69] for a concrete icon of the imaginable outcome of a speculative pedagogy that could be Hegel and more than Hegel. The first two modalities denoting the *performance of memory* are essential to the representational politics of a general economy of the signature Hegel supplies (e.g., the signer actively engaged in authenticating the impression of self-identity, either by conscious intent or by accident, resulting in the leaving of a set of "idiomatic" marks to fulfill the stylistic demands of the genre of transmission).[70] The signature enables the life-writing of memory to allude to two chronological ages, for example, the spatio-temporal figurativization of dissonant modes of subjectivity that exhibit divergent stages of mental development relative to states of being—the wisdom of Hegel, the elder philosopher versus the folly of Hegel, the untutored child. The dialectical synthesis of identity from the interiorizing effects of memory overcomes the symmetrization of the self and anti-self as the false identities of opposites. By resolving this binary structuration of subjectivity that Hegel presents as a thesis versus antithesis construction to the prospect of a third term, the speculative result of what is subsumed within the "force-gesture" of a sublation *(Aufhebung)* is that which "raises, denies, suspends, and preserves the first."[71] The penultimate movement is suspended indefinitely, held in reserve, for reasons that are revealed by Derrida to be not altogether altruistic (ethical), but immanently self-serving and selfishly motivated by the "narrow" interests of the time. The reader is left to ponder over it, to decide what it all means. What *can* we make of the auto-bio-graphical reliability of the life-writing of memory that Hegel signs for, to preserve a philosophical pedagogy?

The representation of pedagogical experience Hegel yields to, incumbently for reasons of argument, is not and could not (ever) be identical to the conceptual tenor of the ideas evoked. Even though a *life-writing-of-the-self* must be responsive to a subjective transcendentality of the memory trace, it is still supplementary to thought itself—a sign of a sign—and not analogous, correlational, motivational, nor iconic of the eidetic workings of the human psyche.[72] The conceptual limits of the exposition *(Darstellung)* Hegel proffers to Altenstein are exceeded by the undecidability of an *already-not-yet (déjà-pas-encore)* reconfiguration of philosophical subjective identity that Derrida introduces to displace, to dis-locate, and to dis-figure *(Enstellung)* the self-confident *prosopopoeia* of the portrayal.[73] The "enjambed" logic of the structure of this neologism connotes the philosophical selfhood of the subject Hegel to be a veritable conundrum of multiply suspended educational beginnings: rather than the assertion of a teleologicality of Being that is re-presented as the likelihood of the first steps to a speculative pedagogy. The destructuration of the "ideal route" to a re-gaining of identity stultifies the absolute certainty of a subjective self-representation the life-writing of memory is wont to warrant. Derrida explains the deconstructive complication:

> At the age of fifty-two, he [Hegel] speaks of his twelfth year. He was already a philosopher. But just like everyone else is, right? That is, not yet a philosopher since, in view of the corpus of the complete works of his maturity, this *already* will have been a *not yet.*
>
> If we don't think through this conceptual, dialectical, speculative structure of this *already-not yet,* we will not have understood anything (in its essentials, as he would say) about the *age* (for example, that of Hegel). Or about any age whatsoever, but especially, and *par excellance* that *of* philosophy or *for* philosophy. . . . Under the cover of the *already-not-yet,* autobiographical confiding enlists the anecdote in a demonstration, treating the issue of (the) age as a figure in the phenomenology of the mind, as a moment in the logic.[74]

It is not a matter of who the "real" Hegel is or was. Such understanding could never be realized *in toto*: the rhizome of actions and events of discourse carried out by or enacted upon a subject do not and cannot concede such accuity of insight. For Derrida, the pedagogical purposiveness of the life-writing of memory Hegel surrenders to is an extant indicator of an intransitory subjectivity, a *coming-into-being-of-the-self* that the signature of the proper name authorizes and is authorized by, to dissimulate identity as a presence feigning absence behind the masks of confiding.[75]

The predisposition of this writing of the identity of self from the ruins of life's memories assures that Hegel will speak only of the deaths of un-named, de-propriated, and ex-propriated younger selves. What is excluded from the representation of being is an intrinsic forgetfulness *(lèthè)* of Being that Derrida acknowledges. It is a *prosopopoeia* that spans the dark recesses of a space-time continuum to veritably undo the mimetological impulse of the life-writing of anamnesis by keeping its structures open to the machinations of *différance,* wherein meaning re-construction is deferred from the traces of differential movements of the signification process away from an intangible source. Derrida explains:

> The powers of *lèthè* simultaneously increase the domains of death, of non-truth, of non-knowledge. This is why writing, at least insofar as it sows "forgetfulness of the soul," turns us toward the inanimate and toward non-knowledge. But it cannot be said that its essence simply and *presently* confounds it with death or non-truth. For writing *has* no essence or value of its own, whether positive or negative. It plays within the simulacrum. It is in its type the mime of memory, of knowledge, of truth, etc.[76]

Hegel's depiction of this pedagogical moment from the "pasts" of childhood must inevitably surrender the living presence of life-writing of the self-sameness of auto-affective presence itself to the contaminating effects of a first out-side—the "monumental" *(hypomnematic)* supplementarity of a form—that is the absence (or death) of "essence" within the economy of memory that incurs a loss of profit(s)—the "up-side" of its meaning potential—due to the very materiality of its production.[77] It is in this sense of the "inscribability" of "psychic life" and "somatic existence" that what is included under the authority of the *sign of Hegel* are the fragments of a thanato-graphical discourse that looks forward, in time, to the ends beyond the impending death of the philosopher and of his philosophical pedagogy, although also insures for or against it. For what is signed remembers the Self to the Other, yet also remembers the death of the Self to the Other and to the Self.

Delimiting the Teachings of Metaphysics

The Pedagogical Institution and the Perils of Philosophy: Deconstruction and GREPH in the Postmodern Age of Hegel

To further the discussion of the nature of educational presentation "adequate" to philosophy education, Derrida turns loose the specters of the Hegelian legacy on the "analogous and contiguous"[78] context of postrevolutionary France. Twenty-two years after the "self-portrait" Hegel sketched out, the (again very public) "confidence" of a progeny of Hegelianism, Victor Cousin, is added to the file. A disciple and friend of the German philosopher (whose release from prison Hegel had secured after six months of incarceration for participation in demon-strations occuring during the period of social unrest involving the university student fraternities of Bavaria [1824]),[79] Cousin expostulated an eloquent argu-ment to oppose the threatened eradication of philosophy from the *collèges* by the powers-that-be in a discourse presented before the House of Peers. Derrida sum-marizes it as follows:

> The jist [sic] of Cousin's reply: Definitely not [in regard to the abolition of metaphysics from the *lycée* curriculum]; since philosophy teaches natural certitudes (for example, the existence of God, the freedom or immortality of the soul), in principle, it can never be too early to begin. In other words, as long as the contents of instruction reinforce, as it were, the predominant forces, it is best to begin as early as possible. And the contradictory unity that reconciles the predominant force with itself and constitutes the basis of historical compromise is a mutually desired contract between secular State and Religion.[80]

On the one hand, by insisting on the "reciprocal independence of philosophy and theology"[81] Cousin attenuates the *liberal* and *neutralist* scope of pedagogy to take on the epistemological demeanor of a national French character in that of a Cartesian Rationalist dreamscape. His mentor Hegel, we must remember, had originally attempted to introduce the German context to the recapitulation of these equivocal motifs, for what "extends the domain of 'general culture'"[82] within curriculum is what "always remains highly determined in the contents it inculcates."[83] Cousin is in some ways more precocious. And he promises to instill at the beginnings of the philosophy curriculum a program of study concentrating on a dualist metaphysics of knowing derivative of a provisional and "methodic" doubt, whereby the *"naturality of truth"* tracks a transcendental route as proceeding from the self-evident resolution of the reflexive sensibilities of Mind realized through the activation of epistemological subjectivity (the *cogito*) to a *perfect* certainty of Spirit. The affirmation of the rational soul of the self, in Cousin's pedagogical revising of Cartesian epistemology, verifies the existence of God to unite religion with philosophy for the eradication of skepticism and for the betterment of the State. By contrast, Hegel denies the gymnasium (the primary grades) entrance to the "Pantheon of Western Metaphysics"[84] by invoking the "limits of schoolteaching"[85] to safeguard against the pedagogical shortsightedness of allowing the material components of instruction—its curriculum—to surpass the mental capabilities of these students.

Regulating the implementation of a prephilosophical (read *non*-metaphysical) content core that Derrida objects to, the Hegelian curriculum is made up of "the humanities (the Ancients, the great artistic and historical ideas of individuals and peoples, their ethics and their religiosity)"[86] as well as other areas (e.g., empirical psychology and logic). The pedagogical aim Hegel pursues here is to seamlessly cultivate a "natural" progressivity of learning to be inaugurated from the first non-contemplative steps of interiorizing memorization *(Erinnerung)*[87] to an outwardly speculative rationality of thought "for, [as he insists in the report] in order to possess knowledge of any kind—even the highest sort—one must have memorized it *(im Gedächtnisse haben)*; regardless of whether this is to be a beginning *or* an end in itself."[88] In "The Age of Hegel," the theo-philosophico-rationalist conceptualization of intellectual maturity Cousin advances for nurturing the mental capacities of the average student to apprehend the "natural truths" of Spirit-Mind is juxtaposed against the organicist archetype of the *mnèmè* of Spirit-Mind Hegel entreats to assert a hierarchy of instructional contents excluding metaphysics. The approach permits Derrida to lay bare the great extent to which both discourses harbor deep-seated ideological compulsions aspiring to pedagogically replicate "nationalistic" or "State-sponsored" assumptions indicative of a "general culture" from which the suitability of subject matter and the appropriateness of instructional maneuvers for the teaching-learning of philosophy are determined. The undertexts of both discourses condone the educational institutionalization of a philosophical knowing that ensures and is ensured by the *reproducibility* of dominant modes of cultural (re)transmission for the perpetuation of the onto-theo-logy of Western metaphysics.

The yielding of contrasting positions with respect to the "correct" age for the teaching-learning of first philosophy is not coincidental; the *"higher reasons"* of Religion, for Cousin (e.g., to placate the skepticism of the Church), and the *"good reasons"* of State, for Hegel (e.g., to appease the power of a government bureaucracy), encroach on the pedagogical methodologizing of epistemology in their search for the *most* appropriate means to *acceptable* ends. From this quasi-eschatological viewpoint, a cross-organizational harmonizing of the structures of the educational organum with those socio-cultural institutions that it must, sooner or later, surrender answers to is metaphorically subsumed in an overcoded symbol of teleology, the "onto-encyclopaedic system of the *Universitas*"[89] as the microcosmic counterpart of the totality of the "real world":

> There is a Hegelian hierarchization [Derrida is referring to the assignment of the "letter" as a minor pedagogical moment in the philosophical canon of Hegel] but it is circular, and the minor is always carried, sublated *(relevé)* beyond the opposition, beyond the limit of inside and outside in(to) the major. And inversely. The potency of this age without age derives from this great empirico-philosophical cycle. Hegel does not conceive of the school as a consequence or the image of the system, indeed, as its *pars totalis*: the system itself is an immense school, the thoroughgoing auto-encyclopaedia of the absolute spirit in absolute knowledge. And it is the school we never leave, hence, an obligatory instruction, which obliges (by) itself, since the necessity can no longer come from without.[90]

Neither Cousin nor Hegel ignore the "conservativism" of the type Derrida abstracts above from the speculative system of dialectics. We are again reminded that the defense of the right to philosophy teaching-learning in the public (dis)course of education must project an ethico-political accountability for the concept of the pedagogical institution and for the lasting results of its curricular ordinances. Unsurprisingly enough, this sense of responsibility to the power of *external forces* contained within the *internal bounds* of the disciplinary infrastructure of the educational system reinforces the "distinction between metaphysics and dogmatic theology"[91] for Cousin and Hegel. The partitionary function of the historical paradigm of the faculties for separating epistemology from religion in both situations allows them to gloss over the prejudices of the curricular prerequisites unique to each context for inculcating the experience of a civic sense of duty in students through the procedures of schooling. The overwhelming irony, however, is that this common goal is also the *stigme* of their departure in judgment when both philosophers are pushed to the limit by the requirement of recommending solutions to the problem of the "age" befitting the teaching-learning of "pure" philosophy.

Of common and singular importance to the strategies of Cousin and Hegel is to keep the philosophical formulations on which their pedagogical propositions depend manifestly "pliable" or ostensibly "open" so as to make the "substance" of their ideas appear favorable to the prevailing doctrines of the day. The political overtones of the criteria they both employ for the setting out of what are oppositional curricula are temporarily defused by a restatement of their respective pedagogical visions in the metaphysical surety of a "post-Cartesianist" meditation. More than likely, the rationalist mannerisms of the style would be perceived to be non-threatening to the ideological predilections of the nineteenth-century state bureaucracies they were presenting them to: either because of the distinctive penchant for perpetuating an effigy of "epistemological nationalism" by transmuting it into the (in)flexible stock of cultural capital or because of the favorable predisposition of an educational methodology toward a benign controllability of the "natural faculties" of thought.[92] Feigning a "rational disinterestedness" for setting the parameters of what *can be* thought and of how thought *is to be* expressed, Cousin and Hegel sufficiently neutralize the political upshot of what could be construed to be, on the one side, "reactionary" or, on the other, "biased" in the meticulous rhetoric of their speculative musings on education.

Derrida reads the ethical coherence of this ideologico-philosophical hedging as a verbal alibi for reinstating many of the well-known naturalist motifs of a pedagogical humanism considered potentially less dangerous to the stability of the *status quo*. Redirecting the critical emphasis to the material conditions of the educational institution inherited from these major dialecticians by contemporary makers of curriculum or educational policy (bureaucrats, public servants, and so on), "The Age of Hegel" directly engages (but has it ever really left?) the post-modern sphere of partisan politics engulfing France during the mid-seventies. Derrida consciously forefronts the relevance of the historical context to tamper with the two complementary poles of nationalism and universalism that Cousin and Hegel eulogize, "not [wanting] to abandon the field to empiricism and thereby to whatever forces are at hand":[93]

> it is always by insisting upon the 'natural,' by naturalizing the content or the forms of instruction, that one "inculcates" precisely what one wishes to exempt from criticism. GREPH must be particularly careful in this respect, since its tactics could expose it to this risk of naturalist mystification; by demanding that the age at which a young person begins the study of philoso-phy be lowered, and that the scope of instruction be extended, there is a risk of being understood (without intending it; but the adversary will do his best to further this impression) as suggesting that once prejudices and "ideolo-gies" have been erased, what will be revealed is the bare truth of an "infant" always already ready to philosophize and *naturally* capable of doing so. Those modes of discourse that are currently held to be the most "subversive" are never entirely free of this naturalism. They always appeal to some sort of return to primitive desire, to the simple lifting of repression, to the unbind-ing of energy, or to the primary process. . . . The natural truths taught by metaphysics proceed from divine writings and will have engraved in the soul of the disciple that which the teacher of philosophy can only reveal through self-effacement: an invisible writing that he causes to appear on the body of the pupil. Are the discourses of the GREPH always free of this schematiza-tion? Does it not return, necessarily, in a more or less disguised form?[94]

"The Age of Hegel" localizes the precipitous complexity of the pedagogical *ideal of progressivity* in respect to the metaphysical genealogy of the Western institu-tion of pedagogy. And it facilitated the point of entry for a radical broaching *(l'entame)* into the heterogeneity of the intense deliberation over state educational policy reform that was needed at the time the text was written and first appeared in *Qui a peur de la philosophie?*,[95] a research manifesto into philosophy teach-ing-learning published under the aggregate authorship of the GREPH. Derrida addresses the *historicity* of these pressing issues very plainly to accent the alac-rity of how the historico-political circumstances preceding the situational consid-erations of the philosophical age Cousin presided over while a member of par-liament and in which Hegel "found himself implicated, advancing or floundering,"[96] are akin to the social climate initiating the pedagogical reform movements of post-1968 France that culminated with the issuance of the Haby Reform (1975).

A state proposal for drastic educational restructuring named after the then newly appointed Minister of Education, René Haby (who served in the "Gaullist" [right-wing] government of Giscard d'Estaing), the Haby Reform promised to reduce the number of classroom hours available for philosophy instruction in the *lycée*. Moreover, the imperatives of the "Giscard-Haby" plan very much threatened the future of the discipline in the university. The consternation that the severity of its edicts bred about the overarching or longer-ranging ramifications of this preemptive intervention on the part of the State into teaching-learning was one of the factors that eventually led to the "official mobilization" of the GREPH against the Haby Reform in January 1975.[97]

Derrida, for his part a founding member and a major force, wished to help move forward the group's avowedly activist involvement in the public debate over "philosophy." In speaking to the GREPH, "The Age of Hegel" provides only one illustration of how to interrogate the ethico-political "decipherability" of the Haby Reform through these metastatic fluctuations of the juridical aegis of epistemology before and since Hegel. That the example—the exemplarity of the example—is itself *"deconstructive"* is incidental (one might also say idiosyncratic) to Derrida's own intricate style of reading and writing. The mission of the GREPH had "defined itself [from the outset] as a locus of work and debate, and not as a center for the broadcasting of slogans or doctrinaire messages"[98] without the benefit of intense research, both empirical and theoretical.[99] To stimulate dialogue that could prove useful for negotiating a consensus within the diversified interests of the group, Derrida did, in fact, formalize the "Preliminary Proposal for the Constitution of a Research Group on Philosophical Education" (the "Avant-Projet")[100] by synthesizing ideas from notes taken at their meetings. But he was not adamant about, nor interested in, transforming the GREPH into a *"deconstructive machine,"*[101] if this were even possible.[102] Derrida has preferred instead—as he has done in "The Age of Hegel" and afterwards—to warn of the likely dangers of confronting the State and its (mis)management of the pedagogical institution "head-on" through a leveling of injunctions that are intended to bring down the structures of the oppressive edifice itself, once and for all. Such a teleologico-eschatological zeal to dismantle a system of education with a view to setting up its replacement *"anew"* could only serve to prohibit the advent of appreciable change within the general composition of the whole.

In referring to the archetype of the university as the "onto- and auto-encyclopaedic circle of the State,"[103] Derrida counsels that "the deconstruction of its concepts, of its instruments, of its practices cannot proceed by attacking it *immediately* and attempting to do away with it without risking the *immediate* return of other forces equally capable of adapting to it. *Immediately* to retreat and make way for the 'other' of the *Universitas* might represent a welcome invitation to those very determinate and very determined forces, ready and waiting, close by, to take over the State and the University."[104] The aftermath of this wasted labor would undoubtedly be to reaffirm the *doxa* of precisely those institutional conventions in question. And the casualness of its *all-or-nothing* mandate will inadvertently fail: given that the totalizing force of the ideal must re-produce the generic organization of standardized forms or models (e.g., utopic, metaphysical, anarchic) whose limits take shape between the dyad of opposing argumentative guardrails *(garde-fous)* marking out the space amid the less than agreeable chimeras of nihilism and despair. For example, by either protecting, on the one side, against the fearful responsibility of misdoing by fostering inaction or, on the other, by provoking irresponsible decision making leading to reckless action.

Where the premise is to appreciatively alter the formal boundaries of the educational system, to make its performative structures more responsive to the alterior qualities of subjective differences, Derrida is most exact about what kind of resistive activity is called for: "In consequence: battling as always on two fronts, on two scenes and according to two ways *(porteé)*, a rigorous and efficient deconstruction must at the same time develop the critique (practice) of the current philosophic institution [from within the enactment of its aberrations] and to engage in a positive transformation, rather affirmative, audacious, extensive and intensive, of the teaching called 'philosophic.'"[105] It is the aporiatic space of the educational system itself—an institutionalized interiority of *pouvoir/savoir* without pure exteriority—that licenses the agonistics of a "double science" Derrida has culled, always taking great care to remind us that the field of oppositions deconstruction criticizes "is also a field of non-discursive forces."[106] The pragmatic territoriality of this space, once cleaved open from the intertwining and doubly invaginated folds of its "inside" and its "outside" margins, reveals a deterritorialized non-space where the counter-hegemonic locality and illocality of deconstruction can bring to light the heteronomous autonomy of the excluded at the peripheries of the institutionalized center.

Of course, the juridico-political stakes of the ethical struggle for equality of educational opportunities that the GREPH has pledged to carry on are an important denouement of this redressing of the performative relation of philosophy and pedagogy, formalized as it is in the praxeological cybernetics of the educational institution.[107] For Derrida, aspiring to rectify the *catachresis* of past injustices requires exposing the hidden fallibility and innate fragility of comforting centers of established order that permitted them in the first place. Showing the unpredictability of play within the seemingly fixed hierarchical structures of a dominating logics breaks the coherence of its autarchic control.[108] "The Age of Hegel" skillfully orchestrates the schematics of this well-known deconstructive compulsion that imminently enables work against the concrete abuses of institutionalized systems of cruel authority or repressive power.[109] By way of reference to the legitimation of the notorious letter Altenstein received, Derrida advocates an audacious transformation of the normative structures of culture that justify and ascribe the privilege of worth to a subject or object.

> What is to be done with this Letter of Hegel's? Where is it to be situated? Where does it take (its) place? Evaluation is inevitable: is it a "major" text or a "minor" one? Is it a "philosophical" text? What status, as they say, do we grant it? What title? One of the tasks of the GREPH could be a critique (not only formal, but effective and concrete) of all existing hierarchies. . . . Without such a reelaboration, no profound transformation will be possible.

The force that dominates the process of classification and the institution of hierarchies allows us to read whatever it is interested in having us read (which it then labels major texts, or texts of "great import"); and it renders inaccessible whatever it is interested in underestimating, and which in general it *cannot read* (describing such texts as minor or marginal). And this holds true for the discourse of the educator and for all his evaluatory procedures (grading; juries for examinations, competitions, theses; so-called supervisory committees; etc.); it is the evaluative standard determining all discourse: from that of the critic and the upholder of tradition to that determining editorial policy, the commercialization of texts, etc. And once again, it is not simply a matter of texts in print or on blackboards, but rather of a general textuality without which there is no understanding and no action.[110]

Beginning with the preliminary phases of "a general reelaboration of the entire problematic of hierarchies,"[111] deconstruction unbalances the deliberate equationing of language and meaning as the only authentic *reading* and *writing* of the concept of the truth of education. It challenges and disrupts the historical continuity of the institution's capability to re-produce its logic through the nurturing of a "pure[ly] egological subject"[112] that has its codic source for "Truth" in the systematic stratification of the meaning of signification and the fixed rules of its evaluation or rendering. But unlike more conventional forms of *"ideology critique,"* deconstruction denies recourse to any intuition or conception of reality unmediated by language from which to glean a glimmer of the "falsity" of consciousness. *"Il n' y a pas de hors-texte"* [113] (There is no outside-text; there is nothing outside of the [con]text), Derrida will insist. That is the "marching order" of deconstruction.

Derrida therefore also places the premises of the GREPH "at risk" in "The Age of Hegel" through a careful expanding upon of the unavoidable pitfalls of a critique of normativity without the cautious reflectivity of an auto-critique of the desire of the self and of the same:

Reread the Preliminary Project of the GREPH: every sentence demands that the censured or devaluaed [sic] be displayed, that the vast holdings of a more-or-less forbidden library be exhumed from the cellars. And that there be a lack of respect for prevailing evaluations: not only to indulge certain perverse bibliographic pleasures (on the other hand, why not?); nor even in order to better understand what links philosophy to its institution, to its institutional underside and recesses *(dessous et envers)*; but rather to transform the very conditions of our effective intervention in them. *Underside or recesses,* because it is not a matter of discovering today, belatedly, what has been known all along: that there is such a thing as a philosophical institution. Indeed, "Philosophy" *("la" philosophie)* has always had a dominant concept to take this into account, and *institution* is at bottom the name it has reserved for this task. Underside and recesses, because we are not satisfied with what the institution reveals about itself: neither with what we can perceive empirically, nor with what we can conceive according to the law of the philosophical concept. Underside and recesses would no longer have a signification dominated by the philosophical opposition that continues to order discourse in terms of a concealed substance or essence of the institution, hidden beneath its accidents, circumstances, phenomena, or super-structures. Underside and recesses would designate, rather, that which, while still being situated within this venerable (conceptual metaphoric) topos, might begin to extricate itself from this opposition and to constitute it in a new manner.[114]

At the border crossings of the transhistorical strife over the praxeological intelligibility of the signifier *"philosophy"* enacted as pedagogy is the discourse of the educational institution, the eternal gatekeeper of the sense of "reason" ordering and translating for the curricular substance of the discipline. Positing an unassailable *oikos* of language as the order *(nomos)* of the "house of Being" has safeguarded the particular directions adopted in the West for the instruction of the subject.[115] And what Derrida calls the cure and poison of this discursive/non-discursive circularity construes the *pharmakon* of a teaching-learning that one can never escape. Language is the symbolic violence that *in-forms* the conceptual-metaphorical schemata of the psyche for dealing with everyday reality.[116] It is within the mastery of the rhetoricized heart of the institution's disciplinarity that the in-grained *habitus* of one's own subjectivity is subject to, and a subjectification of, the flux of language expended upon the ideology of a free-will.[117] Derrida is succinct: "There is no neutral or natural place in education *(l'enseignement).* Here, for example, is not an indifferent place."[118]

To be sure, the institutionalization of knowledge consolidating the philosophical lessons of Western epistemology bears the transcription of a *logoarchy* that intertwines the ontotheological foundations of a metaphysical language with the intellectual backdrop of a pedagogical history inseparable from the truth of its object.[119] The semiotic effectivity of this operative modeling of learning upon a knowledge-centered teaching of closed values is described by Derrida as follows: "Teaching delivers signs, the teaching body produces (shows and puts forth) proofs *(enseignes),* more precisely signifiers supposing knowledge of a previous signified. Referred to this knowledge, the signifier is structurally second. Every university [or general system of education] puts language in this position of delay or derivation in relation to meaning or truth."[120] A pedagogical method patterned after the instrumentality of a Platonic-Hegelian mimetologism of the *eidos* cannot be anything but a laconic dictation of self-obscuring memory. Such an invasive instruction cast of a mechanical repetition that has as its *techne* a retrospective rather than a prospective function is more apt to valorize the reproduction of knowledge than to create the conditions for discovering or inventing it:[121]

> Along the stages that are always idiomatic, we are always guided back to the most durable tradition of the philosophical concept of teaching: revelation, unveiling, the discovered truth of the "already-there" *(déjà là)* according to the mode of "not-yet" *(pas encore),* a Socrato-Platonic anamnesis sometimes taken up by the philosophy of psychoanalysis. Throughout these specific determinations may be found, time and time again, the same scheme, the same concept of truth, of a truth linked to the same pedagogical structure. But the interpretation of these specificities must not succumb to this determination, as though one had to settle for the discovery of the same

beneath all variations. One should never settle for this but also never forget to take its power into account . . . the question at issue is always, as it was for Plato, one of a double metaphoric of inscription: a bad writing *(une mauvaise écriture)*, secondary, artificial, cryptic or hieroglyphic, voiceless, intervenes to obscure good writing *(la bonne écriture)*; it overdetermines, occults, complicates, perverts, makes a travesty of the natural inscription of the truth of the soul. By effacing himself, the teacher *(maître)* is also promoting the unlearning of bad writing. But if this motif retains a certain "Platonic" allure, the specificity of its "age" marks itself by a profound "Cartesian" reference.[122]

The "teaching body"[123] Derrida refers to has a regenerative role in the educational institution fundamental to an ancillary fulfillment of the dominant pedagogical theme of Western philosophy, the "metaphysics of presence" or "logocentrism."[124] Where teaching characterized by the mere delivery and reception of signs "has [as] its ideal, with exhaustive translatability, the effacement of language *(la langue),*"[125] learning is and can be—no more, no less—equivalent in difficulty to the cognitive capabilities of a minimal technical competence required for the "error-free" exchange of transmitted concepts. It presumes, and Derrida is clear on this, that the living spirit of a writing *enfleshed* of preestablished empirical proofs can be actively etched into the conscious *corps* of a passified "student body." This positive value of signifier-signified/sign-referent relations that is exhibited and perpetuated as the traditional discourse of a teaching-learning practice (e.g., a positivistic didactics of total cognition) connects thought to expression to bring about the essential possibility of faultlessly duplicating the content of signification in the contours of the mind. Its transcendental inspiration of a "transportable univocality or of formulizable polysemia"[126] propagates the illusion of a correspondence theory of pedagogical truths. When the presuppositions of the well-known teaching-learning model that Derrida describes above are combined with the absolute idealism of speculative dialectics Hegel supplies for supporting the case of a curriculum driven by the fruits of *mnemosyne,* two things are foreshadowed: the end of pedagogy and the end of philosophy. Nothing remains untheorized outside the oppositional complementarity of this Metaphysical System that could counter the dialectic of its glorious memory, essentially because the conceptualization of "meaning," "truth," and "reality" is sequestered in the liminal scope of the singular, the finite, and the totalizing.

It will follow that the "scene of teaching" alluded to by Derrida via "The Age of Hegel" comprises the student, the teacher, and the institution defined *not only* in and of themselves, with respect to their rights, obligations, freedoms, duties, etc., as the entities of a tripartite division of the educational space.[127] Each "body" is more (and *conceivably less*) than the sum of its accumulative parts as the grounding for the synchrony and diachrony of inter-relations between the principal actors of the *topos* oscillates. Moreover, these educational "entities" are subjectively prone to the "ideological" effects of internally and externally motivated influences upon the situated formations of the scene of teaching that create a specific socio-cultural and ethico-political niche for the possibility of pedagogy. Support for the material conditions of the system's structure so crucial to its *living on* is maintained by the hegemonic entrenchment of legitimating metanarratives justifying, and justified by, an ethos of praxis.[128] The applicability of the general principles of deconstruction to the historical contextuality of the pedagogical institution is due to the fact that the educational bodies comprising the material scene of teaching are themselves mediated by the constructions of discourse. Or of a pervading textuality effectively determinant, as such, of the subjectivation of experience. The discourse infusing the (inter)disciplinarity of this educational site is a fertile ethical and political ground for deconstruction because the "actual" circumstances of a particular pedagogy (e.g., a "philosophical" one) implies the institutional privileging of a set of ideological assumptions toward teaching and learning, the logic of which underlies and guides the prescriptive implementation of a hierarchical frameworking of knowledge in the concrete form of a curriculum. On this point, Derrida is concise: "The university [as both *Umwelt* and schooling organization] is philosophy, a university is always the construction of a philosophy."[129]

To destabilize the centrality of a dominant conception of philosophy to the existing disciplinary structure and valuations of the pedagogical institution, one that has done much to annex its positionality, charges neither a destruction of the "old system," nor a flat-out denial of the conventionality of *epistémè* inherited from the ages before and after Hegel. Deconstruction concedes not to the naïve enlightenment of an EITHER/OR, NEITHER/NOR propositionality simply to be "on the other side" of Reason in all situations despite the circumstances.[130] It obliges a patient and unrelenting resistance from within the system that challenges the arbitrary working-out of its practices through the magnified inconsistencies in the logic of its discourse:

> Following the consistency of its logic, it [deconstruction] attacks not only the internal edifice, both semantic and formal, of philosophemes, but also what one would be wrong to assign to it as its external housing, its extrinsive conditions of practice: the historical forms of its pedagogy, the social, economic or political structures of this pedagogical institution. It is because deconstruction interferes with solid structures, "material" institutions, and not only with discourses or signifying representations, that it is always distinct from analysis or "critique." And in order to be pertinent, deconstruction works as strictly as possible in that place where the supposedly "internal" order of the philosophical is articulated by (internal *and* external) necessity with the institutional conditions and forms of teaching. To the point where the concept of the institution itself would be subjected to the same deconstructive treatment.[131]

As Derrida's deconstruction of the Foucauldian archeology of madness has demonstrated, "all history [of the system of the institution, pedagogy included] can only be in the last analysis, the history of meaning, that is of Reason in general."[132] And if "Reason" and "history" are the only conceivable ends of the institutional structure of pedagogy as an objectification of philosophy, there is a "double bind," or a bi-directional "fold" in the laws of the system and of its philosophical analysis, impinging upon the GREPH's project—as it did upon Foucault's—that makes it difficult, if no precautions are taken, to avoid the dual traps of either reinstating the heterology of an "other" monolith while opposing the privilege of an epistemological reduction of meanings or to escape imposing a willful silence upon the languages of the self while assenting to the "fittingness" of a theoretical posture.

The recommendations Derrida makes to the GREPH regarding a political resistance to the Haby Reform incorporates these deconstructive principles in an effort to regulate the "preconditions of a political practice that seeks to be as coherent as possible in its successive steps, in the strategy of its alliances and in its discourse."[133] What justifies deconstruction to move through and into the arena of discourse to the empirical conditions of "real-world" injustices forged by the architectural "cornerstones" of the *ideologico-conceptual thematisms of the pedagogical institution* is the ethical nature of socio-political effects following any act of criticism:

> One first locates, in an architectonics, in the art of the system, the "neglected corners" and the *"defective* cornerstone," that which, from the outset, threatens the coherence and the internal order of the construction. But it is a cornerstone! It is required by the architecture which it nevertheless, in advance, deconstructs from within. It assures its coherence while situating in advance, in a way that is both visible and invisible (that is, corner), the site that lends itself to a deconstruction to come. The best spot for efficiently inserting the deconstructive lever [the *mochlos*][134] is a cornerstone. There may be other analogous places but this one derives its privilege from the fact that it is indispensable to the completeness of the edifice. A condition of erection, holding up walls of an established edifice, it also can be said to maintain it, to contain it, and be tantamount to the *generality* of the architectonic system, "of the entire system."[135]

More notably, a "deconstructive" rereading of the discursive archive of pedagogy to locate its institutional inclusions/exclusions, its orderings/disorderings, its valuations/devaluations, and so on, must precede the "reconstructive" phase(s) of a rewriting of the existing subdivisions configuring the disciplinarity of epistemological foundations, for a "critical reelaboration of this hierarchy and of this problematics of hierarchy must not be restricted to new 'theorems' in the same language *(langage)*."[136] It requires the heteroglossia of a fresh writing that inscribes and is inscribed by the rules of an unborrowed code following "an other logic,"[137] one that can self-consciously evade the conceits of the metaphysical arrangements it is reacting to or may use in the performance of critique. This would presuppose: firstly, the inversion of the argumentative logics, the hierarchy of which privileges a normative arrangement of concepts from a binarization of terms (good/bad, right/wrong, etc.); and, secondly, a displacement of the epistemological groundwork coordinating the ethical acceptance of the formal structuring of its concepts that organize the "essential" possibilities of thought itself.

Conclusion for an Ending:
A Monstrosity for Which There Is No End

Deconstruction is wary of origins. It does not account for them because it does not believe in reinstating them nor in reinforcing their legitimizing value to celebrate their privileging of an immutable foundation. Yet deconstruction derives its critical force from the differential markings of the chains of signification that emanate from the search for a definitive finality; that last link, always so near, but forever out of sight, that only a Hegel could foresee in the absolute knowledge of a dialectical *u-topos* as the end of meaning and of history, the end of philosophy and of pedagogy. If there can be no end to the situation of deconstruction, it is surely appropriate to ask whether the "strategies" discussed in Chapter 2 are not simply promoting a futile and self-defeating task, especially for pedagogical issues that often beg some sort of resolution. Absolute finality is non-identity signifying the death of being: the death of the subject and the death of meaning, not to mention history. To say that something like a pedagogical issue ends, that is to say that it exists *no more,* is absurd, because then there would be no remainder, only the space of silence and the silence of space. There would be nothing left to say that would not already be known. Discourse will probably never cease to exist until the demise of the last of humanity, but until then we almost certainly will have deconstruction with us, for the expression of ideas initiates responses that seek to understand the complexity of a plethora of motivational factors looming below the surface of any subject position. Identifying what is "right" and what is "wrong" also goes along with discovering how these values are constructed and sometimes, perhaps, why. Deconstruction can certainly help us with that. Minimizing the dangers of forgetting the past would inevitably dull the passion of memory and of the soul's desire for fulfilling a meaningful regeneration of the human spirit or mind, if not the credibility of exercising the freedom of a nascent will as a spur from catalyzing thought to emancipatory action. This glimmer of an Archimedean point that is always already unreachable is what pedagogy should aim for to extend teaching-learning beyond the tendency to merely imitate a brief scholastic adventurousness as one would watch the cascading flicker of a fading memory casting empty shadows on a cave wall.

Notes

1. Jacques Derrida, "The Pit and the Pyramid: Introduction to Hegel's Semiology," trans. Alan Bass, in *Margins of Philosophy* (Chicago: University of Chicago Press, 1982), 102.

2. Citation in Jacques Derrida, "The Age of Hegel," trans. Susan Winnet, in *Demarcating the Disciplines: Philosophy, Literature, Art,* ed. Samuel Weber (Minneapolis: University of Minnesota Press, 1986), 3.

3. Derrida, "The Age of Hegel," 4.

4. Derrida, "The Age of Hegel," 23.

5. See Shlomo Avineri, *Hegel's Theory of the Modern State* (Cambridge: Cambridge University Press, 1972).

6. Derrida, "The Age of Hegel," 11.

7. Derrida, "The Age of Hegel," 23.

8. Derrida, "The Age of Hegel," 23.

9. G. W. F. Hegel, *Elements of the Philosophy of Right,* trans. H. B. Nisbet, ed. Allen W. Wood (Cambridge: Cambridge University Press).

10. Hegel's letter to Duboc, 30 July, 1822 cited in Derrida, "The Age of Hegel," 15.

11. Derrida, "The Age of Hegel," 23.

12. Derrida, "The Age of Hegel," 23-24. See also the account of this complex situation in Avineri, *Hegel's Theory of the Modern State.*

13. Derrida, "The Age of Hegel," 15.

14. Derrida, "The Age of Hegel," 12.

15. Derrida cites extracts from Hegel's correspondence on the subjects of Bavarian lottery tickets and the matter of contributions to the General Fund for Widows, a form of institutional life insurance for professors.

16. See Jacques Derrida, *Writing and Difference,* trans. Alan Bass (Chicago: University of Chicago Press, 1978) and Jacques Derrida, *On the Name,* trans. David Wood, John P. Leavey Jr., and Ian McLeod, ed. Thomas Dutoit (Stanford: Stanford University Press, 1995).

17. Derrida, "The Age of Hegel," 17.

18. Derrida, "The Age of Hegel," 4.

19. Derrida, "The Age of Hegel," 24.

20. Derrida, "The Age of Hegel," 15.

21. Altenstein's Letter of June 6, 1822, cited in Derrida, "The Age of Hegel," 15.

22. Derrida, "The Age of Hegel," 15.

23. Cited in Derrida, "The Age of Hegel," 25.

24. Derrida, "The Age of Hegel," 25.

25. From the letter of G. W. F. Hegel "To the Royal Ministry of Spiritual, Academic, and Medical Affairs" (April 16, 1822), appended to Derrida, "The Age of Hegel,"40.

26. Derrida, "The Age of Hegel," 25.

27. Derrida, "The Age of Hegel," 28.

28. Derrida, "The Age of Hegel," 17.

29. Derrida, "The Age of Hegel," 26.

30. Derrida, "The Age of Hegel," 17-18.

31. See David Farrell Krell, *Of Memory, Reminiscence, and Writing: On the Verge* (Bloomington: Indiana University Press, 1990), especially Chapter 5, and Jacques Derrida, *Margins of Philosophy,* trans. Alan Bass (Chicago: University of Chicago Press, 1982).

32. Derrida, "The Age of Hegel," 17.

33. Derrida, "The Age of Hegel," 8-9.

34. Derrida, "The Age of Hegel," 24. (Emphasis in the original.)

35. See the whole of footnote 1 in Derrida,"The Age of Hegel," 34. More thorough discussions on the problem of rethinking the concept of "ideology" in terms of the "linguistic turn" of intellectual history after poststructuralism and specifically deconstruction that are beyond the scope of analysis conducted here are to be found in Dominic LaCapra, *Rethinking Intellectual History: Texts, Contexts, Language* (Ithaca: Cornell University Press, 1983); George Attridge, Geoffrey Bennington, and Robert Young, eds., *Poststructuralism and the Question of History* (Cambridge: Cambridge University Press, 1987); and Hayden White, *The Content of the Form: Narrative Discourse and Historical Representation* (Baltimore: Johns Hopkins University Press, 1987).

36. Derrida, "The Age of Hegel," 22.

37. Derrida, "The Age of Hegel," 22.

38. Derrida, "The Age of Hegel," 22.

39. Derrida, "The Age of Hegel," 28.

40. Jacques Derrida, "Between Brackets I," trans. P. Kamuf, in *POINTS . . . Interviews, 1974-1994,* ed. Elizabeth Weber (Stanford: Stanford University Press, 1997), 26.

41. Derrida, "Between Brackets I," 26.

42. In Jacques Derrida, *The Ear of the Other: Otobiography, Transference, Translation,* trans. Peggy Kamuf and Avital Ronell, ed. Christie McDonald (Lincoln: University of Nebraska Press, 1988), the question of autobiography and otobiography is interrelated to the problem of the proper name and the signature. Derrida confronts the academic freedom of Nietzschean pedagogy and its reception, interpretation, etc., through a discussion of "how one becomes what one is," one of the central themes underlying "The Age of Hegel."

43. Michel de Certeau, *The Writing of History,* trans. Tom Conley (New York: Columbia University Press, 1988). De Certeau has some interesting insights into the limitations of the Hegelian *Geistesgeschichte* (a "cultural" form of intellectual history) for capturing the ideal of the "spirit of the times," but goes further to set down a theory of the writing of history that incorporates many Derridean features (e.g., writing and death, difference and trace).

44. See David Ingram, *Reason, History, and Politics: The Communitarian Grounds of Legitimation in the Modern Age* (New York: State University of New York Press, 1995).

45. Derrida, "The Age of Hegel," 23.

46. See White, *The Content of the Form.*

47. Derrida, "The Age of Hegel," 23.

48. Vincent Descombes, *Modern French Philosophy,* trans. L. Fox-Scott and J. Harding (Cambridge: Cambridge University Press, 1980), 137.

49. Derrida, "The Age of Hegel," 22-23.

50. Ryan, *Marxism and Deconstruction: A Critical Articulation* (Baltimore: Johns Hopkins University Press, 1982), 118.

51. Derrida, "The Age of Hegel," 25.

52. Derrida, "The Age of Hegel," 24.

53. Hegel, *Elements of the Philosophy of Right,* 321.

54. See also G. W. F. Hegel, *Phenomenology of Spirit,* trans. A. V. Miller (Oxford: Clarendon Press, 1977).

55. Cited in Jacques Derrida, "The Pit and the Pyramid: Introduction to Hegel's Semiology," trans. Alan Bass, in *Margins of Philosophy* (Chicago: University of Chicago Press, 1982), 73.

56. See Martin Heidegger, *Questions Concerning Technology and Other Essays,* trans. William Lovitt (New York: Harper and Row, 1977).

57. Andrew Vincent, *Theories of the State* (Oxford: Basil Blackwell, 1987), 125.

58. Derrida, "The Age of Hegel," 17.

59. Jacques Derrida, *Glas,* trans. John P. Leavey Jr. and Richard Rand (Lincoln: University of Nebraska Press, 1986), 1.

60. See Jacques Derrida, *Glas.*

61. Derrida, *The Ear of the Other,* 56.

62. Jacques Derrida, *Dissemination,* trans. Barabara Johnson (Chicago: University of Chicago Press, 1981), 105.

63. See Derrida, *The Ear of the Other.*

64. Martin Jay, *Downcast Eyes: The Denigration of Vision in Twentieth-Century French Thought* (Berkeley: University of California Press, 1993). This is an unusual twisting of the Derridean neologism "phallogocentrism" because of the anti-phenomenological inferences pointed to by the visual focus of the word "ocular."

65. Jacques Derrida, *The Truth in Painting,* trans. Geoff Bennington and Ian McLeod (Chicago: University of Chicago Press), 19.

66. See Manfred Frank, "Is Self-Consciousness a Case of *Présence à Soi?* Towards a Meta-Critique of the Recent French Critique of Metaphysics," in *Derrida: A Critical Reader,* ed. David Wood (Cambridge: Blackwell, 1992), 218-234.

67. In Jacques Derrida, *Memoires for Paul de Man,* trans. Cecilia Lindsay, Jonathan Culler, and Eduardo Cadava (New York: Columbia University Press, 1986), the experience of memory, subjectivity, and intersubjectivity is probed as the defacement of *autos* or *prosopopoeia.*

68. Derrida, *Dissemination,* 27.

69. Derrida, "The Age of Hegel," 18.

70. See Jacques Derrida, *Signéponge/Signsponge,* trans. Richard Rand (New York: Columbia University Press, 1976).

71. Gayatri Chakravorty Spivak, "Speculations on Reading Marx: After Reading Derrida," in *Poststructuralism and the Question of History,* ed. George Attridge, Geoffrey Bennington, and Robert Young (Cambridge: Cambridge University Press, 1987), 43.

72. See Umberto Eco, *The Role of the Reader: Explorations in the Semiotics of Text* (Bloomington: University of Indiana Press, 1979); and Jacques Derrida, *Of Grammatology,* trans. Gayatri Chakravorty Spivak (Baltimore: Johns Hopkins University Press, 1976).

73. See Fredric Jameson, *The Political Unconscious: Narrative as a Socially Symbolic Act* (Ithaca: Cornell University Press, 1981) and Samuel Weber, *Institutions and Interpretation* (Minneapolis: University of Minnesota Press, 1987.

74. Derrida, "The Age of Hegel," 3-4.

75. See Jean Baudrillard, *Simulacres et simulation* (Paris: Galilée, 1981).

76. Derrida, *Dissemination,* 105.

77. See Derrida, *Dissemination.*

78. Derrida, "The Age of Hegel," 5.

79. See Avineri, *Hegel's Theory of the Modern State.*

80. Derrida, "The Age of Hegel," 5.

81. Cousin cited in Derrida, "The Age of Hegel," 9.

82. Derrida, "The Age of Hegel," 29.

83. Derrida, "The Age of Hegel," 29.

84. Derrida, "The Age of Hegel," 22.

85. Hegel cited in Derrida, "The Age of Hegel," 26.

86. Derrida, "The Age of Hegel," 26.

87. See Derrida, "The Pit and the Pyramid."

88. Hegel cited in Derrida, "The Age of Hegel," 26.

89. Derrida, "The Age of Hegel," 11.

90. Derrida, "The Age of Hegel," 33.

91. Derrida, "The Age of Hegel," 6.

92. See Jacques Derrida, "Languages and Institutions of Philosophy," trans. Sylvia Söderlind, Rebecca Comay, Barbara Havercroft, and Joseph Adamson, *Recherches Semiotique/Semiotic Inquiry* 4, no. 2 (1984): 91-154.

93. Derrida, "The Age of Hegel," 33.

94. Derrida, "The Age of Hegel," 6-7.

95. GREPH, *Qui a peur de la philosophie?* (Paris: Aubier-Flammarion, 1977).

96. Derrida, "The Age of Hegel," 5.

97. The GREPH originally banded together in 1974. See Derrida, *Du droit à la philosophie* (Paris: Galilée, 1990).

98. Derrida, "The Age of Hegel," 19.

99. See GREPH, *Qui a peur de la philosophie?*

100. Included as appendix in Jacques Derrida, "Où commence et comment finit un corps enseignant," in *Du droit à la philosophie* (Paris: Galilée, 1990).

101. Personal conversation with Jacques Derrida, Paris, July 1994.

102. See also Jacques Derrida, "The Time of a Thesis," trans. Kathleen McLaughlin, in *Philosophy in France Today,* ed. Alan Montefiore (Cambridge: Cambridge University Press, 1983), 34-50.

103. Derrida, "The Age of Hegel," 33.

104. Derrida, "The Age of Hegel," 33.

105. Derrida, "Où commence et comment finit un corps enseignant," 120-121. Cf. Jacques Derrida, *Dissemination.*

106. Derrida, *Margins of Philosophy,* 329.

107. Opening the philosophical door to a possible alliance of the GREPH with Marxist politics, Derrida writes in "The Age of Hegel": "If the current French State is afraid of philosophy, it is because its teaching contributes to the progress of two types of threatening forces: those wanting to change the State (those, let's say, belonging to the left wing of Hegel) and to wrest it from the control of those forces currently in power, and those which, on the other hand or simultaneously, allied or not with the foregoing, tend toward the destruction of the State. These two forces cannot be classified according to the prevailing divisions. They seem to me, for example, to cohabitate today within the theoretical and practical field known as 'Marxism.'" (33-34)

108. See Jacques Derrida, "Structure, Sign, and Play in the Discourse of the Human Sciences," in *Writing and Difference.*

109. See, for example, Thomas E. Wartenberg, ed., *Rethinking Power* (Albany: State University of New York Press, 1992).

110. Derrida, "The Age of Hegel," 19-20.

111. Derrida, "The Age of Hegel," 19.

112. Derrida, "Mochlos; or, The Conflict of the Faculties," trans. Richard Rand and Amy Wygant, in *Logomachia: The Conflict of the Faculties,* ed. Richard Rand (Lincoln: University of Nebraska Press, 1992), 11.

113. Derrida, *Of Grammatology,* 158. (The form of the original has been modified.)

114. Derrida, "The Age of Hegel," 20.

115. Gilles Deleuze and Felix Guattari, *A Thousand Plateaus: Capitalism and Schizophrenia,* trans. Brian Massumi (Minneapolis: University of Minnesota Press, 1987).

116. See Pierre Bourdieu and Jean-Claude Passeron, *Reproduction in Education, Society and Culture,* trans. Richard Nice (London: Sage Publications, 1977). The violence of writing as the letter of the law of exclusion is the focus of the second half of Jacques Derrida's *Of Grammatology.*

117. See Pierre Bourdieu, *Language and Symbolic Power,* trans. Gino Raymond and Matthew Adamson (Cambridge: Polity Press, 1991).

118. Derrida, "Où commence et comment finit un corps enseignant," 114.

119. This is the motivating premise of Derrida's, *Of Grammatology.*

120. Derrida, "Où commence et comment finit un corps enseignant," 130.

121. Bourdieu and Passeron, *Reproduction in Education, Society and Culture.*

122. Derrida, "The Age of Hegel," 7-8.

123. See Jacques Derrida, "Où commence et comment finit un corps enseignant" for further elaboration on the role of the teaching body in the forms of reproduction that saturate and amplify the contradictions of the scene of teaching, its field.

124. See Jacques Derrida, *Of Grammatology.*

125. Jacques Derrida, "Living On: Border Lines," trans. James Hulbert, in *Deconstruction and Criticism,* ed. Harold Bloom, Paul de Man, Jacques Derrida, Geoffrey Hartman, and J. Hillis Miller (New York: Continuum, 1979), 93-94.

126. Derrida, "Living On: Border Lines," 93.

127. See Gregory Ulmer, *Applied Grammatology: Post(e)-Pedagogy from Jacques Derrida to Joseph Beuys* (Baltimore: Johns Hopkins University Press, 1985).

128. See Jean-François Lyotard, *The Postmodern Condition: A Report on Knowledge,* trans. Geoffrey Bennington and Bernard Massumi (Minneapolis: University of Minnesota Press, 1991).

129. Derrida, "Où commence et comment finit un corps enseignant," 119.

130. See Jacques Derrida, "On Colleges and Philosophy," in *Postmodernism: ICA Documents,* ed. Lisa Appignanesi (London: Free Association Books, 1989), 66-71.

131. Derrida, *The Truth in Painting,* 19-20.

132. Derrida, *Writing and Difference,* 308.

133. Derrida, "The Age of Hegel," 30.

134. See Derrida, "Mochlos."

135. Derrida, *Memoires,* 72.

136. Derrida, *Memoires,* 20.

137. Derrida, "Où commence et comment finit un corps enseignant," 121.

Chapter Three

Technologies of Reason

Academic Responsibility beyond the Principle of Reason as the Metaphysical Foundation of the University

> Would it not be more "responsible" to try pondering the ground, in the history of the West, on which the juridico-egological values of responsibility were determined, attained, imposed? There is perhaps a fund here of "responsibility" that is at once "older" and—to the extent it is conceived anew, through what some would call a crisis of responsibility in its juridico-egological form and its ideal of decidability—is *yet to come,* or, if you prefer, "younger." Here, perhaps, would be a chance for the task of thinking what will have been, up to this point, the representation of university responsibility, of what it is and might become, in the wake of upheavals no longer to be concealed from ourselves, even if we still have trouble analyzing them. Is a new type of university responsibility possible?
>
> —Jacques Derrida, "Mochlos; or, The Conflict of the Faculties"[1]

Chapter 3 extends the range of the "dominant metaphorical register"[2] of the Derridean call for the deconstruction of the institution—after the memorious professing of the pedagogical ends of the dialectical reason of Hegelianism—through its attending to the critical presuppositions of "a certain architectural rhetoric"[3] of a post-Kantian type that retranslates the rational ground of the systemic technologies of the classic interdisciplinarity of knowledge constructions within the university as the basis for the possibility of the articulation of a "new" ethics of academic responsibility. It presents a reading of "The Principle of Reason: The University in the Eyes of Its Pupils," the text of a public lecture given by Jacques Derrida before an assembly at Cornell University in April 1983. The chapter itself is composed of two parts. The first part engages the reason of the occasion of the discourse itself, the motivation provided for the institutional conventionality of the text-context encounter, that generates the simplicity and the complexity of the "rules of exchange" governing the axiology of the gift-counter-gift logic structuring the reality of the moment, its ethics, and its politics. The purpose here is to analyze how the lecture—being essentially of an inaugural "type" to honor the precise moment of Derrida's symbolic "ascension" to an endowed chair of philosophy—works both with and against the formal limits of the situation to gauge the epistemic and empirical "values of responsivity" implied or expected from the "participants" involved at the scene. Continuing on this theme of the constation and performativity of academic responsibility, the first part also examines the metaphorical parameters of the topology of Cornell University, how the actual landscaping (artificiality) and setting (naturalistic) of the campus, e.g., the bridges and the abyss, forge the figure and ground of the *scopic structures* that impress Derrida as being the "literal example" for the *oto-bio-graphic* stipulations placed in the discourse on *how one should not speak of the university.* The second part deals with the deconstruction of the metaphysical foundation of the principle of reason. Or, what is the logic of the ground of the being of the modern university itself as the cultural product of the unification of philosophy and technology. The ramifications of the *idea of the principle of reason* are explored through an extended meditation on its pragmatic and hermeneutic consequences for the *instrumental and poietic aims of research.* Chapter 3 finishes by way of a critical probing of some of the suggestions Derrida makes for "re-awakening" or "re-situating" the ethics of the responsibility of the *academic community-at-large.*

Performative Contradictions

In Apologia *Quid Juris:* Broaching the Responsibility of Dangerous Confessions

> Today, how can we not speak of the university?
> I put my question in the negative, for two reasons. On the one hand, as we all know, it is impossible, now more than ever, to disassociate the work we do, within one discipline or several, from a reflection on the political and institutional conditions of that work. Such a reflection is unavoidable. It is no longer an *external* complement to teaching and research; it must make its way through the very objects we work with, shaping them as it goes, along with our norms, procedures, and aims. We cannot speak of such things. On the other hand, the question "how can we not" gives notice of the *negative,* or perhaps we should say *preventative,* complexion of the preliminary reflections I should like to put to you. Indeed, since I am seeking to initiate discussion, I shall content myself with how one should not speak of the university. Some of the typical risks to be avoided, it seems to me, take the form of a bottomless pit, while others take the form of a protectionist barrier.
> Does the university, today, have what is called a *raison d'être*?
> —Jacques Derrida, "The Principle of Reason:
> The University in the Eyes of Its Pupils"[4]

Allowing for the temporary suspension of a "false start."

We must pause prior to directly engaging these initial, preparatory and vigilant, propositions submitted at the beginning of a lecture addressing the question of the being of the university—the reason of its methods of research, teaching and learning—to remind ourselves of a startling confidence Jacques Derrida permits us access to, "taking the floor [at Cornell University] to speak [for the first time] as an Andrew Dickson White Professor-at-Large":[5]

> Before preparing the text of a lecture, I find I must prepare myself for the scene I shall encounter as I speak. That is always a painful experience, an occasion for silent, paralytic deliberation. I feel like a hunted animal, looking in the darkness for a way out where none is to be found. Every exit is blocked.[6]

It is a generous, but *timely,* confession of a secret truth. The sudden revelation outlines a course of habit, that in an unfeigning (heartfelt) rendition of the *aporia* of the situation of deconstruction, does much to shed light on the veiled passion of a writer's craft and a philosopher's life, both of which are at the least germane, if not crucial, to a rereading of "The Principle of Reason: The University in the Eyes of Its Pupils." The originating source of the "psycho-sensible" discomfiture Derrida describes—as the affectivity of reactions to situational distractors experienced in advance of the actual process of the writing of the text of this lecture—is quite thoroughly based in the projected reality of having to meet the contextuality of factual circumstances surrounding the empirical event of its enunciation to the Other. So, the disclosure of the personal trauma of these disturbing feelings of disorientation forefronts how conceding to the overpowering "virtuality" of the limits of comprehending a possible "state-of-affairs" within the irreducible specificity of unforeseen conditions can only impede recourse to the *freeing-up* of a train of thought and language.[7] In other words, to draw out the Kantian line of Derrida's description of *hesitation,* when confronted with this immensity of the magnitude of an Idea (to invoke this supra-sensible essence of the "purely rational," the "*sur*-real") that exceeds the synthetic powers of intuitive estimation, the imagination experiences the inadequacy of this maximum and, thus, the violence of its own stretched limitations, causing it to recoil on itself.[8] For the pain and pleasure of these reasons and those to come, Derrida readily concedes, "In the [then] present case, the task [of writing a lecture 'on the subject—quite properly sublime—of the essence of the University,'[9] its reason for being] seemed triply impossible."[10] Let us re-begin here then. At the edge of possibility.

    1. To reiterate what has already been noted above, in passing: "this was not to be just a lecture like any other."[11] But rather, to fulfill the sobering propriety of a certain "pre-setting" of requirements suitable to the determinative constraints of the occasion, the constative disposition of its written text, as it produces the performativity of itself by speaking "self-reflexively" about the operative value of itself,[12] "had to be ['stylistically' consistent with the general specificity of a genre] something like an inaugural address"[13] in order to demonstrate a "genuine" appreciation for the conferment of a venerable title. According to this "academi-

cized" tradition of "meritocracy," of the divisible exchange of the "giving-and-receiving"of prestige, within the grander system of the university,[14] the lecture demanded an ethico-political obligation of the act of speech itself and of the speaker, Derrida. And by extension, I would also say, of the *"work" of deconstruction* for the institutional honor of the *gift of recognition*: regarding the implied pledge of an appropriative reconciliation of the advent of its subjective inscription of expression with the abiding strictness of "standards of adherence" to the conventions of a more or less commonly used rhetorical archetype of formal recitation we would be most tempted to call a *"discourse of ingratiation."* A manner of presentation at once fitting to the hyperstylized decorum of the situation, the "crux" of its ritualism, and not egregiously parasitic on the conditional guidelines[15] of the delimiting contextuality the philosopher, as well as his interlocutors, must not self-consciously betray or knowingly abuse to neatly execute the discreet ordinance of tribute to the high seriousness of the moment. So, preceding the actual instance of the performative re-animation of the written text, there is an unspoken, yet duly acknowledged, "responsibility" expected, in principle, on the part of Derrida,[16] for a public re-exhibition of gratitude that, *in the equity of its re-circulation of the exchange of "thankfulness,"* would obey, by both theoretical and practical necessity, the etiquette of the structure of an ethical supplementarity supportive of the unbending logic of the rules of response affecting the co-incidental appropriety of the truth value of the lecture.[17] The covenant of the obligation to reciprocate, qualified as such, distributively structures the *symbolic order* of the line of credit extended from university to professor, and back again, in the circular geometry of a prescribed calculability of "rightful" exchange. The *"interest"* of a fair paying-back of the debt owed (entailed, to be given back, *re*-turned) the institution by Derrida, while adopting and carrying out one of the ceremonial functions of "epistemic subjectivity,"[18] *in his name before the Other,* is accruable out of the bond of "friendship" and "politeness" for its gracious entitlement of him to the duties to come of the chair he will most willingly bear *in the name of Another as Other of the Other.* The requirement of the writer-speaker, philosopher-teacher, individual-scholar can only be the *possibility* of doing *"nothing-but-justice"*—in the sense of being *juste* or "right"[19]—to the self-reaffirming "spirit" of the laws of measurable indemnity and "mutual indebtment" constructing the overdetermined stabilizability (saturability) of the situation. No "fallibility" or "ineptitude" in the pre-reading of the occurential determinants of the responsibility of the discourse is tolerable that puts the *intention of duty* into default.

Moderating for the potentiality of negative effects arising from what might be perceived as "inopportune" or "ill-judged" comments, Derrida scans over the mutually amicable history of a long association with the institution now granting him a status of distinction—"the first American university [he] ever taught for"[20]—to ask the obvious and overwhelming question: "Was this inaugural lecture a well-chosen moment to ask whether the University has a reason for being? Wasn't I about to act with all the unseemliness of a stranger who in return for noble hospitality plays prophet of doom with his hosts, or at best eschatological harbinger, like Elijah denouncing the power of kings or announcing the end of the realm?"[21] Wondering out loud, with a self-deprecating air of benevolent curiosity, whether the matter of the discourse should be presented to the audience defuses and heightens the implicit angst of the situation; quelling and accenting the potentially catastrophic violence of its gnawing uncertainty of outcome by radicalizing the homogeneity of the code of its laws the "saturated" context of the lecture proclaims for its "major" and "minor" participants. Derrida—in speaking candidly of the ethics of communication and of the deconstructive "sufferance"[22] of a superseding of the responsibility to "say-the-right-thing"—exhibits a keen awareness of the irrecuperability of the perils to be assumed for exceeding the known bounds of charity that are allowable to "the donee" and "the doner" by the conditional "ritualizing" of the rules of a faithful exchange of obligation to the Other.[23] Failing to even *appear to uphold* the promise of the cycle of restitution threatens to annul the intentionality of the "gift-counter-gift" axiology particular to the precomprehension of the situation we have been outlining, by estranging the solemn temper of the moment. Still, the gesture of forthright non-avoidance Derrida performs by seizing the chance to complicate the normative insolvency of a "discourse of consensus" unquestioning of the being and function of the university as it sponsors this "gift event" suffices to abate the imminent jeopardy of what could be construed as the *non-excusability of a missed opportunity for the ethical surrendering of a subjective position to the fixed duty of a calculable exchange of obligation.* But is that the end of it? Derrida, by admitting to a "hesitance about speaking without hesitation,"[24] while making painstakingly sure to maintain an unqualified humility for the tenor of the situation, manages to arouse feelings of respect or even admiration in the Other.[25] Are the "options" of response so easily exhausted, the *invention* of deconstruction so glibly stifled, with the polite declaration of a collateral awareness of both a transgression of neutrality and a questioning of injunction? I do not think so.

The "other side" of the responsibility Derrida more than infers here, participating fully, at this time, in the topological programmatics of the intra-university, inter-institutional event, through the enactment of these irruptive words, is not an irresponsibility posed as a *typology of defiance.* A "faulty" ingratitude avoiding the debt of restitution that flies in the face of "good conscience" by flagrantly doing the discourtesy of "violence" to the "logic" of the *rendezvous.* The deconstructive incentive (motivation) of the discourse, "of such force and desire as it may have [being neither *on* the side of 'right' nor simply *against* it], is a certain experience of the impossible,"[26] an infinite *aporia* of the possible that increases the responsibility of the obligation to the Other *as* Other. The incalculable anteriority of its *ethics of singularity,* Derrida has shown often enough,[27] comes to take the interventive form of a decision to a hazardous commitment of an *absolute risk* one must make to speak and think, freely and openly, without limits or the necessity of a punctilious abiding to the normative rules or categorical laws of a "proper" (ritual or statutory) responsiveness to the determination of a call to duty in the deliberate service of a self-regulating, noncritical ego.[28] Pushing the conventionalized borders of/to thought and experience beyond the established frontiers of inherited prohibition is a willingness to step over the compromising edge *(arête)* of the univeralized "case" of possibility itself.[29] To respond, as Derrida does, for example, to the *invitation of the gift,* neither in the *"language of ritual* and the *language of duty,"*[30] nor out of obligation to the jurisprudence of generalized rules of "friendship" and "politeness." Doing so would prevent us from cutting ourselves off from a "boundless gratitude" that is the hyper-responsibility of the "subject" (empirical and epistemic) to the value and justice of truth, *"the right to say everything."*[31] To ex-pose our discourse to the questioning of the Other, not by devolving it into a *rhetoric of autonomy,* but by welcoming its resistances to a dialogue of the Self to the *self-same,* is to open oneself to the play of learning through queries and objection that empty the subject to infinitize and to enrich its heteronomy.[32] "One must not be friendly or polite out of duty"[33] is but one side of the adage, *the rule of the non-rule,* Derrida obliquely ventures to bring to the fore through this discourse, *without exactly saying it,* against the regulative decidability of a Kantianist ethics. For a deconstructive re-newing of the infinite responsibility owed the alterity of the Other, the reverse would, at the same time, also be true of a response to obligation, *to be just, above all, in the language of the Other.* As Derrida notes elsewhere, "It is insufficient to say that the 'ought' [*'il faut'*] of friendship, like that of politeness, must not be the order of duty."[34] To consider oneself beyond reproach, with frivolity and arrogance, before all law and all obligation, destroys the possibility of a hope to justice yet to come *(à-venir).*[35] Recalling the determinate conditions under which Derrida *has to speak,* the horizon of the discourse situated, as it is *"in the history"* of the institution of the university, "gives voice" to the *vouloir-dire* of the text, its *wanting-to-say-something-meaningful,* not as the realization of intentionality (or the *telos* of its plenitude), but as the undecidability of what remains to be thought by the Other.[36] And at this dissembled or inverse hinging of the secret of "translation" that pulls apart univocity by suspending the silence of the speaker's *right of decision qua the singularity of the communicative value of signification,* there is heralded more than a hint of a "double affirmation."[37] The paradox of knowing what one must do and its opposites in the *aporia* of the desire to do both. What makes us quiver with fear is the dread of "scandal," the ethical danger of "not managing to accede to the [traditional] concept of responsibility in the process of *forming* it."[38] For Derrida, specifically, *on the one hand,* it is a wanting-to-say the "right thing" for the discourse to remain responsibly conducive, *accountable,* in answering-for-itself (hence for its speaker) to the specificity of the general demands of that place and time without compromising the singularity of the "impossible" ethics of deconstruction and the multiplicity of its obligation to the iterative trace of "Otherness" within the Same. *On the other,* there is the desire to satisfy personal conscience regarding the philosophical exposition of arguments on matters educational with respect to the founding of the university, its *reason for being,* and to show the required deference to an academic institution by neither undermining nor condemning the auto-logic of its existence. We will return to the more immediate implications of this *aporetic point of passage* again shortly. How it is tied to the plethora of meanings issuing forth from the "phrase 'at large,' as in 'professor at large,'"[39] the descriptor used to discern the unspecified locality of the academic position, the obligations, freedoms, and responsibilities, that Derrida will hold and be held to.

2. Then, there is the *mise en scène* of the lecture, Cornell University, and the question of the view of its divided self across the bridges spanning the abyss

(Abgrund). As Derrida surveys the "natural" scene of the performance, the themes of origin and self-assertion, of being and spirit[40]—in echo of Martin Heidegger's infamous rectoral address[41]—become essential to this occasion for reflection on the interminable obligation of the promise of beginnings: "A second cause for worry is that I find myself involved already, quite imprudently, that is, blindly and without foresight, in an act of dramaturgy, writing out the play of that view in which Cornell, from its beginnings, has felt so much to be at stake. The question of the view has informed the writing-out of the institutional scene, the landscape of your university, the alternatives of expansion and enclosure, life and death. From the first it was considered vital not to close off the view."[42] What is the nature of the view, exactly, that so fills the philosopher with "shudders of awe,"[43] making his soul tremble by feeding the fear of mediocrity with an oppressive sense of "inadequacy," before the glorious void? "Beneath the bridges linking the university to its surroundings, connecting its inside to its outside, lies the abyss."[44] The peculiar "dia-synchrony" of the "tell-tale" portrait Derrida sketches—its belonging and non-belonging to the *tableau vivant* of Cornell—effuses an allegorical radiance, its signs emblazoning on the surface of reality a spatio-temporal immemoriality always before us. The style of the phraseology is simple, however, not at all unimportant or unremarkable for the *coup de théâtre,* the dramatic twist, of the *impression of truth* that is to be excavated from the institutional archive made reference to. Even though the physical view is truly magnificent because of the imposing phenomenality of its own spectacular attributes (e.g., natural and corporeal placements, "negative" relationships of infinite magnitude), the inspirational sensibilities evoked by the openness of its chorographic spacing definitively mark, feverishly *im-print,* the history of the founding of Cornell University.[45] On the one hand, we know that the *good reason* given for its being constructed on/across the split-site of a gorge was to secure the availability of room for the expansion inevitably needed to facilitate later growth. On the other, as Derrida reinforces, quoting James Siegel—whose text, "Academic Work: The View from Cornell,"[46] he is rereading in this lecture, "decipher[ing] that parable in [his] own way"[47]—the acumen of the institution's *namesake,* the primary influence on the decision taken, was not "simply on the side of life":[48] "[F]or Ezra Cornell the association of the view with the university had something to do with death. Indeed Cornell's plan seems to have been shaped by the thematics of the Romantic sublime, which practically guaranteed that a cultivated man [or woman] in the presence of certain landscapes would find his [or her] thoughts drifting metonymically through a series of topics—solitude, ambition, melancholy, death, spirituality, 'classical inspiration'—which could lead, by an easy extension, to questions of culture and pedagogy."[49] I will step in verily here to wax psychoanalytic on the dangerous beauty of these "recollections made in tranquillity" (to paraphrase William Wordsworth) and their significance. Where the inspiration of the view is palliative to the soul's need for terrible musings and self-alienation: the psychic distortion of an unconscious displacement of meaning relations penetrating the movement of the mind from *word-to-word* brings on "the exalting, desperate sense of the sublime"[50] in the *throwing-back* of Being to reality where, confronting the *ever-present-absence* of the gorge, being finds itself "suspended between life and

death."[51] Derrida says as much of his own ethical predicament of writing and speaking. Where the daemonic substrate of this compulsion of attraction and repulsion is involuntary and perpetually in the transference of displaced repetition, the affective delay *(Nachträglichkeit)* inhibiting the *sending of being* by eclipsing its *thrownness (Geworfenheit)* back to the light of the living ghost of itself: there is cause to worry.[52] The administration of Cornell University said as much of *their* predicament, in 1977, when it proposed to put up protective railings on the two bridges joining the great divide, "to check thoughts of suicide inspired by the view of the gorge."[53] The scheme, no doubt, brought protest, as the historical record shows us. And Derrida offers an anecdote of the defensible basis of this dissension to the very idea of these additions that is key to the interpretability of the debate: "In testimony before the Campus council, one member of the faculty did not hesitate to express his opposition to the barriers, those diaphragmatic eyelids, on the grounds that blocking the view would mean, to use his words, 'destroying the essence of the university.' What did he mean? What *is* the essence of the university?"[54] What the view portends for the continuity of both an anterior and a future concept of Cornell is inextricable from the institution's vision of its own historicity, *the reason for its being and the pursuant ambitions of its destination scoping-out the pragmatological parameters of its destiny.*[55] For Derrida, the philosophico-noematic complexity of the *panorama* as it relates to the initiating act of the foundation of the university—e.g., the localized example of Cornell and the greater idea of the *Universitas*—announces itself through the negative form of an affirmation that takes shape in the abyss *(Abgrund)*, a *topos* without *topos,* a place of no discernable grounding of limits, of no reason. How are we to read this, justify it? "An event of foundation can never be comprehended merely within the logic that it founds."[56] That is, to search out the *essence* of the university from the reason of *its* ground is to avoid questioning the *value* of the rationality presupposing the organization of the institution. For logic finds only that which it seeks. Putting the ethics of the *law of right* to the test demands, Derrida will state elsewhere, a *"surplus* of responsibility."[57] Or, as we explained earlier, the *double duty* of deconstruction.[58] An accounting of/for a position from which to challenge the single-sided boundaries of a reason of principle and of the principle of reason underlying the tranquil institutionalization of knowledge "within" the university and "outside" of it *"without renouncing the classical norms of objectivity and responsibility, without menacing the critical idea of science and of philosophy and thus without renouncing knowledge."*[59]

3. Considering the vulnerability of the position Derrida finds himself in, being an "insider" and an "outsider" to the academic community of the institution now paying him homage, it is imperative in such an atmosphere of "mixed" emotions (not to mention allegiances) to create a bearable space from within which to speak without reservation and yet also to be able to also leave something behind. The distasteful alternative to *not* situating these controversial remarks in the way I have been driving at—that is, by *responding responsibly* to the authority of the conventionalized code of citationality, *the philosophemes of metaphysics* that brought about the possibility of the university, while pursuing a *"graphics of iterability"*[60]—is self-censorship and self-deception. (Also a poten-

tial "byproduct" of the hierarchization of knowledge valuations in the system of the university. That is, a result of visible/invisible coercion of the disciplines upheld by the intimidation of a force *(Gewalt)* with power. The belligerence of authority outweighs and denies the real complexity of such an organization.)[61] The languishing tone of nostalgia permeating the scattered reflections of the early phases of the discourse helps to establish the precedent (something like a "negative assurance") for the tentative contract of "good faith" between speaker and listener Derrida must have, to say the things he does. It facilitates for the metalocution of a sense of *"blind trust"* where one, a philosopher by chosen profession, "unaware of the context, the proper rituals, and the changed environment,"[62] has been "given leave to consider matters loftily, from afar."[63] But ethical responsibility is not abdicated as far as the *telling of truth supposes justice.* Under the aegis of these friendly ruminations among colleagues and friends (perhaps some enemies also), the discourse emphasizes that the ethico-political and historico-institutional ramifications of the ceremony as a symbolic act of self-renewal and acceptance for both professor and university *cannot, could not, should not, be held in abeyance.* And Derrida does not prove too shy or uncontentious for an efficacious interference: "To ask whether the University has a reason for being is to wonder why there is a University, but the question 'why' verges on 'with a view to what'? What is the University's view? What are its views? Or again: what do we see from the University, whether for instance, we are simply in it, on board; or whether, puzzling over destinations, we look out from it while in port or, as French has it, *'au large,'* on the open sea, 'at large'?"[64] Couched in the language of the *coup d'envoi,* the sendoff, the questions converge toward "the category or the theme of DESTINATION";[65] in a word, it translates the "unity" of the *"topoi"* fashioning the philosophical augury of the meditation (as deliberative of "cause, purpose, direction, necessity, justification, meaning and mission.")[66] The dramatic slide of the subject of the "rite of passage," and its "right," Derrida explicitly refers to—e.g., changing the focus from the in-corporate location or site of the university to the "travelling mass" of its human alter ego or body politic subsumed in the fragile anonymity of the collective pronoun "we"[67]—includes a witnessing of departure that bemoans a loss of filiality and the welcoming of arrival that awards the gift of new life. The "promise of destination" is the catalyzing agent for the possibility of a "future-to-come" accompanied as it is by a prophetic omen of the "gift of death" without which one cannot speak about a time after the past and the present of the institution.[68] Playing metaphorically (metonymically) on the relational ambivalence of perspectives of affiliation with/in the "onto-totality" of the university itself and the "ideo-logical" origins of the reason of its systemic model (e.g., its organismic sense of "compartmentality" and "professionalism"), the thematic drift of the discourse displays the ethical undercurrent of the deconstructive resignation of thought about the generative form of a new kind of academic responsibility to be negotiated both among the extant community of its scholarly body and with those to whom the highly problematic "we" of "higher" education are more or less ultimately accountable: the State and the political constituency of public society. A relentless questioning of the complacency of the tranquil assurances of "so many 'clean consciences'"[69] for the unfolding of the being of the institution merges the concerns of "theoretical consciousness (that is also thetic or thematic consciousness) to [those of] 'practical' consciousness (ethical, legal, political)"[70] in the complexity of a continually transformative obligation within alternate states of a changing field of reality. Subjecting the *reason of the university* to the *"trial of deconstruction,"* Derrida calls for the *anabasis* of an affirmation of uncompromising responsibility; "a sort of promise of originary alliance [before the language of any and all contracts made, past, present, and future] to which we must have in some sense already acquiesced, already said *yes,* given a pledge [*gage*], whatever may be the negativity or problematicity of the discourse to follow."[71]   Still, the *apostatic* desire of the attempt of deconstruction to challenge the "rational" foundation of higher education built as it is on the artifacts of an older, "outdated," or somewhat "antiquated" groundwork cannot break completely with the normative laws of epistemic tradition for the potentially rejuvenating act of moving learning and understanding to other passageways and places waiting to be discovered or explored. As Derrida has frequently stated, there is no use or sense in doing without the conceits of metaphysics to critique the "trappings" of metaphysics, and, thereby, irresponsibly arresting avenues to the giving engagement of the subject to thinking.[72] The "hyper-responsibility" or the "ultra-ethics" of a deconstructive intervention into the "reason" and "unreason" of the university protects the possibility of its *living on*—its conscious self-renewal of direction, of being and of existence, after *"the now"*—only by a reflective working through of the oppressive restrictions of the system itself. Bolstering the chances of achieving a restructuring of the general code of the institution and of "institutionality" beyond the solitary rules of a comprehensive "univerticality"[73] of order means addressing the open question of the destination of knowledge across the "give-and-take" of existing disciplinary lines and politics. Why and how it is that the historicity of the pyramidic organization of the knowledge hierarchy (e.g., as "science," "technology," "philosophy," "poietics," "theory," "law," "practice") puts limitations on the extent of the freedom of play in the latitudes and lassitudes allowable the pursuit of teaching and research. The example I have been occupied with touches, in an obvious way, on the multiplicity of the philosophical idioms of the Heideggerian term *"Geschick"* (often translated as "destiny") to trope on the dispensation of the University *Dasein.*[74] The "post-Cartesian" idea of the reflective structure of the *envoi-renvoi,* the sending-sending-back, of Being at the root of the "ob-ject" of being translates easily for Derrida to the mis-guided plight of an institution ready to re-present the abyss of the reason of itself (the groundlessness of its grounding) without a meticulous questioning of academic responsibility or ethics, *a questioning of the ethics of its ethics.*[75] Leveraging the leveling force of the contradictory yet reciprocal dualities of the concept of destination as location/dislocation, orientation/disorientation, departure/arrival, end/beginning, and so on, safeguards against the irresponsibility of securing arbitrary separations of knowledge within the collocution of a constative and performative, theoretical and pragmatic space of teaching and learning. Not to resolve the contradictions of a determinant concept of "the University" that is at odds with the reality of itself as it sends itself outside of itself and back again to preserve and transmit knowledge (*a question of translation*) while transforming the sphere around it (*a problem of displacement*), but to probe the paradoxes of the *ur-ground* of its idealized structurality, the principle of reason, the metaphysical foundation for the development of the dual obligation of the institution.

The legitimacy of the opportunity (a chance?) Derrida takes to exercise a right of academic freedom by "speaking his mind" on the ethics of academic responsibility for those residing within the space of the university is not an unearned privilege: "In my teaching in Paris [he says] I have devoted a year-long seminar to the question of the university. Furthermore, I was recently asked [1982, early on] by the French government to write a proposal for the establishment of an International College of Philosophy, a proposal that for literally hundreds of pages considers all of the difficulties involved."[76] The text of the lecture we are presently rereading was one of many composed during this intense period of thinking and writing, of *praxis,* about the arduous enterprise of founding an "autonomous" (e.g., degree-granting and self-regulating) institution of advanced study unlike any other in the groundbreaking provocation of the initiative of its programs to encourage "inaugural incursions"[77] into areas foreign to the context of the *academic* tradition of research science. While many of us have undertaken the obligation of trying to reform flawed pedagogical infrastructures to better education or to improve the equity of access to it, few of us, like Derrida, have accepted the *co*responsibility of thinking and working through the *polemos* of establishing what is, more or less, comparable in formal stature to a "University" and yet goes beyond it, by pushing the practico-conceptual limits of the standard outward toward the reality of inventing new research possibilities. A formidable and risky undertaking to say the least. As such, these reflections engaging the problems of presiding over the reconceptualization and reconstitution of a scholastic destination—the phantasmagoric *coup de force* of transforming the metaphysical legacy of the ethico-juridical tradition of agency regulating academic responsibility that Derrida discourses on—are *not* exclusively theoretical, but are the tangible result of the wisdom of personal experiences. *A phronesis of deliberation achieved through the prism of deconstruction.* We cannot take this entwining of thought and action, constation and performativity, that is embedded in the finely sedimented textures of the lecture's devising at all lightly. How then do we resolve the ambiguous con-figurations of the opening citation to the discourse and *speak of the university by not speaking of it* in a certain fashion? It follows from the *ethics of deconstruction.* How can we not?

Toward a Metaphorology of the Sublime: The Uncanny, the University, and the Abyss

To return then, once again, to this interrupted beginning anew, though more deliberately now, and from somewhere near "the top." *"Today, how can we not speak of the university?"* Derrida draws attention to the *"negative"* or *"preventative complexion"* of the grammatical clause coordinating the syntactic composition of the guiding question serving as the opening of the discourse. Given that the spatio-temporal vista of the presentation so valorizes the mnemonic field of reflection in preparation for the implicature of the metaphorical grounding of figure in the tropology of the lecture, the explanation of the rationale behind the schematization organizing the conceptual network of the argument to be made "in favor of a new university Enlightenment *(Aufklärung)*"[78] anticipates both what is lost and what is gained in the "tutelary value" of the example *(paradeigma)*. Samuel Weber (having Søren Kierkegaard's *Repetition* in mind) explains how the "inherent tension" in the concept of *paradeigma* is etymologically (historico-ideologico-lexically) legible: "What is *ex-emplary* is *taken out* of its initial context, and this in a double sense. It is taken to an *extreme* and yet, at the same time in so being transported, it appears to be *more itself* [and I would add *more than itself*] than ever before."[79] The lecture, we should recall, is an attempt made by Derrida to *en-gage* the Other in the *critical promise* of an active portrayal of a form of deconstructive (re)reading converging on the question of the university's reason for being, *the grounding of its ground.* It therefore patently awaits the responsibility of a response to its pedagogical patterning of possibilities of repetition, *repeatability.* To entice the "viewer-listener" to enter into the reciprocity of an impending dialogue, be it polyphonous or cacophonous, regarding the ground of reason and its location within the space of the university, there are figural delimitations imposed on the discourse that obligate *an answering-back.* As memory remembers ahead as a *living-forward of past experience,* this is the "risk" involved for Derrida, for deconstruction: How to explain how one *ought not* to speak of the university. It implies, no, *expects,* limits to build, at the very least, the shadow of an argument on. For to know what one is or is not teaching, working to avoid or to embrace, requires reflection on the groundedness of one's thought as *productive negativity* or the reversal of finitude, an instant of madness. Not to mean, however, that Derrida cannot endeavor to exceed or to collapse those outer *frontières* of reason's boundaries into each other. Deconstruction must and will: unhindered as it might be by "a certain *usure* [*pthora*] of metaphorical force in philosophical exchange."[80] The tropological milieu—through which to deliberate the being of the university and its Being—thus enframed, betwixt the *phragma* and the abyss of reason, fulfills more than the role of "pedagogical ornament."[81] Derrida's serious play within the economy of formal sign-values tracing the empirico-denotative structurality of these figures of closure and non-closure will cause them to incur an essential redefinition and a semantic extension of what they represent compared with what they are for a deconstructive re-thinking of the sense of their differences. But here, at the point of separation, there is predicated a metaphorical *trans*-ference of semantic properties from the contrariety of dissimilar "objects" supplied the complementarity of these negative forms to the oppositionality of politico-institutional forces occupying the "higher" site of teaching and research. This subjective aspect of value relegation, in its turn, affects the perception of the "opening" and "closure" of knowledge within the classical system of the university. So, the tropic horizon inflecting the predicative restatement of the motivating intensions around which the thematic articulations of the discursive topic itself revolve (how *not* to speak of the university), isolates the *double-handed* imperatives of the deconstructive moves that will inform the "working out" of the original purpose of the query. Derrida can then elucidate the critical responsibility of the prospective line of inquiry to be enacted thereafter (while doing it all along!) in the "lecture proper":

> There is a double gesture here, a double postulation: to ensure professional competence and the most serious tradition of the university even while going as far as possible, theoretically and practically, in the most directly underground thinking about the abyss beneath the university, to think at one and the same time the entire "Cornellian" landscape—the campus on the heights, the bridges, and if necessary the barriers above the abyss—and the abyss itself.[82]

The occurential significance of the (previously highlighted) imagistic leitmotiv carried through the text of the lecture would surely not be lost on the audience at Cornell. The referential images of "the abyss, and bridges, and boundaries"[83] situating the proleptic aura of the "propaedeutical remarks"[84] put forward "to designate the teaching that comes before teaching"[85] are, of course, very real "signs," or *ec-topic* indicators recalling the appreciably conspicuous structuration of external formations inhabiting the existing landscape of the campus. The rhetorical flourish of these overt, although furtively suggestive, allusions to easily identifiable features of the physical layout and architectural design of Cornell, purposefully registers—within the spatio-temporal dimensions of an instantly recognizable representation of "empirical facticity"—the perlocutionary aspects of this constative discourse that are indispensable to achieving the performativity of its illocutionary presentation. Said another way, the text must needs *say what it does* and *do what it says* to counteract its "wearing off" or its "giving way" to the invasive excrescence of conditional detractors that would impinge on the residual impact of its expression.

The appurtenance of the figuration is uncanny *(Unheimliche)*,[86] oscillating as it does across the conceptual fluidity of a semiological space (yawning, rift, breach) opened up amid the reverse polarity of complementary and contradictory images of topological features from the reality of Cornell's dwelling that coordinate the tropic framework of the lecture. The metaphoricity en-joining and disjoining the non-mutually exclusive parameters of the antithetical analogues of reason setting up the "ideality" of the semantico-syntactic axes of the discourse as the inexhaustible formlessness of an abyss and the solid refuge of a barrier intercedes for the pure difference of the substantive meaning of their sensible exteriority. Weaving the texturing of ideas on the being of the university around the elemental propriety and *techno-logical* aspects of landmark formations prominently visible at Cornell—obvious images of ocular reference that *take in* the meanings of these conceptions of rationality defining "how one should not speak of the university"—promotes a *speculative caesura,* a "pausing-thought effect," making the familiar *environs* of the philosopher's performance seem unknown and strange. It is the clearing *(Lichtung)* of a "faint light" shattered.[87] An appropriative event *(Ereignis)* of truth[88] where the intimacy of understanding *(entendement)* degenerates, withdraws, so as to become ephemerally blurred from the erasure of the distinctions separating the sensory (object) and the non-sensory (idea).[89] Clusters of polyvalent meaning surrounding the *re*-presentation of the

imagery as it is continued during the succeeding sections of the discourse commence to take shape in the *unconcealment* of previously unnoticed, hence non-
evident, connections made between differing objects via a metaphorical translation conducted through "the passage from one existent to another, or from one
signified meaning to another, authorized by the initial *submission* of Being to
the existent, the *analogical* displacement of Being."[90] The *quality of feeling* is
comparable to having unearthed something hidden and menacing from what is
otherwise *"homely" (Heimliche)*. The quasi-epiphany of this *étrangeté* comes at a
time when such morphological considerations of the "bioarchitectural totality,
nature and artifact"[91] of a system of institutional organization (the *reason* of its
being) are not only appropriate, but concomitant to a questioning of the governing concept of the Western university (the reason of its *being*), e.g., how the
biotechnological rationality of its topological singularity writes out the formula-
tive synthesis of its constitution topographically.[92] From the doubling power of
fabulation not stolen away by the *similitudo* of metaphor, the geographical setting of Cornell becomes the "literal example"[93] of the contentions Derrida ex-
pounds in the lecture, through the writing of language, about the groundless
ground of the being of the modern university (the capricious [in]transitoriness of
its destination, *sending* or Being) as it is founded on and instituted through the
principle of reason:

> To have a *raison d'être,* a reason for being, is to have a justification for ex-
> istence, to have a meaning, an intended purpose, a destination; but also to
> have a cause, to be explainable according to the "principle of reason" or the
> "law of sufficient reason," as it is sometimes called—in terms of a reason
> which is also a cause (a ground, *ein Grund*), that is to say also a footing and
> a foundation, ground to stand on. In the phrase *raison d'être,* that idea of
> causality takes on above all the sense of final cause, in the wake of Leibniz,
> the author of the formulation—"the Principle of Reason."[94]

We are now ready to be moving more away from metaphor on a transversal trajectory that will get us closer to metaphysics. But is not one a part of the figure
of speech of the other?[95] Nevertheless, we shall circle back on the *reason of philosophy,* near the sun of its origins, amid the situatedness of ontology and the
ontic, *to see.*

The question we will have been attempting to answer all along is the one
Derrida asks the congregation at Cornell about (its) institutional "topoli-
tics"—"the exemplary nature of the topology and politics of th[e] university, in
terms of its views and its site,"[96] in sum, its point of view and reason *"to be"*:
"What can the University's body see or not see of its own destination, of that in
view of which it stands its ground?"[97] The query on the opening of the ethics of
the reason of its being and the responsibility to be assumed for it comes, in the
discourse, at the conclusion of a short, but entertaining, rhetorical foray on Aristotle, just before the perspective of that incisive "detour" is closed off "quick as a
wink and in the twinkling of an eye."[98] Working backwards from there, we find
the site of deconstruction to be a segment of an ancient text Derrida is concerned

with, again for the purpose of leading to a point of metaphorical illustration, an anatomizing of philosophy and education, *spoude/paideia*:

> Starting with its first words, Metaphysics associates sight with knowledge, and knowledge with knowing how to learn and knowing how to teach. I am of course referring to Aristotle's *Metaphysics*. I shall return presently to the political import of its opening lines; for the moment, let us look at the very first sentence: "All men, by nature, have the desire to know."[99] Aristotle thinks he sees a sign of this in the fact that sensations give pleasure, "even apart from their usefulness." The pleasure of useless sensations explains the desire to know for the sake of knowing, the desire for knowledge with no practical purpose. And this is more true of sight than of the other senses. We give preference to sensing "through the eyes" not only for taking action, but even when we have no praxis in view. This one sense, naturally theoretical and contemplative, goes beyond practical usefulness and provides us with more to know than any other; indeed, it unveils countless differences. We give preference to sight just as we give preference to the uncovering of difference.[100]

The commentary seems straightforward "theoretically," *"deconstructively,"* almost aloof. Derrida, paralleling the logic of Aristotle, attributes a visual ardor to knowing that is compatible with the metaphysical rendering of what it is. An identification of aspect *(eidos)* achieved through the gleaning of difference among forms *(Gestalten)*. But the conceptual locus for problematizing the totality of the sense of sight is contained in the passage: the profusion of references to the self-fulfillment of the faculty. "The metaphysical domination of the concept of form," Derrida has shown, "cannot fail to effectuate a certain subjection of the look."[101] An ocularcentric knowing infers the sticky matter of a physical-noumenal saturation point to the power of sight—the "now" and "not-now" of experience infusing the present-time of perception[102]—that circumscribes the confusion of alterity always already at the origins of the most basic constellations of a visual encounter bringing together a subject *(hypokeimenon)* with an object *(antikeimenon)*. *What we think we see is not the total reality of what we think we are looking at.* Once the formality of exteriority is "scoped out" by a subject in relative accordance with the functioning of perceptual variables acting on the mechanics of a field of vision and the phenomenology of apperception is absorbed in the symbolicizing zone of (pure) interiority, these gaps of *presence lacking* are multiplied. The Other is not known as Other but as a sign of a sign of the Other that is not itself. It is a difference doubled and re-doubled again; the sign-impression of an absent presence. A de-centering of the subject follows the breakdown of the positive intelligibility of being. *The absence of presence as the illusion of plenitude is the downfall of a pedagogy of the gaze.* The solipsism of a sheer pleasure enjoyed in the pursuit of knowledge with no guide or intent beyond satiating the intellect's appetite for finitude: the absolute happiness and blindness of only "the desire to know" and not the passion to learn.

For Derrida, the pedagogical urgency of transforming the university, to renew the magnitude of its ethical responsibility to the Other reflecting out of the selfsame difference of itself, arises from the monodimensionality of this self-satisfying aspect of sight:

> But is sight enough? For learning and teaching, does it suffice to know how to unveil differences? In certain animals, sensation engenders memory, and that makes them more intelligent and capable of learning. But for knowing how to learn, and learning how to know, sight, intelligence and memory are *not* enough. We must also learn how to hear and how to listen. I might suggest somewhat playfully that we have to know how to shut our eyes in order to be better listeners.[103]

Beckoning for a movement away from the *metaphysics of vision* that nurtures a *"state of knowledge"* in and of itself, deconstruction calls not for the end of seeing as some onlookers would have it, but for a transition to the productive interdependence of an *oto-scopic sensibility* and the beginning of *a learning to think, a thinking to learn.* A harmonizing of eyes and ears, no less. It is a subjunctive comparison (read metaphoral) that is translated effortlessly to the situation of the university's reason for being:

> Opening the eyes to know, closing them—or at least listening—in order to know how to learn and to learn how to know: here we have the first sketch of the rational animal. If the University is an institution for science and teaching, does it have to go beyond memory and sight? In what rhythm? To hear better and learn better, must it close its eyes or narrow its outlook? In cadence? What cadence? Shutting off sight in order to learn is of course only a figurative manner of speaking. No one will take it literally, and I am not proposing to cultivate an art of blinking. [104]

And why not? Consider the alternative we are presented with as Derrida extends the "figuration a little farther in Aristotle's company":[105]

> In his [Aristotle's] *De Anima* (421b) he distinguishes between man and those animals that have hard, dry eyes [*ton sklerophtalmon*], the animals lacking eyelids, that sort of sheath or tegumental membrane [*phragma*] which serves to protect the eye and permits it, at regular intervals, to close itself off in the darkness of inward thought or sleep. What is terrifying about an animal with hard eyes and a dry glance is that it always sees. Man can lower the sheath, adjust the diaphragm, narrow his sight, the better to listen, remember, and learn. What might the University's diaphragm be? The University must not be a sklerophthalmic animal, a hard-eyed animal; when I asked, a moment ago, how it should set its sights and adjust its views, that was another way of asking about its reasons for being and its essence.[106]

The description of the "sklerophthalmic university"—a panopticon of bestial proportions—might well be read as a re-translation of sorts, an adaptation made from grotesque caricatures of Nietzschean formulation displaying the devastating results of a disequilibrium of the faculties. Those bizarre, "de-natured" (read allegorical) creatures of *Thus Spoke Zarathustra*—"inverted cripple[s]"[107]—that satirize obsessive overreliance on a single sense to justify the "right" of claims to knowledge, the truth of "Truth." Before the discourse we are currently reading, in "Otobiographies: The Teaching of Nietzsche and the Politics of the Proper Name," Derrida referred to one of these monstrous organisms—a giant ear with a body attached—to elaborate the perils of an *acroamatic method of education*: the preferred technique of the master *lectoris,* a genius of dictation, unleashing the violence of encrypted words to be replicated by a student body using the uncritical rudiments of a 'stenographic' transcription of the *logos* tying its listeners to the *omphalos* of the "paternal belly of the State."[108] Here, the caveat Derrida espouses is less subtle philosophically, more psychoanalytically arresting: "Dream this umbilicus [to the university, 'the mother—the bad or false mother whom the teacher, as functionary of the State, can only simulate':][109] it has you by the ear."[110] The *metathesis* of analogy from the sense of hearing in the earlier text (similarly a discourse) to the sense of sight and their *oto-oratic* combination in the latter, punctuates the contradictions underlying the axiology of both a high-fidelity teaching of the ear and a myopic pedagogy of the eye.

Demarcating the essential realm of knowledge to be manifest in the perfect translatability of a representational axiomatics of teaching and learning, be it visual or aural, lexematic or acoustic, has ethico-political import for pedagogy and the university. As Derrida clarifies in "Living On: Border Lines," the stability of the institutional firmament—the metaphysical foundation convening the legitimation of its "inside" and its "outside"—is held together by a tight control over the difference of language and meaning:

> What this institution [the university] cannot bear, is for anyone to tamper with [*toucher à*; also "touch," "change," "concern himself with"] language and meaning *both* the *national* language *and,* paradoxically, an ideal of translatability that neutralizes this national language. Nationalism and universalism. What this institution cannot bear is a transformation that leaves intact neither of these two complementary poles. It can bear more readily the most apparently revolutionary ideological sorts of "content," if only that content does not touch the borders of language [*la langue*] and of all the juridico-political contracts that it guarantees. It is this "intolerable" something that concerns me here. It is related in an essential way to that which, as it is written above, brings about the limits of the concept of [univocal] translation on which the university is built. . . .[111]

The symbolic power of the university depends on, subsists and thrives on, an ideological overcoding—a curricular overdetermination, overt and covert—of the intelligibility of concepts within the classificatory morphology of its disciplinary configuration, a structural microcosm homologous to the philosophico-scientific and ethico-political struggles of civil society.[112]

The careful planning of the institution as a cultural organization of sophisticated but instantly reproducible qualities of value mediates in advance for the meta-communicative possibility of aberrant readings or misinterpretations of the expression of its rationality. It represents a "wanting-to-neutralize" or significantly reduce the likelihood of resistance to the authority of the system to which it belongs by internalizing within the structure of a set of working assumptions and goals the "semiotic resources" of a second-order violence assaying to ensure the predictability of language forms. As it is supported by a "rhetoric of naturalism, organicism, or vitality"[113] thematizing the staunch ethics of a post-Kantian posturing for "the complete and interdisciplinary unity of knowledge,"[114] the classical tradition of the university reduces the figural play of the oppositional markedness of (subjective) difference within the non-interpretative enclosure of a decidable frame of reference. The sense of its pedagogy—the instituted way of its *reason for being*—is restricted to a regulative stipulation of instrumentalizing procedures that function to occlude, or to subordinate, the dissonance of perceptual effect(s) relative to a universalizable ideal of "truth" revealing only the means to the ends of itself. *A priori* any conception of the *will to knowledge* is the model of the "educated" individual predicated on the basis of a theory of truth. A subject whose competences do not exceed the limitations of the system of representing and representation. An orthodoxy of teaching and learning dismissive of the negativity of difference (particularity, singularity, otherness) and for the positivity of similarity *(homoiosis)* ignores the effects of cognitive and affective variance that potentially influence modes of apperception and being. Inculcating, thereupon, in the inflexible patterning of their pre-calculated interactions, is the means for conceiving both a unified (centered) subject and a sterile (unmoving) object. The objectification of the value of knowledge/power connections that Pierre Bourdieu has analyzed as the ethico-political transfigurations of the cultural logic of a sign or symbol system to/from the onto-encyclopaedic reason of the university "contribut[es], in Weber's terms, to the 'domestication of the dominated.'"[115] Between universalism and particularity—the overzealousness of the "nationalism" Derrida specifies—is the injustice of hegemony. The *proper name,* we could say, of the seductive state of a dystopic incredulity to reason cast from the euphemizing[116] of an ideology-based ordering of evaluative relations offering no room for the freedom of difference or a straying from normativity. Flattening out the authentic "peaks" of the code of responsivity to a monovalent attenuation of standards of responsibility makes possible the institutionalization of a "distinction *(Unterscheidung)* between friend and enemy,"[117] to use Derrida's quasi-ethical reaccounting of political oppositionality from the work of Leo Strauss. The Law of "the Same" is the reason of injustice: for the inclusion of a subject *that belongs* and the exclusion of an Other *that does not.* But the auto-present logic of the Idea of the old architecturality of the university cannot defend against the radical re-translatability of the encoded signs of the institutional system achieved from the iterability of the difference of interpretative reconstructions of ambiguity. That is, for the progressive degradation of the "right" of the meaning of its officious "babble" as it tries to decree the law of the full-form univocity of its *reason for being.* The institution of the university can account neither for the ineluctability of the deferred traces of the signs of knowledge differing at the fundamental ontology of the truth of their origin, nor for the explanation of their deconstructability, *différance.*

Reason Unbound

The Principle of Reason: The Institutional Ground of Modern Rationality

The analytic direction that I intend to follow hereafter takes its strategic cues from the *meta-reflexive* reverberations of a question Derrida asks during the discourse we have been reading closely, letting the critical timbre of its message resound noisily in the ear of the nameless, faceless Other within us: "Is the reason for reason rational?"[118] Coloring the post-metaphysical positionality of the attitude expressed therein, a modicum of ludic indiscretion enhances the deconstructive resonance of the appeal the philosopher makes for a reappraisal of the self-insulated myth of the innocuousness of the disarming logic of *"ratio sufficiens, ratio efficiens."*[119] Derrida, we will have glimpsed earlier, is strikingly clear about the peculiar *retro-spectivity* of the lexico-conceptual lineage leading to the formulation of the principle of reason during the seventeenth century—the protracted time-lag of its epistemic genealogy as it is played out from a *looking-back-on* the "Aristotelian requirements"[120] of all future science, "of metaphysics, of first philosophy, of the search for 'roots,' 'principles,' and 'causes'"[121]—that gave rise to the original *idea* and *ideal* of the university and its modern-day re-institution in the revisionist model constructed by Wilhelm von Humboldt:

> As far as I know, nobody has ever founded a university *against* reason. So we may reasonably suppose that the University's reason for being has always been reason itself, and some essential connection of reason to being. But what is called the principle of reason is not simply reason. We cannot for now plunge into the history of reason, its words and concepts, into the enigmatic scene of translation that has shifted *logos* to *ratio* to *reason, Grund, ground, Vernunft,* etc. What for three centuries now has been called the principle of reason was thought out and formulated, several times, by Leibniz. His most often quoted statement holds that "Nothing is without reason, no effect is without cause" *("Nihil est sine ratione seu nullus effectus sine causa").* According to Heidegger though, the only formulation Leibniz himself considered authentic, authoritative, and rigorous is found in a late essay, *Specimen inventorum*: "There are two first principles in all reasoning, the principle of non-contradiction, of course . . . and the principle of rendering reason." *("Duo sunt prima principia omnium ratiocinationum, principium nempe contradictionis [. . .] et principium reddendae rationis.")* The second principle says that for any truth—for any true proposition, that is—a reasoned account is possible. *"Omnis veritatis reddi ratio potest."* Or, to translate more literally, for any true proposition, *reason can be rendered.*[122]

There is a "cost" of economizing due the principle of reason that cannot be left unanalyzed or unheeded. Especially if we do not wish to construe its "cardinal" and "secondary" mandates *solely* as aphorisms for the "rational faculty or power"[123]—the ability of mind and of speech—attributive of the sacred dignity of the human animal *(zoon logon ekhon)* by Aristotelian metaphysics. Doing so, Derrida warns, would be an unfortunate mistake: "The principle of reason installs its empire only to the extent that the abyssal question of the being *(l'être)* that is hiding within it remains hidden, and with it the question of the grounding of the ground itself, or of grounding as *gründen* (to ground, to give or take ground: *Boden-nehmen*), as *begründen* (to motivate, justify, authorize) or especially as *stiften* (to erect or institute, a meaning to which Heidegger [on whose analysis the interpretation given here relies] accords a certain pre-eminence)."[124] The *phoronomy*[125] of the *principium rationis* demands something more profound of the subject's thought and action than the self-aggrandizing hyper-relativism of the *doxa* of merely changing "opinion" emboldening itself on the excesses of itself. And that is an element of accountability *(Rechenschaft)* for the "truth-value" of the representation *(Vorstellung)* of judgments made about "an object [*Gegenstand*—'that-which-stands-over-against'] placed and positioned *before* a subject,"[126] an ego who, now more than ever, sure of its self, thinks "I" *(sum)*. The justification *(Rechtfertigen)* of the certainty of such a self-grounding of the ground of knowledge yielded of the *cogitabilis* rests on the security of demonstrating the proof of the "evident correctness" of an explanation. It grounds a reversal of the logic of the *percipio* as it is set back on the source of the response directed to language. Reason is sufficiently rendered, "given back,"[127] and *it has to be* for the determinacy of the *ens rationis* (intellect) to piece together an *idea of reality* in lieu of "esoteric" principle, only if and when a "representation that judges"[128] can display the "truth" of its propositional outcomes by re-directing the ground of the "connection" of subject and predicate—the "what" of "is"—back to a cogitating "I."[129] This structure of repetition orders the chain of consequence organizing the syntagm of language in the coming-back of its re-turning of presence to the "double effigy" of the sign/picture for concept *(Begriff)*. It has the function of "holding" or "keeping" the world of beings firmly-fixed *(fest-gestellt)* in the bright light of "objectivity" *(Gegenständlichkeit)*,[130] over and against the underlying filter of the projecting self-consciousness of the "knowing self"[131] as *subjectum* or *hypokeimenon,* "that-which-lies-before" *(qua* prior). The firmament of the truth of experience depicted as such bears an anthropocentric foundation and the unmistakable mark of a *metaphysical humanism.*[132] For, as Derrida explains, "This relation of representation [between subject and object]—that in its whole extension is not merely a relation of knowing—has to be grounded, ensured, protected [by making the subject an object]:[133]] that is what we are told by the principle of reason, the *Satz vom Grund.*"[134] To expand in a slightly different way. On the one hand, the productive reflexivity of a presuppositionless egoity sustains the "purity" of the ground of its reasoning by its "power-of-bringing-back-to-presence"[135] the self-presence of the *truth of representation* from within the abiding swells of an inwardly spectating imago of mind. But this is not enough. On the other, a collective form of the responsibility to *give an account of reason (logon didonai)* is co-affirmed outright by the *autopoietic* reflexivity of a self-consciousness of self and self-*hood* disengaging of itself from empirical reality to set apart Sub-ject from Ob-ject, Self from Other, in its subordination of nature to a mortgaging of its fore-closure that is always ready-to-hand *(das Zuhanden).*[136] Taking these together: the sense of *ratio* understood in the affirmative form of the principle of reason, *Omnes ens habet rationem* (Every being has a reason), is interpretable as a reckoning to account *for* the calculability *(Berechenbarkeit)* of entities *(Seinden).*[137] Subjectivism thus precedes objectivism in and ensuing the Cartesian age of modernity Derrida believes to be a portentous omen of philosophical innovation that prepares the way to the development of the university as we know it today.

Vouchsafing the ground of the predictable equationing of beings, the principle of reason convenes the primacy of calculation as the fate of Western thought. The *techne* of this amenability of the *ratio reddendae* we have outlined is the characterizing feature of the historicity of the evolution of "philosophy" to "science" that after the epistemological trailblazing of the early Greeks (not the pre-Socratics) stimulates the onto-genesis of modern "TECHNO-science" without which there would be no contemporary university.[138] The method of its "Reason" as "the structure and closure of representation"[139] is not, nor could it ever be, outside the *scope of deconstruction,* but rather is a precursor of and, moreover, integral to *the necessity for a critical questioning of the grounding of the foundation of the institutional frameworking of knowledge.* The metaphysical (logocentric) assumptions behind the objective setting of the value of truth are reductive, autarchical and protective, of the *practical ends of the task of thinking. Reason and the technologies of Reason are not without interest, not without ground or a grounded grounding that withdraws, refracts, is concealed.* And in this solicitation of a "crossing-over" from *theoria* to *praxis* where normative levels of the "optimal performance" of ideas have to be met to the utmost satisfaction of "rationality," there is hidden the *opening of the non-ethical violence of the universal.* "Beyond all those big philosophical words—reason, truth, principle—that generally command attention," Derrida tells us, "the principle of reason also holds that reason *must be rendered.*"[140] "Deconstruction"—and there cannot be just *one*—is not exempt from the responsibility of answering the obligation of thinking through this obdurate call to grounds *in full,* albeit in the profusive singularity of its own distinctive ways.[141] But the issue of the "properness" of response becomes more radical in conjunction with what has become a *post*-modern "crisis of representation," a suspiciousness of reference and referentiality formed as a question of the *"Question of Reason"* and its "must." How are we then to comprehend the ramifications of the ethical aim of this modal behest unto being Derrida recognizes to be *nothing but essential,* convoking as it does at the thematic fissures of its deepest openings toward education the Socratic problem of the "(un)examined life" or *how one ought to live*? And therefrom, to unravel why "one cannot *think* the possibility of the modern university, the one that is re-structured in the nineteenth century in all the Western countries, without inquiring into that event, the institution of the principle of reason."[142] The road we will take, to move on, with Derrida and after him (as we have endeavored to do from the start) will lead us from the metaphysical immanence of a ground of decidability to the deconstructive provenance of an abyss of undecidability; or from the rectitude of the techno-scientific rationalism of (late) modernity to the amplitude of the limitless responsibility of deconstruction.

The "moralizing" disbursement of the rendering of reason—the practical objectives of its empirically conditioned "must" as the volitional basis of the causality of the freedom of being—Derrida says, "seems to cover the essence of our relationship to principle, it seems to mark out for us requirement, debt, duty, request, command, obligation, law, the imperative."[143] Who would want to deny this or be willing to reject it out of hand? Nihilism and anarchy would arguably be the negative forms of a plausible repercussion of "unschooled" reactions to opposing the welcoming of a responsibility to reason. Given that, in all likelihood, the obscuration of intentionality or the meaninglessness of violence can irrevocably dampen the vitality of the human subject in the abject despairing of its *being-in-the-world*. But is not an uncritical servility to the principle of reason also a denial of the liberating statute of its *law of right, the right of its law*? The regulated "objectiveness" of a prescriptive responsivity is of dubious integrity because it conflates the logic of the universal with that of the particular to override any justification of the heteronomous ground of subjective differences of judgment. Reason lays down the law *(Gesetz)*. Yes. And the *principle* of reason must be "obeyed." No objection. Yet can we still respond with responsibility to reason without giving up the right to question to a not so automatically benign thought-less-ness?[144] And without duping the natural law of judgment—its capacity to exercise *uncompromising* discernment—by relinquishing the free will of conscience to the power *(Macht)* and authority of a violent means leading to what could be nothing else but unjust ends? Derrida asks, "Who is more faithful to reason's call, who hears it with a keener ear, who better sees the difference, the one who offers questions in return and tries to think through the possibility of that summons [of the principle of reason], or the one who does not want to hear any question about the reason of reason?"[145] The *irrationalism* of cleaving to hasty assumptions based on the self-deceiving conviction that we both completely know and agree on what the essence of the axiom is (e.g., its *quiddity,* "whatness,")[146] or what it "wants- to-imply," along with what is expected of us, is brought out in the *irresponsibility* of a thought-less obedience to decree.[147] Although Derrida appropriates the deontological expressionism of a Kantian order of classifications to show how, by the categorical law of universalizability, "pure practical reason continually calls on the principle of reason, on its 'must,'"[148] the prelude to an aggressively deconstructive questioning of the teleology of the self-accounting ground of reason and of the being of the university the conclusion will later point to, is seriously Heideggerian:

> A responsibility is involved here, however. We have to respond to the call of the principle of reason. In *Der Satz vom Grund* [*The Principle of Reason*], Heidegger names that call *Anspruch*: requirement, claim, request, demand, command, convocation; it always entails a certain addressing of speech. The word is not seen, it has to be heard and listened to, this apostrophe that enjoins us to respond to the principle of reason.
>
> A question of responsibility, to be sure. But is answering *to* the principle of reason the same act as answering *for* the principle of reason? Is the scene the same? Is the landscape the same? And where is the university located within this space?[149]

How are we to hear and grasp the ethical presumption of the invocation of the principle of reason? According to Heidegger: by way of the collected awareness of Being to the open realm of language (its "home," "abode," "in-dwelling")[150] through which the fundamental difference of mind and body is united over time in the ecstatic broadening of hermeneutical countenance realized experientially—via the *circumspective immediacy* of meditative consciousness—as the "piety" of a "gathered hearkening"[151] that composes the authenticity of itself out of the giving of itself to a listening with a view to the "releasement" *(Gelassenheit)* of the originary thinking of being toward the mystery of the "letting be" of things.[152] A rejection of the epistemological opposition of "intelligible" and "sensory" knowing deeply undercuts the foundation of the self-legislating self-groundedness of subject centered reason and clears the way for the procreative resolve of effectuating a "new autochthony"[153] out of the past. It is this comportment of fused sensibilities directed to a *future-not-yet-realized* that carries with it the hope of building, through the *act of thought,* a better place to dwell *(Aufenthalten).*[154] This radical re-positioning of thinking as *poiesis* (making or producing) and *praxis* (acting or doing) liberated from the strangle hold of a modernist theory of representation collapses the "noetic/somatic" duality of the Cartesian problematic of truth at the pre-ontological ("lived") threshold of the *ego cogito* where the material ambiguities of the everyday play of "world" and "things" are brought together and borne apart. That said: these theoretical premises of Heidegger's that my rereading of the call of the principle of reason hinges on will capacitate Derrida in the discourse to play the *logic of rationality* against the *method of science* while reflecting on the ethics and politics of the work of research within the university.[155] As we shall see.

To provoke the philosophical imagination into judging the merits of reconstituting a fictional interchange between Charles Sanders Peirce and Heidegger on the tehno-rational birth of the modern university from the self-accounting normativity of the principle of reason, Derrida cites a telling excerpt from the American proto-pragmatist, already having begun to refrain from initiating such a *tête-à-tête*:

> discuss[ing] the purpose of [higher] education, without once alluding to the only motive [reason] that animates the genuine scientific investigator. I am not guiltless in the matter myself, for in my youth I wrote some articles to uphold a doctrine called pragmatism, namely, that the meaning and essence of every conception lies in the application that is to be made of it. That is all very well, when properly understood. I do not intend to recant it. But the question arises, *what is* the ultimate application; and at the time I seem to have been inclined to subordinate the *conception* to the *act,* knowing to doing. Subsequent experience of life has taught me that the only thing that is really *desirable* without a reason for being so, is to render ideas and things reasonable. *One cannot well demand a reason for reasonableness itself.*[156]

At first blush, the leap of thought from "application" to "reason," grounded fully in the interest *of-itself, for-itself,* seems greatly at odds with the tenets of Peircean pragmaticism. However, as Christopher Norris has correctly noted, what distinguished Peirce from his philosophical contemporaries (John Dewey and William James) was the "belief that every intellectual discipline requires some ultimate cognitive faith, some idea (as Peirce expressed it) of 'truth at the end of inquiry.'"[157] Where one would expect an altogether oppositional stance toward the value of reason for the utility and "practicality" of research, it is an "epistemological lapse" that has left Richard Rorty a less than enthused advocate of Pragmaticism.[158] And yet why does Derrida forgo the chance of pursuing the matter of this dialogical intercourse of "pragmatism" and "phenomenological hermeneutics" any further in "The Principle of Reason"? To arbitrarily force an encounter (from the breaks of what would be and are admittedly bracketed textual fragments) the sharp discordance of a theory of practice and a practice of theory separating Peirce and Heidegger. Is it simply because the sum and substance of the supposititious disquisition placed firmly in question could never *really* have happened anyway? There being, after all, no discernable compulsion for the one to *"speak-to"* the other *in* these terms or *on* these terms of the *reasonable* ground of the University. The desiderata of this hypothetical repartee are obliquely displayed in "The Principle of Reason" by Derrida's strategic use of exemplarity that we have dealt with in the first part of this chapter to show how the discourse itself is a *praxeology of theory,* taking its philosophical inspiration, as it does, somewhat precipitously from the difference between Heidegger and Peirce. What is to be garnered from the suspension of this *all-but-chimaerical agon,* it being, *in the last analysis,* very much under the *cull* and *sway* of a deconstructive (in)direction, if you will?

Well, for Derrida, "[T]o bring about such a dialogue between Peirce and Heidegger [around what he describes as 'the compound theme, indeed, of the university and the principle of reason,']"[159] we would have to go *beyond* the conceptual oppositions between 'conception' and 'act,' between 'conception' and 'application,' theoretical view and praxis, theory and technique."[160] And this is what "The Principle of Reason," more or less, does, *works at,* achieves. But does not a fundamental irreconcilability continue to persist and so to inhibit a bridging together of the *aporias* of meditative reflection consuming the *impracticable idea* with the apodicticity of habitual determination particularizing the *sensible event*?

The incommensurability between "thinking" and "doing," as such, accentuates *a fortiori* the methodological differences that both philosophers hold dearly to in the very heart of their dissatisfactions with the legislations of "pure reason" for the facilitating of educational aspirations.[161] Or, what is, *pace* Immanuel Kant, the ground proposition *(Grundsatz)* of the being of the university;[162] where the ideal of a calculable rationality secures the *sine qua non* for a motive of a principle of (collective) action undergirding the law of its *practical essence*[163] and the viability of its autonomy as a public institution.[164] According to Derrida, "What Peirce only outlines," and willingly takes for granted by virtue of a theoretical impasse at work within the self-professed objectives of his own version of pragmatism that cancels out the fortuitous contingency of even a *rudimentary* examination of the vested interests of Reason's institution, "is the path where Heidegger feels the most to be at stake, especially in *Der Satz vom Grund [The Principle of Reason]*."[165] We have already begun in this journey and are on the way *(Unterwegs)* to "fleshing out" the labyrinth of its trails through the playfulness of a "poetic license" we might well be tempted to refer to here plainly enough, as *a basic right of academic freedom.* But to return to a familiar crossroads, retreading it lightly, to go on in a different direction, we would have to ask here an important question: What warrants deconstruction to in-vade the space of the university as "an institutional practice for which the concept of institution remains a problem"?[166] Looking elsewhere for an answer brings us to Heidegger who is—like Derrida was, in an earlier quotation—succinct: "The university is grounded on the principle of reason. How are we supposed to conceive this: the university grounded on a principle? May we venture such an assertion?"[167] We may and we must. For Derrida, and I am paraphrasing here, *institutions are in deconstruction before deconstruction is in institutions.* It is that simple and that complex.

We would have to forgo then, as Derrida does, that: the principle of reason lies positioned, rather awkwardly, between the "strange and necessary dialogue"[168] of Peirce and Heidegger on the epistemological foundations of an institution of higher education.[169] Each philosopher, in his own turn, gives testimony to strong convictions that cleave open the otherwise invisible contours of the chasm of Western thought, a most intractable void waiting to be filled by the "spirit" and "action" of philosophy, by extending the general realm of analysis across the continuum of a conceptual dichotomy pitting "interpretation" against "application." And like the paling chiaroscuro of a prophetic abyss, the *principium rationis* haunts the preoccupations of these, let us call them (for the sake of convenience), *"complementary figures"* within the epistemological ground *(Grund)* and non-ground *(Ab-grund)* of the history of metaphysics. Their propositions are—to differing degrees—expressive of the need for an assertive questioning of the rationalizing force *(Gewalt)* that authorizes the systemic organicity of the hierarchization of knowledge within the established composition of the modern university.[170] But in the sublimating of the immediately "given phenomena" of being *(Seiend)* to "abstract concepts" *(Verstand)* of ideas of Being *(Dasein),* these proclamations are overtures of nothing less than faithful judgments indicative of deeply divergent philosophical allegiances that have affected the university. Fateful disclosures, consciously or unconsciously, ill at ease with the unforgiving dictates of the principle of reason. This is why the abrupt un-staging of this extraordinary confrontation *(Auseinandersetzung)* of Peirce and Heidegger that Derrida suggests *must* occur, but refrains from illuminating *stricto sensu,*[171] leaves "us" dangling precariously, at altogether loose ends, as it were, over a most contested philosophical divide. Drifting freely along the interminable fluctuations of these oppositional limits of epistemic irresolution constructing the *khora* (literally the "'place,' 'location,' 'region,' 'country'"[172] or metaphorically the provisional movement and ephemeral stases)[173] of the truth of reason and the "untruth" of its other, *unreason,* within the institution. The *plus d'une langue*[174] of deconstruction, meanwhile, asserts itself amid the unlimited complexity of these tensions and repulsions that only appear to coalesce, however unhappily, toward the ambiguous mediality of a thin line separating "pure theory" from "pure practice" reproduced arbitrarily as the placeholder of techno-scientific interests within the interdisciplinary model of the university.[175] That is, across the paradigmatic interspaces of this institutional struggle where the differential gamut of a range of "post-Kantian" philosophizing vies for the justifiable "right" to express a skepticism of the truthfulness of *a priori* knowledge claims.[176] It lies between, *on the one hand,* an idea of "pure reason" from which the *compartmentality* synthesizing the form *(Bild)* of the programmatic structure of the university evolves[177] and, *on the other,* an idea of "pure practical reason" from which the *ethicity* orienting the employment of the first principles of a system of scientific knowledge surfaces. How can we assert this judgment? Because, as deconstruction has shown, there is no recourse to what would inevitably *have to be* the moderating code of a master language capable of bringing together the "inner world" of the *res cogitans* with the "outer world" of the *res extensa* to mercifully undermine, once and for all, the troubling diffraction of conflicting faculties of "reason."[178] We cannot count on a veritable "Purveyor of Truth"[179] whose peremptory capacity for *semiotic reductionism* could clarify the inter-phenomenal terms of otherwise unpredictable pronouncements made from the ideolect of "sign-thing" correlations, *viz.* ideational constructions of a life-world *(Lebenswelt)* by and within the refracted self-consciousness a de-centered subject.

In this respect of the institutionalization of "interpretative finitude" or "hermeneutic universalism" Derridean deconstruction runs counter to, the elocution of the principle of reason codifies the obligation of thinking to the quasi-mystical eschatology of a Will to Truth by providing in itself the expletive out-let through which to achieve a consolidation of the *conditions of the possibility* of the course of Western knowledge and pedagogy after the ethical predisposition of that which Plato had specified through the so-called doctrine of Ideas as the quest for the good "beyond being" *(epekeina tes ousias).*[180] *By Law* and *by Right,* the performative dimension of the ("professional") field of human endeav-ors (philosophic-scientific-aesthetic) *"within"* and *"without"* the university is tied to the necessity of a theoretical justification of the decision supporting actions taken or abstained from. That is, a response or "even a non-response is charged *a priori* with responsibility"[181] to the principle of reason as a *fundamental princi-ple of Being and beings,* and thence of *poiesis* and *praxis,* because the effects of the metaphysical exigency of "explain[ing] effects through their causes, ration-ally,"[182] are inescapable for *the living of the good life.* Here, in the wake of Heraclitus and the demise of the *logos*—from *legein* (to say), to which the Word is sent back to its roots in the *apophainesthai,* "to bring forward into appear-ance"—and with this, the shining of a light on Platonism, the first decisive steps are taken toward a calculable rationality that initiates the modern epoch of "representational thinking."[183] Or what is the periodic culmination of an episte-mological transmigration of philosophy and science away from a basic question-ing of the ground of Being *(Seinsfrage) meta ta physika* and toward the intracta-ble manipulation of ends through the mediation of techno-science.[184] The mantle of modernity rests on the directives of the principle of reason that pave the way—through Cartesian representationalism—for the instrumental logic of "purposive rationality" *(Zweckrational)* because the empire of metaphysics can-not abandon the "destinality" of being to the mystagogy of ill-calculation. There is no safety in the lack of a well-planned abode, the careful forging of a place for the in-stalling of *homo faber* to rule as undisputable master "of the totality of what is."[185] Even if—in the challenging forth *(Herausfordern)* of what is revealed of the raw materiality of the human world as "standing-reserve" *(Bestand),* a re-source always present-at-hand *(Vorhandenheit)* and ready to be used—the artifici-ality of a ready-made "techno-ecology" bringing nature and beings to the order of a standstill by the enframing *(Gestell)* of a world picture *(Weltbild)* contributes to feelings of alienation and homelessness *(Unheimlichkeit).*[186] A withdrawing from Being cast in the spectral emptiness of a "calculable and representable sub-jectivity"[187] allows us to see into the *oblivion of metaphysics,* not to dispense with its language or its stratagems, but to accept it for what it is, *a violence of light.*

My rereading of the "institution of modern technoscience that is the university *Stiftung* [foundation],"[188] like Derrida's, relies on the later philosophy of Heidegger after the infamous turn *(Kehre).* And the point is this: "[W]e can no longer dissociate the principle of reason from the very idea of technology in the realm of their modernity."[189] For the *self*-definition and *self*-presencing of the sovereign subject of "metaphysical humanism"[190] there is no other viable option than the commanding of the power of the Will to Will. And all that that means. When "Man" is the measure *(metron)* of the reason of the being of all things, metaphysics and technology, it stands, are largely equivalent terms. Not the same, but interconnected and intertwined, in their refusal to think Being *(Dasein).*[191] Let us continue to deal with the question of the institutional re-transcription of the principle of reason Derrida poses, to inquire further into the "the origin of that demand for grounds,"[192] while referring to the general problem of instrumentalism, a technologizing strand of metaphysics the text of our discourse will have only foreshadowed until now.

The significance of "end-oriented thinking" to the development of the modern university cannot be underestimated, justifying, as it does, the unity of the rationale for the organizational division of teaching and research among and within the disciplines. Inasmuch as the "verbal formulation" of the principle of reason "provides the impetus for a new era of purportedly 'modern' reason, metaphysics and technoscience,"[193] the objectification of its needs as universalizable goals to be achieved without fail comes to dominate the requirements for the "surety" of the "truths" that pervade the institution. For Derrida, questioning the neutrality of the epistemological foundation of claims to knowledge constrains, but also opens up, the larger purview of academic responsibility beyond the appeal to rationality. Once the "Originary Ethics" of the call of the principle of reason are entrenched within the representational ground of meaning so as to obligate a reproducing of the normative value of response, there is the problem of a conflict of self-interest that deconstruction *must* and *can* address:

But to answer *for* the principle of reason, and thus for the university, to answer *for* this call, to raise questions about the origin or ground of this principle of foundation *(Satz vom Grund),* is not simply to obey it or to respond *in the face of* this principle. We do not listen the same way when we are responding to a summons as when we are questioning its meaning, its origin, its possibility, its goal, its limits. Are we obeying the principle of reason when we ask what grounds this principle that is itself a principle of grounding? We are not—which does not mean that we are disobeying it, either. Are we dealing here with a circle or an abyss? The circle would consist in seeking to account for reason by reason, to render reason to the principle of reason, in appealing to the principle in order to make it speak of itself at the very point where, according to Heidegger, the principle of reason says nothing about itself. The abyss, the hole, the *Abgrund,* the empty "gorge" would be the impossibility for a principle of grounding to ground itself. This very grounding, then, like the university, would have to hold itself suspended above a most peculiar void. Are we to use reason to account for the principle of reason?[194]

Up to this point, my own rereading of the "why" and "not-why" (the because) of the response demanded of being for a "proper" answering to the responsibility of the call to reason has turned on the lexico-hermeneutical axis of a Heideggerian *double-shifting* of the tonality common to the "popular" phrasing of the dictum, *nihil est sine ratione.* Derrida briefly mentions this "given the limits of [his] talk."[195] Such a moving away from the "cognitive" phase of the principle that places the emphasis on the first and third words of its abbreviated statement "**nothing** is **without** reason" in contradistinction with the modulated pitch of a newly conjugated register stressing "nothing **is** without **reason**" brings about the *perception* of an accord of Being *(Sein)* and ground *(Grund).*[196] Far-reaching conclusions follow from this.

The latter, "transposed," version of the principle of reason as a *principle of Being* seems to collide with the former as a *principle of beings.* There is no common denominator of logic or language that can relieve the tension of this ontico-ontological difference in the magical euphoria of a dialectical synthesis of opposing terms. *Leaving reason to account for the principle of reason obviates the problem of the essence of its ground.* For it reinforces the metaphysical pre-supposition of a conceptual unity—the redundant movement of a self-authorizing ascription—sealing the distance between *the proximity of being that has value and Being that has none.* Taking the argument one step further, for our purposes, a paradox ensues: *if the principle of reason must ground itself on the essence of itself (reason) to have any grounding at all, then it would seem to have no grounding given the tautological structure of the foundation.* What does this have to do with the university? Everything and nothing.

The university is founded on the principle of reason and on "what remains hidden in that principle,"[197] the "Other" of reason (not its opposite): an un-grounded grounding, the place and non-place of the abyss. This is very strange. One might even say that it reveals, already *in* metaphysics, a certain love of "ir-rationality." And yet, within the academic community of the institution, Derrida observes, "nowhere is th[e] [historicity of] this principle [or its 'instrumental-ity'] thought through, scrutinized, interrogated as to [the sources of] its ori-gin."[198] Nothing could surprise us less. The university is a cultural artifact of the principle of reason that we will have *always already* existed in, ever since and even before the Academy of Plato or the Lyceum of Aristotle. A pleasing fic-tion—akin to how Kant described it[199]—of the philosophical anthropologism (read "humanism") of the West. Symbolizing the "place" where all knowledge and non-knowledge can be found or is housed, the *Panepistemion* is an enigmatic construct of both imaginary concord and very real resilience indistinguishing of the difference between an appearance of totality and an idea of infinity.[200] A flexibly self-correcting system of persistent re- and de-orchestrations that have overcome the short-sighted density of human time.[201] As the *reason for its being* objectifies the valuation of an idealized vision of *"the good life"* that self-validates the auto-nomic "Right" of the institution through the *indispensable lie* of an intersubjective sharing of common interests among its collective rank and file,[202] the "archive of its archives"[203] remains haunted from the start by a specter of the past and a dream of the future. A daimon of multiple eyes and ears and hearts more at war than at peace with the *rational essence of the university.* Or the "ethico-ideologico-philosophical" grounding of its knowledge politics and the technocratizing subdivisions of its inter-disciplinarity. "The university is a (finished) product," Derrida has said elsewhere, "I would almost call it the child of an inseparable couple, metaphysics and technology."[204]

Deconstruction and the Ethics of Science and/as Research:
The (Dis)Orienting of a New Academic Responsibility

The principle of reason "as principle of grounding, foundation or institution"[205] tends to guide the *science of research* to techno-practical ends. The politics of academic work and the role "the ['modern'] university may play"[206] in helping to construct the arena experiencing the application of results or the "pay off"[207] of pre-directed outcomes of inquiry is fed by competing interests situated outside of the rationale of the institution itself or the ideals of the nation-state. The "orientation" of research "programmed, focused, organized"[208] on the expectation of its future utilization, Derrida insists, is "centered instead on [the desires of] multinational military-industrial complexes of techno-economic networks, or rather international technomilitary networks that are apparently multi- or transnational in form."[209] Forces wielding the power of "investment"—not necessarily monetary—are always wanting to control the mechanisms of creative production to commodify knowledge. And with these "external" influences affecting and reflecting the purposes of the university that are found more and more in not obvious but strategic areas within the confines of the institution thanks to the "channel of private foundations"[210] sustaining the direction of research through the irresistable lure of funding and other incentives (power, status, career advancement, etc.), the "pragmatic" interests of an "applied science" are set adroitly in opposition to the "disinterestedness" of "fundamental" (basic) inquiry. A distinction of "real but limited relevance"[211] given the deferred dividends of the "detours, delays and relays of 'orientation,' its more random aspects,"[212] that are either incalculable or go unrecognized until a suitable situation of advantageous use presents itself. For Derrida, it is naive to believe there are some "basic disciplines ['philosophy,' 'theoretical physics,' and 'pure mathematics' are the examples he gives] shielded from power, inaccessible to programming by the pressures of the State or, under cover of the State, by civil society or capital interests."[213] That thought has now been unthinkable for some time since the dawning of the "post-critical" age of nuclear politics and the wake of the informativizing function of science as research "[a]t the service of war."[214] What is at stake concerning the "control" of knowledge pivots around the "higher priority" issue of protecting "national and international security"[215] interests, however heterogeneous the calculation of a plan of insurance or the lack of it is to the logic of "peace" or "democracy." The differentiation of the aims of research, Derrida contends, is not that discreet an indicator of its "use-value" so as to clearly distinguish between the profitability of application and the destructive effects of misappropriation, despite the usual "factoring in" of "reasonable" margins of error:

research programs have to [in the sense of *are made to*] encompass the entire field of information, the stockpiling of knowledge, the workings and thus also the essence of language and of all semiotic systems, translation, coding and decoding, the play of presence and absence, hermeneutics, semantics, structural and generative linguistics, pragmatics, rhetoric. I am accumulating all these disciplines in a haphazard way, on purpose, but I shall end with literature, poetry, the arts, fiction in general: the theory that has all these discipline as its object may be just as useful in ideological warfare as it is in experimentation with variables in all-too-familiar perversions of the referential function. Such a theory may always be put to work in communications strategy, the theory of commands, the most refined military pragmatics of jussive utterances (by what token, for example, will it be clear that an utterance is to be taken as a command in the new technology of telecommunications? How are the new resources of simulation and simulacrum to be controlled? And so on . . .). . . . Furthermore, when certain random consequences of research are taken into account, it is always possible to have in view some eventual benefit that may ensue from an apparently useless research project (in philosophy or the humanities, for example). The history of the sciences encourages researchers to integrate that margin of randomness into their centralized calculation. They then proceed to adjust the means at their disposal, the available financial support, and the distribution of credits. A State power or forces that it represents no longer need to prohibit research or to censor discourse, especially in the West. It is enough that they can limit the means, can regulate support for production, transmission, diffusion.[216]

Within the "concept of information or informatization"[217] the ethics and the politics of research take shape as the conservative ideal of "science" the university stands on is overtaken by a sacrificing of the autonomy of its own self-regulating measures of knowledge advancement to the real-world pressures of securing a future for itself. And that is understandable, although it may not be acceptable to even those unquestioning defenders of the dominant (or onto-teleological) interpretation of the principle of reason and its "integrat[ing of] the basic to the oriented, the purely rational to the technical, thus bearing witness to that original intermingling of the metaphysical and the technical."[218]

The "responsibility" Derrida wishes to "awaken or resituate"[219] is "in the university or before *(devant)* the university, whether one belongs to it or not."[220] *Its double gesture bridges the ungrounded space of the conditions of possibility over which positions on ethics and responsibility, reason and rationality are thought out and taken.* Derrida begins to elaborate the difficulty of this "new responsibility" by opposing the "prohibiting limitations"[221] that "presses, [public and private] foundations, mass media,"[222] and other "interest groups" place on the act of research within the institution: "The unacceptability of a discourse, the non-certification of a research project, the illegitimacy of a course offering are declared by evaluative actions: studying such evaluations is, it seems to me [he emphasizes], one of the tasks most indispensable to the exercise of academic responsibility, most urgent for the maintenance of its dignity."[223] To intervene decisively in the business of the university is to appeal (to) reason, to ask for the concession of reasons out of which to judge judgments. The medium in question that relates the obligation and responsibility of ethics to politics and the practices of the institution is language and two ways of thinking about the *value of language.* Derrida defines these in relation to the principle of reason as "instrumental" (informative) and "poetic" (creative) by associating their contrasting methods of semiological effect (e.g., representation/undecidability) with research-type, end-oriented and fundamental. And on the basis of the difference of values of finitude that must not proceed from knowledge but always head toward the possibility of its invention is grounded the deconstructive attempt to define a new academic responsibility "in the face of the university's total subjection to the technologies of informatization."[224] The cross-contamination between the "instrumental" and the *"poietic"* aims of research science is obvious "at the outer limits of the authority and power of the principle of reason"[225] where the specificity of goals or purposes is blurred by the shared logic of *praxis.* Derrida situates this antinomic responsibility—of "the experience and experiment of the *aporia,*"[226] more or less—within the general domain of a hypothetical "community of thought"[227] that is committed to the "sounding [of] a call to practice it."[228] The *"group-at-large"* referred to is not one "of research, of science, of philosophy, since these values [of 'professionalism' and 'disciplinarity' no matter how 'radical'] are most often subjected to the unquestioned authority of the principle of reason"[229] and can be absorbed into the homogeneous magma of intra-institutional discourse (e.g., the standardization of Marxism and psychoanalysis). Elsewhere Derrida has named this loosely gathered consortium a "community of the question"[230] after the death of philosophy, a chance for safekeeping the possibility of the question of the *violence of metaphysics,* onto-theo-logical and proto-ethical. How would it function? Derrida explains as follows:

> Such a community would interrogate the essence of reason and of the principle of reason, the values of the basic, of the principial, of radicality, of the *arkhe* in general, and it would attempt to draw out all the possible consequences of this questioning. It is not certain that such a thinking can bring together a community or found an institution in the traditional sense of these words. What is meant by community and institution must be rethought. This thinking must also unmask—an infinite task—all the ruses of end-orienting reason, the paths by which apparently disinterested research can find itself indirectly reappropriated, reinvested by programs of all sorts. That does not mean that "orientation" is bad in itself and that it must be combatted, far from it. Rather, I am defining the necessity for a new way of educating students that will prepare them to undertake new analyses in order to evaluate these ends and choose, when possible, among them all.[231]

Less than a year after this lecture on the principle of reason, the Collège International de Philosophie (CIPH) would open its doors to students and scholars (during January1984), providing perhaps a much anticipated answer to the abiding question of a "community of thought" and the suggestion of a rethinking of the institution of "higher" education.[232] Derrida was its first "acting director," to be followed by Jean-François Lyotard and others in a succession of one-year appointments. The international makeup of the CIPH was and is reflected by the composition of the membership of its "governing bodies," the result of an open letter reprinted on the French Ministry of Research and Industry letterhead and circulated around the world in May 1982, to invite the participation of interested parties in its planning and operation.[233] There were more than 750 replies to the epistle Derrida drafted on behalf of the Socialist government of François Mitterand, who, on the eve of his election to office, had promised the GREPH to protect the discipline of philosophy within the organization of the public school and university curricula. All responses were evaluated, and the four members of the mission (Derrida, François Châtelet, Jean-Pierre Faye, and Dominique Lecourt) issued the lengthy *Rapport pour le Collège International de Philosophie*.[234] The expressed intention or "regulating idea" of that document was to interrogate and displace "the ontological encyclopaedic model by which the philosophical concept of the *universitas* has been guided for the last two centuries"[235] as was originally stated in the letter:

> The International College of Philosophy is to give *(doit donner)* priority to themes, problems, experiences that do not yet find a legitimate or sufficient place in other institutions, whether they concern philosophy or the relations between philosophy, sciences, techniques, and artistic productions. Beyond simple interdisciplinarity, it will be oriented toward new intersections and will work to open *(frayer)* other paths between constituted or compartmentalized disciplines *(savoirs)*. In order to undo traditional isolations, the college will be broadly open, according to new modes, to exchanges from abroad.[236]

That the institution was to be a "College of Philosophy" is not incidental, secondary or superfluous, to the context of this lecture we are rereading on the principle of reason and the being of the university. The semiologico-symbolic interground of any and all potential articulations of academic responsibility is, for Derrida, an irreducible dimension of "thought" and "thinking" analogous with the poststructural meta-criticality of deconstruction. An intellectual practice of grafting, confrontation, and productive interference that transgresses the fixed borders of "the arts" and "the sciences" for the transformative redistribution of knowledge values and the founding of new fields of research at the inter-spaces of philosophy and science. This is made explicit by Derrida's (quasi-)deconstruction of the interdisciplinary schematicism of the Kantian university model:

> One can no longer distinguish between technology on the one hand and theory, science and rationality on the other. . . . [A]n essential affinity ties together objective knowledge, the principle of reason, and a certain metaphysical determination of the relation to truth. . . . One can no longer maintain the boundary that Kant, for example, sought to establish between the schema that he called "technical" and the one he called "architectonic" in the systematic organization of knowledge—which was also to ground a systematic organization of the university. The architectonic is the art of systems. "Under the government of reason, our knowledge in general," Kant says, "should not form a rhapsody, but it must form a system in which alone it can support and favor the essential aims of reason." To that pure rationality of the architectonic, Kant opposes the scheme of the merely technical unity that is empirically oriented, according to views and ends that are inci-

dental, not essential. It is thus a limit between two aims that Kant seeks to define, the essential and noble end of reason that gave rise to fundamental science versus the incidental and empirical ends that can be systematized only in terms of technical schemas and necessities.[237]

Kant had observed in *The Conflict of the Faculties (Der Streit der Fakultäten,* 1798*)*[238] that the university was created by the *enactment of an idea.* An objectivation of the Will to Reason as ceded, in principle, from what is *de jure* a metaphysical incipit *a priori* the inscription of being. Or a *fatum* of the time-less-ness of Being, the ground and abyss of its infinity. That is, the *principle of reason.* Kant, as only he could, attempted to re-theorize the insights and short-comings of such a novel idea as the university in an architectonic division of intellectual labor pure and practical. A uni-form system of knowledge designa-tions starting from "the idea of the whole field of what is presently teachable *(das ganze gegenwärtige Feld der Gelehrsamkeit).*"[239] But the irony is that owing to the "artificiality" *(Künstliche)* of the institutional architecture "one would [have to] treat knowledge a little like an industry *(gleichsam fabrikenmässig)*"[240] and be committed to reproducing the rigid partitions of unsurpassable limits of separa-tion between disciplines. A development related to the themes of "profession," "professionalism" or "professionalization," Derrida views as "regulat[ing] univer-sity life [and research] according to the supply and demand of the marketplace [not excluding the institution itself] and according to a purely technical idea of competence."[241] Any "sociology or politology"[242] policing these borderlines of the Academy—regardless of method (e.g., "Marxist or neo-Marxist, Weberian or neo-Weberian, Mannheimian, some combination of these or something else en-tirely")[243]—in responding to the necessity of justifying the value of its own ex-istence and acceptance to the structural logic of the organic whole "never touches upon that which, in themselves, continues to be based on the principle of reason and thus on the essential foundation of the modern university."[244] Even the most underground thinking—"deconstruction"—can be rehabilitated or reappropriated to serve a "highly traditional politics of knowledge"[245] if the conditions of expo-sition ("historical, techno-economic, politico-institutional, and linguistic")[246] are not analyzed with a vigilant wariness, a radical suspicion. Rather than encourag-ing the open harmony of higher- and lower-level orders of theory and practice Kant envisions, wants, or presumes, the attempt to separate and compartmental-ize interests is the source of the conflict of the faculties itself and an omen of the history of canonical battles, among and within them, for control over the charted and uncharted territory grounding the "economy and ecology"[247] of the institu-tion.

Insofar as "no experience in the present allows for an adequate grasp of that present, presentable totality of doctrine, of teachable theory,"[248] Derrida, in re-reading these idealist presuppositions of this seminal text on the straining inter-relations of the disciplines, argues elsewhere that: "An institution—this is not merely a few walls or some outer structure surrounding, protecting, guaranteeing or restricting the freedom of our work; it is also and already the structure of our interpretation."[249] The ethics of the ground of that edifice of the university is what is being questioned here, in "The Principle of Reason," along with the responsibility to be taken for it, and who this "our" *does* or *can* refer to exactly. This is not to aver, as Kant would have it, that philosophy—the faculty from which the "Great Model of the University" acquires the academic legitimacy of its ideal autonomy— is completely "outside" and "above" any hierarchization of knowledge due to a "higher" responsibility it claims to answer for/to Reason and Truth. There is another side to it.[250] Concurrently, philosophy (unlike other disciplines) would also need to be "inside" and "below" the structure of the institution, filling out the reason of the lower ground on which its being stands. But what of the originary violence of a *faculty of Right?* Is the "mystical foundation of its authority" as a legislator of "Reason" and "Truth" for the university assuaged by an inverted mirroring of its stature? Could it be?

Even if we choose to believe Kant, there is a minimal security, if any at all, to the tautological notion of "the essence of knowledge as knowledge of knowledge":[251] the s(t)olid (meta-philosophical) ground of university autonomy. It is "justified [Derrida stresses] by the axiom stating that scholars alone can judge other scholars."[252] But this still says nothing of academic responsibility. And by this we do not mean the obligation of the institution, a mere husk or shell, a clever figment of a living entity. It goes deeper. The responsibility we are speaking of is that of the teaching body *(le corps enseignant),* the soul of the university.

On both the personal (I/me) and the communal (us/we) planes of the ethico-juridical strata of the norms of responsibility epistemic or empirical subjectivity submit to, the *first* and *final* law of being is preserved by the ground of reason as the fundamental logic of an institution, *the right of its Right.* But the founding and conserving violence complicit with the historicity of the university does not *wholly* ensnare the inspirited bodies of "those who teach"[253] either. Derrida explains how an uncomplicated philosophy of language is the cause for the ambiguity Kant is blind to:

> Kant defines a university that is as much a safeguard for the most totalitarian of social forms as a place for the most intransigently liberal resistance to any abuse of power, resistance that can be judged in turns as most rigorous or most impotent. In effect, its power is confined to a power-to-think-and-judge, a power-to-say, though not necessarily to say *in public,* since this would involve an *action,* an executive power denied the university. How is the combination of such contradictory evaluations possible for a model of the university? What must be such a model, to lend itself thus to this? I can only sketch out an answer to this enormous question. Presuppositions in the Kantian delimitation could be glimpsed from the very start, but today they have become massively apparent. Kant needs, as he says, to trace between a responsibility concerning truth and a responsibility concerning action, a linear frontier, an indivisible and rigorously uncrossable line. To do so he has to submit language to a particular treatment. Language is an element common to both spheres of responsibility, and one that deprives us of any rigorous distinction between the two spaces that Kant at all costs wanted to dissociate. It is an element that opens a passage to all parasiting and simulacra.[254]

The radical breakdown of the architectonic system of the ethical reference of knowledge arising from within the Kantian conception of the Law and the Right of Reason's institution becomes perceptible when the philosophical endowment of the limit of its Truth is projected outside of itself "between [the chain of] language and something other than itself."[255] That, for deconstruction, is but one measure of the injustice of the *universality of the university*. The inconsistency of the supplication of reason to its ground—the accounting of justification itself—surpasses the metaphysical fastidiousness of what Kant presents as an uncorrupted philosophy—of the Idea of Reason—always willing to aid the judgment of a subject "capable of deciding [as it] tries to limit the effects of confusion, simulacrum, parasiting, equivocality and undecidability produced by language."[256] Wanting to close off the university's inside from its outside (and what this means in a larger context) is a utopian flight of fancy, a fearful withdrawal from responsibility to the Other. As is the dream Kant had for a universal language of philosophy uncorrupted by a natural tongue. A wish to keep reason pure. But the freedom of decision to choose among manifold options of undecidable possibilities is not responsibility abdicated nor obligation ignored; it is responsibility multiplied, obligation intensified. Ethics is crystallized in the education of experience manifest of a subjective "trial of passage" wrought from the difficulty of knowledge. A decision without the possibility of choice, in this sense of achieving an informed optation spurring to performance, can be no decision at all. And that also implies a political dimension adducible of the laws of right and Right. For Derrida—like Kierkegaard before him—the ordeal of decision is an instant of madness, it "always risks the worst,"[257] especially, as concerns us here, in relation to the ungrounding of the pre-conditions of the violence of an existing foundation like the idea of the university's reason for being by defining a new educational problematics:

> It is not a matter simply of questions that one *formulates* while submitting oneself, as I am doing here [in the discourse], to the principle of reason, but also of preparing oneself thereby to transform the modes of writing, approaches to pedagogy, the procedures of academic exchange, the relation to languages, to other disciplines, to the institution in general, to its inside and its outside. Those who venture forth along this path, it seems to me, need not set themselves up in opposition to the principle of reason, nor give way to "irrationalism." They may continue to assume *within* the university, along with its memory and and tradition, the imperative of professional rigor and competence.[258]

The meta-logic of deconstruction—the double-sided responsibility of its "to" and "for" peripatetic—aims at a *Verwindung* of the principle of reason, a "going-beyond that is both an acceptance and a deepening"[259] as Gianni Vattimo has argued of the postmodern experience, not to get over, overcome, or to distort the principle by outbidding it into submission, but to resign the compliance of thought to a rethinking of it.[260] And thus to effectuate a change in the thinking of the being of the University. To avoid reproducing the classical architectonic of the Kantian institution, thereby entrenching it still further, Derrida asserts, "'Thought' requires *both* the principle of reason *and* what is beyond the principle of reason, the *arkhè* and an-archy."[261] The creation of a chance for the future by keeping the memory of the past alive. It is at the inter-spaces of knowledge constructions beyond the grasp of "meaning" or "reason" that risks are taken by endeavoring to put what may appear to be the grounded or static system of a multi-stratified and interlocking hierarchy of disciplinary subdivisions into motion, play, *kinesis*. The institutional meeting place of a deconstructive ethics and politics would be where the undecidability of interpretative links are forged between those faculties speaking a constative (theoretical) language of a Kantian type and others who make performative (interventive) statements of an Austinian type. Like a bridge across an abyss of reason.

A Doubled Closure

There is no ambivalence about the threat of resistance deconstruction poses to reason. For some, the analytical situation Derrida annotates, we could say "of deconstruction," is an equivocatory non-sense of self-cancellations, a being-on-both-sides of the issue betraying a lack of ethical or political resolve; for others, its complexity consigns the *"coups nouveau"* of a *post*modern responsivity to an ineffectual rejection of the totality of what has come before in the hopes of improving what will come after. Few concerned will have no appraisal to offer. The gamut of judgments arising from within the general distinctions of perspective I have made begs the question of the "Other of Reason" depicted as "irrationality" without classifiably reducing the content or the *mal*content of arguments under the qualitative dichotomy of a "good" versus "bad" opposition. That is because the open obligation of the academic reponsibility of deconstruction is of the order of rationality, but not of the metaphysical standards of "critique." For as reason internalizes the difference of its Other within the *subjectivism* of itself, steadfastly determining the rules of its own activation, its delimitations, and its ends, we are, or at the least *we should be,* compelled to inquire about the ground of its *objectivism.* The immanent force of a deconstructive questioning succeeds in collapsing the oppositional logics of metaphysical self-substantiation that excludes, *sui generis,* the relative independence of the subalterned voice of an overlooked middle. And this is where the politics of ethics and ontology, of "first philosophy," lies. Submitting the principle of reason to the hermeneutical conundrum of its own *in-itself, for-itself* structurality so as to interrogate the grounds of its meaning, its origin, its possibility, its goal, its limits, yields tensions commanding neither an obeyance to its unforgiving precepts nor a rejection of them. And here we will give the last word to Derrida:

> The time of reflection is also the chance for turning back on the very conditions of reflection, in all the senses of that word, as if with the help of a new optical device one could finally see sight, could not only view the natural landscape, the city, the bridge and the abyss, but could view viewing. As if through an acoustical device one could hear hearing, in other words, seize the inaudible in a sort of poetic telephony. The time of reflection is also another time, it is heterogeneous with what it reflects and perhaps gives time for what calls for and is called thought.[262]

Notes

1. Jacques Derrida, "Mochlos; or, The Conflict of the Faculties," trans. Richard Rand and Amy Wygant, in *Logomachia: The Conflict of the Faculties,* ed. Richard Rand (Lincoln: University of Nebraska Press, 1992), 11. (Original translation has been modified.)

2. Jacques Derrida, *Memoires for Paul de Man,* trans. Cecilia Lindsay, Jonathan Culler, and Eduardo Cavava (New York: Columbia University Press, 1986), 72.

3. Derrida, *Memoires,* 72.

4. Jacques Derrida, "The Principle of Reason: The University in the Eyes of Its Pupils," *Diacritics* 13, no. 3 (Fall 1983): 3.

5. Derrida, "The Principle of Reason," 5.

6. Derrida, "The Principle of Reason," 5.

7. See Jacques Derrida, *Limited Inc.,* trans. Samuel Weber and Jeffrey Mehlman, ed. Gerald Graff (Evanston: Northwestern University Press, 1988), especially the first "chapter," "Signature Event Context," on the constative and performative dimensions of discourse and the ethical involubility of the speech act and the irreconcilability of indication with the expressive intentionality of consciousness. A theme also approached—in a different manner—in Jacques Derrida, *Speech and Phenomena: And Other Essays on Husserl's Theory of Signs,* trans. David B. Allison (Evanston: Northwestern University Press, 1973).

8. See Immanuel Kant, *Critique of Aesthetic Judgment,* trans. James Creed Meredith (Oxford: Clarendon Press, 1911).

9. Derrida, "The Principle of Reason," 6.

10. Derrida, "The Principle of Reason," 5.

11. Derrida, "The Principle of Reason," 5.

12. See Jacques Derrida, "Psyche: Inventions of the Other," trans. Catherine Porter, in *Reading De Man Reading,* ed. Lindsay Waters and Wlad Godzick (Minneapolis: University of Minnesota Press, 1989), 25-66.

13. Derrida, "The Principle of Reason," 5.

14. See Jacques Derrida, *Given Time: I. Counterfeit Money,* trans. Peggy Kamuf (Chicago: University of Chicago Press, 1991).

15. See Jacques Derrida, *Aporias,* trans. Thomas Dutoit (Stanford: Stanford University Press, 1993) for the themes of ritual, gift, death in the "trans-cultural-specificity" of their law.

16. On the obligation "to speak," see Jacques Derrida, "How to Avoid Speaking: Denials," trans. Ken Frieden, in *Derrida and Negative Theology,* ed. Harold Coward and Toby Foshay (Albany: State University of New York Press, 1992), 73-142.

17. See Derrida, "Psyche: Inventions of the Other," *Memoires for Paul de Man,* and Jacques Derrida, *The Gift of Death,* trans. David Wills (Chicago: University of Chicago Press, 1995).

18. See Pierre Bourdieu, *Homo Academicus,* trans. Peter Collier (Stanford: Stanford University Press, 1988) for the concept of "epistemic subjectivity" in relation to "empirical subjectivity."

19. Jacques Derrida, "Force of Law: The 'Mystical Foundation of Authority,'" trans. Mary Quaintance, in *Deconstruction and the Possibility of Justice,* ed. Drucilla

Cornell, Michael Rosenfeld, and David Gray Carlson (New York: Routledge, 1992), 27.

20. Derrida, "The Principle of Reason," 5.

21. Derrida, "The Principle of reason," 5. Elijah is Derrida's Hebrew name.

22. I am using this word deliberately to call up the risk of deconstruction. See Derrida, "Force of Law" for an expansion of the subject of responsibility, sufferance, and the violence of translation, addressing the work of Walter Benjamin.

23. See Jacques Derrida, *Given Time I.*

24. Simon Critchley, *The Ethics of Deconstruction: Derrida and Levinas* (Cambridge, Mass.: Blackwell, 1992), 42.

25. For an ethical perspective of Heidegger's notion of *Mitsein,* "Being-for-others," see Steven Connor, *Theory and Cultural Value* (Cambridge, Mass.: Blackwell, 1992), 198.

26. Derrida, "Psyche: Inventions of the Other," 36.

27. See Richard Kearney, "Derrida's Ethical Re-Turn," in *Working Through Derrida,* ed. Gary B. Madison (Evanston: Northwestern University Press, 1993), 28-50.

28. See Jacques Derrida, *The Other Heading: Reflections of Today's Europe,* trans. Pascale-Anne Brault and Michael Naas (Bloomington: Indiana University Press, 1992).

29. Every border has two sides, and inside and an outside. One is both separate and part of the other. See Derrida, *Aporias.*

30. Jacques Derrida, "Passions: 'An Oblique Offering,'" trans. David Wood, in *Derrida: A Critical Reader,* ed. David Wood (Cambridge, Mass.: Blackwell, 1992), 8.

31. Derrida, Passions, 23.

32. See Emmanuel Levinas, *Totality and Infinity: An Essay on Exteriority,* trans. Alphonso Lingis (Boston: Martinus Nijoff Publishers, 1979).

33. Derrida, "Passions," 8.

34. Derrida, "Passions," 9.

35. This is the general focus of Rodolphe Gasché, *Inventions of Difference: On Jacques Derrida* (Cambridge, Mass.: Harvard University Press, 1994).

36. See Derrida, *Limited Inc.*

37. See Derrida, "Force of Law."

38. Derrida, *The Gift of Death,* 61.

39. Derrida, "The Principle of Reason," 6.

40. See Jacques Derrida, *Of Spirit: Heidegger and the Question,* trans. Geoffrey Bennington and Rachel Bowlby (Chicago: University of Chicago Press, 1987).

41. Martin Heidegger, "The Self-Assertion of the German University: Address, Delivered on the Solemn Assumption of the Rectorate of the University of Freiberg; The Rectorate 1933/34: Facts and Thoughts," translated with an introduction by Kartsen Harries, *Review of Metaphysics* 38 (March 1985): 467-502.

42. Derrida, "The Principle of Reason," 5.

43. Derrida, "The Principle of Reason," 6.

44. Derrida, "The Principle of Reason," 6.

45. See Gregory L. Ulmer, *Heuretics: The Logic of Invention* (Baltimore: Johns Hopkins University Press, 1994).

46. James Siegel, "Academic Work: The View from Cornell," *Diacritics* 11, no. 1 (Spring 1981): 68-83.

47. Derrida, "The Principle of Reason," 4.

48. Derrida, "The Principle of Reason," 6.

49. Derrida, "The Principle of Reason," 6.

50. Derrida, "The Principle of Reason," 6.

51. Derrida, "The Principle of Reason," 6.

52. See the discussion of Sigmund Freud's, *Beyond the Pleasure Principle* and "The Uncanny" in Jacques Derrida, *The Post Card: From Socrates to Freud and Beyond,* trans. Alan Bass (Chicago: University of Chicago Press, 1987).

53. Derrida, "The Principle of Reason," 6.

54. Derrida, "The Principle of Reason," 6.

55. See Jacques Derrida, "Sendoffs," trans. Thomas Pepper, *Yale French Studies* 77 (1990): 7-43.

56. Derrida, Mochlos," 30.

57. Jacques Derrida, "Canons and Metonymies: An Interview with Jacques Derrida," trans. Richard Rand and Amy Wygant, in *Logomachia: The Conflict of the Faculties,* ed. Richard Rand (Lincoln: University of Nebraska Press, 1992), 202.

58. See Derrida, *Aporias.*

59. Jacques Derrida, *Du droit à la philosophie* (Paris: Galilée, 1990), 107. (All translations from this text are my own.)

60. Derrida, *Du droit à la philosophie,* 88.

61. On this subject see also Jacques Derrida, "Languages and Institutions of Philosophy," trans. Sylvia Söderlind, Rebecca Comay, Barbara Havercroft, and Joseph Adamson, *Recherches Semiotique/Semiotic Inquiry* 4, no. 2 (1984): 91-154.

62. Derrida, "The Principle of Reason," 6.

63. Derrida, "The Principle of Reason," 6.

64. Derrida, "The Principle of Reason," 3.

65. Derrida, "Sendoffs," 14.

66. Derrida, "The Principle of Reason," 3.

67. See Derrida, "Mochlos," on the rationality of the pronoun "we."

68. See Derrida, *The Gift of Death,* especially Chapter Three, "Whom to Give to (Knowing Not to Know)."

69. Derrida, *The Gift of Death,* 25. See also Derrida, "Canons and Metonymies," for a more animated discussion of deconstruction, ethics, and responsibility in light of the discovery of the wartime writings of Paul de Man.

70. Derrida, *The Gift of Death,* 25. (Original translation has been modified.)

71. Derrida, *Of Spirit,* 129. See footnote 5.

72. See Martin Heidegger, *On Time and Being,* trans. Joan Stambaugh (New York: Harper & Row, 1972), especially the "chapter" entitled "The End of Philosophy and the Task of Thinking."

73. Derrida, "Sendoffs," 16.

74. See Jacques Derrida, "Sendoffs." The larger version of the proposal in which "Sendoffs" is included is called "The Blue Report" by Derrida and those at the International College of Philosophy. Approximately 245 pages (with the table of contents), it is worth consulting on these issues of institutional direction and destination.

75. See Jacques Derrida, "Sending: On Representation," trans. Peter Caws and Mary Ann Caws, *Social Research* 49, no. 2 (1982): 295-326 and Jacques Derrida, "Violence and Metaphysics: An Essay on the Thought of Emmanuel Levinas," trans. Alan Bass, in *Writing and Difference* (Chicago: University of Chicago Press, 1978), 79-153.

76. Derrida, "The Principle of Reason," 6.

77. Derrida, "Sendoffs," 13.

78. Derrida, "The Principle of Reason," 5.

79. Samuel Weber, "Upping the Ante: Deconstruction as Parodic Practice," in *Deconstruction is/in America,* ed. Anselm Haverkamp (New York: New York University Press, 1995), 63.

80. Jacques Derrida, "White Mythology: Metaphor in the Text of Philosophy," trans. Alan Bass, in *Margins of Philosophy* (Chicago: University of Chicago Press, 1982), 209.

81. Derrida, "White Mythology: Metaphor in the Text of Philosophy," 221.

82. Derrida, "The Principle of Reason," 17.

83. Derrida, "The Principle of Reason," 6.

84. Derrida, "The Principle of Reason," 6.

85. Derrida, "The Principle of Reason," 6.

86. See the discussion of the Freudian uncanny in the chapter on Jacques Lacan, *"Le Facteur de la Vérité,"* in Derrida, *The Post Card.*

87. See Martin Heidegger, *Poetry, Language, Thought,* trans. Albert Hofstader (New York: Harper Colophon Book, 1971).

88. See Martin Heidegger, *The Question Concerning Technology and Other Essays,* trans. William Lovitt (New York: Harper & Row Publishers, 1977).

89. The transference of the invisible to an image unveils the invisible visible.

90. Jacques Derrida , "Force and Signification," in *Writing and Difference,* 27.

91. Derrida, "Languages and Institutions of Philosophy," 134.

92. Derrida, "Languages and Institutions of Philosophy," 134.

93. I am using this idea of the "literal example" in the sense of Bill Martin, *Humanism and Its Aftermath: The Shared Fate of Deconstruction and Politics* (Atlantic Highlands, N. J.: Humanities Press, 1995).

94. Derrida, "The Principle of Reason," 3.

95. See Derrida, "White Mythology" about the "photo-dia-logico-synthetics" of Western metaphysics, its imagery of light and darkness equated with knowing.

96. Derrida, "The Principle of Reason," 4.

97. Derrida, "The Principle of Reason," 5.

98. Derrida, "The Principle of Reason," 5.

99. See French version of Jacques Derrida, *"Le principe de raison et l'idée de l'Université"* in *Du droit à la philosophie* (Paris: Galilée, 1990), 463. The Aristotelien expression is: *"pantes anthropoi tou eidenai oregontai phusei."* Derrida translates it as *"tous les hommes, par nature, ont le désir du savoir."*

100. Derrida, "The Principle of Reason," 4.

101. Derrida, *Speech and Phenomena,* 108.

102. Derrida has dealt with the problem extensively in *Speech and Phenomena.*

103. Derrida, "The Principle of Reason," 4.

104. Derrida, "The Principle of Reason," 5.

105. Derrida, "The Principle of Reason," 5.

106. Derrida, "The Principle of Reason," 5. (Translation has been modified.).

107. Jacques Derrida, *The Ear of the Other: Otobiography, Transference, Translation,* trans. Peggy Kamuf and Avital Ronnel, ed. Christie McDonald (Lincoln: University of Nebraska Press, 1988), 35.

108. Derrida, *The Ear of the Other,* 96.

109. Derrida, *The Ear of the Other,* 35-36.

110. Derrida, *The Ear of the Other,* 35.

111. Jacques Derrida, "Living on: Border lines," trans. James Hulbert, in *Deconstruction and Criticism,* eds. Harold Bloom, Paul de Man, Jacques Derrida, Geoffrey Hartman, J. Hillis Miller (New York: Continuum, 1979), 94-96.

112. See Pierre Bourdieu, *Language and Symbolic Power,* trans. Gino Raymond and Matthew Adamson (London: Polity Press, 1991).

113. Derrida, "The Principle of Reason," 4.

114. Derrida, "The Principle of Reason," 4.

115. Bourdieu, *Language and Symbolic Power,* 167.

116. See Bourdieu, *Language and Symbolic Power.*

117. Jacques Derrida, "Politics of Friendship," trans. Gabriel Motzkin, Michael Syrotinski, and Thomas Keenan, *American Imago* 50, no. 3 (1993): 355.

118. Derrida, "The Principle of Reason," 9.

119. John D. Caputo, *Radical Hermeneutics: Repetition, Deconstruction, and the Hermeneutic Project* (Bloomington: Indiana University Press, 1987), 231.

120. Derrida, "The Principle of Reason," 8.

121. Derrida, "The Principle of Reason," 8.

122. Derrida, "The Principle of Reason," 7. (Translation has been modified.)

123. Derrida, "The Principle of Reason," 8.

124. Derrida, "The Principle of Reason," 10.

125. See Derrida, "Languages and Institutions of Philosophy."

126. Derrida, "The Principle of Reason," 10.

127. Derrida, "The Principle of Reason," 8.

128. Martin Heidegger, *The Principle of Reason,* trans. Reginald Lilly (Bloomington: Indiana University Press, 1991), 119.

129. See Derrida, "Sending: On Representation."

130. See Heidegger, *The Question Concerning Technology.*

131. Derrida, "The Principle of Reason," 10.

132. See Heidegger, *The Question Concerning Technology.*

133. See Heidegger, *The Question Concerning Technology.*

134. Derrida, "The Principle of Reason," 10. (Translation has been modified.)

135. Derrida, "Sending: On Representation," 307.

136. See Heidegger, *The Principle of Reason.*

137. See Heidegger, *The Principle of Reason.*

138. See Heidegger, *The Question Concerning Technology.*

139. Derrida, "Sending: On Representation," 304.

140. Derrida, "The Principle of Reason," 8.

141. See Derrida, "Force of Law," for the two "types" of deconstructive approaches—the one following the trails of an idea or concept, the other using a text as a springboard to reading and writing—and the "whole subjectal axiomatic of responsibility" (25).

142. Derrida, "The Principle of Reason," 8.

143. Derrida, "The Principle of Reason," 8.

144. See Martin Heidegger, *Discourse on Thinking,* trans. John M. Anderson and E. Hans Freund (New York: Harper & Row Publishers, 1966).

145. Derrida, "The Principle of Reason," 9.

146. See Heidegger, *The Question Concerning Technology.*

147. See Heidegger, *Discourse on Thinking.*

148. Derrida, "The Principle of Reason," 8.

149. Derrida, "The Principle of Reason," 8.

150. See Heidegger, *Poetry, Language, Thought.*

151. Heidegger, *Discourse on Thinking,* 65.

152. On this aspect of *Gelassenheit,* see Jacques Derrida, "Heidegger's Ear: Philopolemology *(Geschlecht* IV), trans. John P. Leavey Jr., in *Reading Heidegger: Commemorations,* ed. John Sallis (Bloomington: Indiana University Press, 1993) 163-218.

153. Heidegger, *Discourse on Thinking,* 55.

154. See Heidegger, *Poetry, Language, Thought.*

155. See Heidegger, *The Question Concerning Technology.*

156. Cited in Derrida, "The Principle of Reason," 9.

157. Christopher Norris, *Derrida* (London: Fontana Press, 1987), 160.

158. The preference Richard Rorty has for John Dewey is stated in *The Consequences of Pragmatism* (Minneapolis: University of Minnesota Press, 1982): "To lump Dewey with Peirce, James, and Quine is to forget that he was swept off his feet, and into a new intellectual world, by Hegel's and Compte's visions of our past." (46)

159. Derrida, "The Principle of Reason," 9.

160. Derrida, "The Principle of Reason," 9.

161. See Derrida, "Force of Law."

162. See Derrida, "Mochlos."

163. See Immanuel Kant, *Critique of Practical Reason,* trans. Lewis White Beck (New York: Macmillan Publishing Company, 1956) and Immanuel Kant, *The Conflict of the Faculties/Der Streit der Fakultäten,* trans. Mary J. Gregor (New York: Abaris Books, 1979).

164. See Derrida "Mochlos."

165. Derrida, "The Principle of Reason," 9.

166. Derrida, *Du droit à la philosophie,* 88. (Translation is my own.)

167. Heidegger, *The Principle of Reason,* 24. Also included in a slightly different translation in a footnote to Derrida's text.

168. Derrida, "The Principle of Reason," 9.

169. Derrida, "Languages and Institutions of Philosophy," 134.

170. See Jacques Derrida, "Languages and Institutions of Philosophy."

171. See the comments on ghosts, specters, apparitions, etc., in Derrida, "Passions." An theme that appears in other texts such as *The Gift of Death,* "The Force of Law," *Specters of Marx: The State of the Debt, the Work of Mourning, & the New International,* trans. Peggy Kamuf (New York: Routledge, 1994).

172. Jacques Derrida, *On the Name,* trans. David Wood, John P. Leavey Jr., and Ian McLeod, ed. Thomas Dutoit (Stanford: Stanford University Press, 1995), 93.

173. The semiotic facet of the *khora* as an aspect of the theory of poetic language and the psychoanalytic drives of the subject is found in Julia Kristeva, *Revolution in Poetic Language,* trans. Margaret Waller (New York: Columbia University Press, 1978).

174. See the chapter entitled "Mnemosyne" in Derrida, *Memoires for Paul de Man.*

175. See Derrida, "Sendoffs."

176. On guarding against the trans-lation of skepticism to mystagogy, see Jacques Derrida, "On a Newly Arisen Apocalytic Tone in Philosophy," trans. John P. Leavey Jr., in *Raising the Tone of Philosophy: Late Essays by Immanuel Kant, Transformative Critique by Jacques Derrida,* ed. Peter Fenves (Baltimore: Johns Hopkins University Press, 1993), 117-171.

177. Derrida, "Languages and Institutions of Philosophy," 132.

178. See Derrida, *Speech and Phenomena.*

179. See Derrida, *The Post Card.*

180. See Jacques Derrida, *Dissemination,* trans. Barbara Johnson (Chicago: University of Chicago Press, 1981).

181. Derrida, "Mochlos," 3. (Translation has been modied, my emphasis.).

182. Derrida, "The Principle of Reason," 8.

183. See Derrida, "Sending."

184. And, in fact, we can follow a trail that leads from the transformation of the pre-Socratic notion of Being as *physis* and *aletheia* into the conception of Being as *eidos* and *idea* from Plato to Being as humanity's idea to technology.

185. Derrida, "The Principle of Reason," 10.

186. See Heidegger, *The Question Concerning Technology* for the discussion of technology as a mode of *aletheuein,* revealing—the essence of technology being nothing "technological" but *poietic.*

187. Derrida, "Sending," 317.

188. Derrida, "The Principle of Reason," 10.

189. Derrida, "The Principle of Reason," 12.

190. Martin Heidegger, "Letter on Humanism," trans. David Farrell Krell, in *Basic Writings,* ed. David Farrell Krell (New York: Harper Collins, 1977), 193-242.

191. See Martin Heidegger, *The Question Concerning Technology.*

192. Derrida, "The Principle of Reason," 10.

193. Derrida, "The Principle of Reason," 8.

194. Derrida, "The Principle of Reason," 8.

195. Derrida, "The Principle of Reason," 9.

196. See Heidegger, *The Principle or Reason,* Chapters 5 and 6.

197. Derrida, "The Principle of Reason," 10.

198. Derrida, "The Principle of Reason," 10.

199. See Kant, *The Conflict of the Faculties.*

200. See Levinas, *Totality and Infinity.*

201. See Derrida, *Du droit à la philosophie,* especially pages 99-100.

202. See Jürgen Habermas, "The Idea of the University—Learning Processes," trans. John R. Blazek, *New German Critique* 41 (Spring-Summer 1987): 3-22.

203. Derrida, "Mochlos," 3.

204. Derrida, "Mochlos," 15.

205. Derrida, "The Principle of Reason," 11.

206. Derrida, "The Principle of Reason," 11.

207. Derrida, "The Principle of Reason," 12.

208. Derrida, "The Principle of Reason," 11.

209. Derrida, "The Principle of Reason," 11. "The Principle of Reason" we must remember was written and presented in April 1983. At the time—the peaking of the Cold War—this is a fair description of the homogeneous "conditionality" of the Western "nation-states"—most conspicuously exemplified by America and Russia—that according to Derrida were spending in total upwards of "two million dollars a minute" on the manufacture of armaments alone.

210. Derrida, "The Principle of Reason," 14.

211. Derrida, "The Principle of Reason," 12.

212. Derrida, "The Principle of Reason," 12.

213. Derrida, "The Principle of Reason," 12.

214. Derrida, "The Principle of Reason," 13.
215. Derrida, "The Principle of Reason," 13.
216. Derrida, "The Principle of Reason," 13.
217. Derrida, "The Principle of Reason," 14.
218. Derrida, "The Principle of Reason," 14.
219. Derrida, "The Principle of Reason," 14.
220. Derrida, "The Principle of Reason," 14.
221. Derrida, "The Principle of Reason," 13.
222. Derrida, "The Principle of Reason," 13.
223. Derrida, "The Principle of Reason," 13.
224. Derrida, "The Principle of Reason," 14.
225. Derrida, "The Principle of Reason," 14.
226. Derrida, *The Other Heading,* 41.
227. Derrida, "The Principle of Reason," 16.
228. Derrida, "The Principle of Reason," 16.
229. Derrida, "The Principle of Reason," 16.
230. Derrida, "Violence and Metaphysics," 80.
231. Derrida, "The Principle of Reason," 16.
232. Two excellent discussions of the Collège International de Philosophie are Vincent B. Leitch, "Research and Education at the Crossroads: A Report on the Collège International de Philosophie," *Substance* 50 (1986): 101-114 and Steven Ungar, "Philosophy after Philosophy: Debate and Reform in France Since 1968," *Enclitic* 8, nos. 1-2 (1984): 13-26.
233. The open letter was published in the United States in *Substance* 35 (1982): 80-81.
234. Jacques Derrida, François Châtelet, Jean-Pierre Faye, and Dominique Lecourt, *Rapport pour le Collège International de Philosophie* (Paris: Ministre de la Recherche et de l'Industrie, 1982).
235. Derrida, "Sendoffs," 13.
236. Cited in Leitch, "Research and Education at the Crossroads," 103-104.
237. Derrida, "The Principle of Reason," 12.
238. See Kant, *The Conflict of the Faculties.*
239. Derrida, "The Principle of Reason," 6.
240. Derrida, "Mochlos," 5.
241. Derrida, "The Principle of Reason," 17.
242. Derrida, "The Principle of Reason," 16.
243. Derrida, "The Principle of Reason," 16.
244. Derrida, "The Principle of Reason," 16.
245. Derrida, "The Principle of Reason," 17.
246. Derrida, "The Principle of Reason," 17.
247. Derrida, "The Principle of Reason," 16.
248. Derrida, "The Principle of Reason," 6.
249. Derrida, "Mochlos," 22.
250. See Derrida, "Languages and Institutions of Philosophy."
251. Derrida, "Mochlos," 5.
252. Derrida, "Mochlos," 5.
253. Derrida, "The Principle of Reason," 5.
254. Derrida, "Mochlos," 18.
255. Derrida, "White Mythology," 216.

256. Derrida, "Mochlos," 18.

257. Derrida, "The Principle of Reason," 19.

258. Derrida, "The Principle of Reason," 17.

259. Gianni Vattimo, *The End of Modernity: Nihilism and Hermeneutics in Post-modern Culture,* trans. Jon R. Snyder (Baltimore: Johns Hopkins University Press, 1988), 172.

260. See Rodolphe Gasché, *Inventions of Difference.*

261. Derrida, "The Principle of Reason," 18-19.

262. Derrida, "The Principle of Reason," 19.

Chapter Four

Teaching the Other the Limits of Philosophy

Face-to-Face with the Violence of Difference

> Those who look into the possibility of philosophy, philosophy's life and death, are already engaged in, already overtaken by the dialogue of the question about itself and with itself: they always act in remembrance of philosophy, as part of the correspondence of the question with itself.
> —Jacques Derrida, "Violence and Metaphysics: An Essay on the Thought of Emmanuel Levinas"[1]

Chapter 4 looks into the future through the historicity of the past by looking at what has been constructed—after the hermeneutical violence of deconstruction upon the archive of Western epistemology—as "the death of metaphysics." It presents a reading of Jacques Derrida's writing on the subject that seeks to resist and alter this contention with respect to the ethical question of the right to philosophy—why we should protect and conserve the past and present of metaphysics while building upon the horizons of its excesses and limitations in order to look forward to a future for thinking. The first part of the chapter deals with the question of what philosophy is and how it includes the Other within the historicity of its *corpus* to betray the image of itself as Western ideology. The attempt here is to breakdown the misinformed generalizations and stereotypes of deconstruction, e.g., that it leads the call for a recognition of the end of metaphysics, when it does exactly the opposite by acting upon the desire to bring its history into the future. This, of course, involves an ethics of practice, a teaching and a learning that does not recognize the end of philosophy but does acknowledge its *closure* as metaphysics. The problems of community, democracy, and representation are addressed with respect to the reconfiguring and rechanneling of the violence against the archive of the West beyond the act of false mourning and a mocking remembrance of a simple, teleological death without the persistence of memory in the spatio-temporal hereafter. The second part of the chapter continues variations upon this theme but brings it back to its foreshadowing of pedagogical implications as it presents a reading of a Derrida lecture presented at the first International Conference for Humanistic Discourses hosted by UNESCO in Paris during the month of April 1994. "Of the Humanities and the Philosophical Discipline: The Right to Philosophy from the Cosmopolitical Point of View (the Example of an International Institution)" is a meditation on the ethical ramifications of who should ask the question of the right to philosophy and where, in what space and place. The analysis focuses upon how UNESCO is used by Derrida to represent a post-Kantian institution that both imbibes philosophy and is the practice of philosophy. And how it extends this intermingling of thought and action toward the generating of a vision of what the international community of nations, states, and peoples is and should be beyond a separation between particular interests and universal aims or goals. Its combining of constation with performativity gives rise to the possibility of its re-visioning of the global condition from a cosmopolitical point of view as an institution that is at the crossroads of a past historicity and a future history. Immanuel Kant had predicted the possibility of its founding, but this is only of secondary importance given the magnitude of its mission to safeguard democracy and access to public education, and therefore also, the right to philosophy. In this sense, the second part of the chapter concentrates upon how deconstruction can help an institution to reconfigure itself for the better by causing those who are part of it, are it, to question the grounding of the concepts they hold most dear as the keys to the perfectibility of human being. Chapter 4 ends with a consideration of some specific headings of principle and of practice, of ethics and of politics, that Derrida suggests would move us beyond the opposition of Eurocentrism and anti-Eurocentrism and the binary basis for an exclusionary thinking that threatens the right to philosophy from the cosmopolitical point of view.

The Deaths of Philosophy:
Of Metaphysics and Mourning for the Archive

That philosophy died yesterday, since Hegel or Marx, Nietzsche, or Heidegger—and philosophy should still wander toward the meaning of its death—or that it has always lived knowing itself to be dying (as is silently confessed in the shadow of the very discourse *which declared philosophia perennis*); that philosophy died *one day, within* history, or that it has always fed on its own agony, on the violent way it opens history by opposing itself to non-philosophy, which is its past and its concern, its death and wellspring; that beyond the death, or dying nature of philosophy, perhaps even because of it, thought still has a future, or even, as is said today, is still entirely to come because of what philosophy has held in store; or, more strangely still, that the future itself has a future—all of these are unanswerable questions.

—Jacques Derrida, "Violence and Metaphysics: An Essay
on the Thought of Emmanuel Levinas"[2]

To mourn the death of philosophy, or metaphysics, after deconstruction reso-
nates as premature. For the "work"—or the economy of the internal emotional
and psychic labor—that sustains the logic driving the motivational force of this
hyperintellectualized (theoretical) act of grieving is inopportune. Its effectivity
mistakenly presupposes a common and universal recognition of the end of an
epistemic tradition rooted in the rise of the Occident as an archive of teaching and
learning. The *force* of this mourning of philosophy mobilizes and is mobilized
by a lamentation of the violence perpetrated against the Archeology of the Letter,
its *arkhe and telos,* the beginning and the finale of the history of metaphysics.
Regret for the "pure loss,"[3] as Jacques Derrida has called it, of an *ideal consignment of knowledge* leaves a space *(kenosis)* for the possibility of an assembling
or *gathering (Versammlung), a coming together,* of that which would mark the
scene of a new beginning onto the futures of thinking with no programmable
end in sight. What will therefore arise *from within* the irreducible anteriority of
the somatico-psychic experience of "philosophy" is the ineffable opening of
metaphysics itself unto the threshold of an impossible unfolding.[4] And yet there
is no sense when dealing with an unforeseeable futurity *within* and *without* the
body of the textual field of the *logos* to philosophize *"à corps perdu,"*[5] passion-
ately, impetuously, with desperation, Derrida would say, so as to attempt to
master the outside limits of knowledge and the inexhaustive multiplicity of its
sub-versive domain:

> Which does not amount to acknowledging that the margin maintains
> itself within *and* without. Philosophy says so too: *within* because phi-
> losophical discourse intends to know and to master its margin, to de-
> fine the line, align the page, enveloping it in its volume. *Without* be-
> cause the margin, *its* margin, *its* outside are empty, are outside: a nega-
> tive without effect in the text *or* a negative working in the service of
> meaning, the margin *relevé (aufgehoben)* in the dialectics of the Book.
> Thus one will have said nothing, or in any event done nothing, in de-
> claring "against" philosophy that its margin is within or without,
> within and without, simultaneously the inequality of its internal spac-
> ings and the regularity of its borders.[6]

A hyper-idealized vision—that in its mad rush of looking forward to an epistemological breakthrough of infinite possibility beckons a restoration of order
beyond the encyclopedia of tradition bereft of any connections to "a past" by
leaving behind or ignoring the historicity of a body of thought and thinking—can only be a "natural" (read uncritical) reaction. The *phthora,* a fraying,
untangling or wearing-away in degradation, of the spatio-temporal organization
of the structurality of the archive, after all, destabilizes the dimensions of the
decisive and indivisible set of points tracing the hieratic lineage of the *meaning
of metaphysics, the metaphysics of meaning,* and in the process minimizes the
already myopic perspective and perspicacity of those hoping to actualize those

first steps of faith toward the enactment of an impossible time—a post-philosophical era.[7]

A word of caution, however, is worth mentioning here as it distinguishes the two horns of the dilemma of the *ouverture* of metaphysics and the fathomability of its Other. To conjugate the problem of the *mal d'archive,* once again, both as the pathology and as the madness of the repetition compulsion, though in a different manner, concerned more with the philosophical and less fixated on the altogether moribund mourning of a philosophical death. On the one hand, all expeditures made to secure a future (for) thinking after the recognition of the impermanence, or *the lack,* of an absolute thought must rely on the aim to "co-ordinate a single corpus, in a system or a synchrony"[8] of repeatable structures, and hence to settle the foundation of a a soci-ety, its com-mun-ity, its laws and institutions, what it values and teaches, protects: in short, to *make real* the desire to consummate, once again, the hospitality of THE DOMICILE *(oikia),* where "we" could live and *be-at-home-in-being.* On the other, the reconstruction of the ground of the public sphere—the cosmopolitical[9]—is compelled to take place with and against the recesses of memory *(mneme, anamnesis, hypomnema)* after the work of mourning is done, though not yet finished, and provides solace in relief of what the *an-archontic,* an-archival, tendency toward a dismantling of the system of hierarchical order leaves us open to,[10] *the impression of a "clean-break," a breach or rupture, of the history of the archive, of philosophy and its teaching.* The contradiction of attempting to "close-off" or put metaphysics "between brackets" *(entre crochets),*[11] to try to exclude it while still having to retain *ipso facto* the mnemonic trace of its operating principles in order to move beyond metaphysics, to OVERCOME it,[12] soon becomes evident. And so there is a false consciousness of the loss of the archive. Its self-deluding internalization of a condition of separation as a self-limiting idea supporting the turmoil that feeds the fever of a mourning for the death of philosophy is destructive, because the focus is put on *the end* rather than *the closure* of philosophy.[13] There is no sense of respect for the alterity of what *may* or *could* come after the prolonged completion of metaphysics, after the trace of repetition wrought by time and difference. What was inaugurated through the extended path of the ontological quest to counter the forgetting of Being, sought to bring about its unconceal-ment, *aletheia,* its unforgetting, by attempting to recall back into cultural and epistemic memory the conceptualization of the Spirit of being and its perfected essence defined after early Greek thinking as the self-presence of presence totally present to itself.[14] For this well-rounded circularity was the beginning and the end of philosophy. Tensions between the "unknowable weight"[15] of competing desires set to fill the chaos of the apocalyptic impression of a lack of a secure ground, and hence the absence of meaning, lead to the seductive awakening of a reconstructive drive singularly bent toward facilitating a "return to order" as an escape from a state of *athesis, non-positionality,* limbo.[16] All of these words most certainly are synonyms for death, the non-being of Being, and the *agon* of its metaphysical *aporia.*[17] A denegation of the genealogy of "the Idea" and its ideo-logy does not recognize, however, that the legacy of philosophy can never be fully erased from cultural memory because the *imprimatura* of its diachronic sign traces the borderlines of Western thought on both sides of the limit of its dividing line. The *agonia* of fighting against the renunciation of that which we desire to *keep close to home* because it is familiar *(heimliche)*, familiarity itself—where "we" live and dwell—is saturated with the sense of the need to identify a metalanguage for externalizing the experiential loss of a stable center of meaning in the *syntagmata* of metaphysics and to facilitate the releasing of an excessive melacholia resulting from the (post)modern subject losing faith in its semiotico-psychic attachments to an ordered conception of life-world *(Lebenswelt)* "bit by bit" *(Einzeldurchführung)*.[18]

And yet neither Derrida nor deconstruction—*the one not being the same as the other*—has ever acknowledged, called for, or celebrated the death of philosophy—if such a thing could indeed be "celebrated," welcomed in its popularization. Since the enclosure of metaphysics in a frame of perfect finitude places restrictions on the possibility and impossibility of engaging thinking at the outer limits of truth. And for good reason. Taking the *step (not) beyond (pas audelà)* philosophy cannot likely be accomplished (from) without philosophy, if it can be accomplished at all (which is really another way of saying it cannot!). This is the *aporia of passage* that must be negotiated with the aid of deconstruction and its risky strategy of an *ex-orbit-ant* modality of reading that marks the double bind of the logic of each and any attempt to *transgress* or even, in some instances, *arrest the progress of metaphysics, whatever this may mean to a future of thinking that has always already been in a perpetual state of closure and therefore without end.* The route to new forms of knowledge is characterized by this *ethical* problem of the paradox of the lack of an outside: *paradox,* from its rootedness in the Greek, *paradoxon,* meaning a thinking beyond popular opinion *(doxa)* yet placed within the hyper-teleology of duty, the right *(orthotes),* of what can or cannot be *justly glorified,* deserves to be held up as an exemplary model to be emulated because it is at once a singular exception, a rare or impossible occurrence, worthy of praise, *doxastic.* The law of this antinomy represented by the image of the *"hors-texte,"* whose double reading Derrida has used to identify the illusion of exteriority, the *Il n'y a pas* of an "out-text"/the non-presence of an *"outside-of-the-text,"* thus structures the inconsolability of the mournful desire to *withdraw from* philosophy so as to regain the essence of subject-ivity and reclaim the spirit of Being in the name of difference and its radicalization of heterogeneity: e.g., the multitudinal guises of a negative and relational locality actualized by the term "Otherness."[19] And this may seem a strange and perhaps scandalous indictment, especially to those who have struggled in good faith, yet blindly, to overturn universalism for the purpose of instating particularity, only to find that via the cultural/material space of an inscription of identity for its own sake, essentialism quickly dissipates the ethical necessity of recognizing and responding to the alterity of an Other with/in the Selfsame. The struggle to escape metaphysics, however precautionary its measures and forthrightness of purpose (good faith, ethicity, openness), will always fail outright because its closure is by definition interminable, a process of repeated repetitions, alterity, a variegation without ending or end. The incommensurability between this lack of an opening and the overzealous push to enforce a moment of finality becomes the enigmatic center of the paradox that suspends philosophy amid mirrored images of its past achievements and the impossible dreams of its future glory. But

then, the ethical questioning of the trajectory of metaphysics and its hyper-
genealogical aftermath beyond end and closure still persists. It proceeds: mainly,
along the *peras* or axis of these guiding lines. Questions persist. Is the fate of
philosophy doomed to pursue in vain the eschatological struggle of attempting
to efface the traces of itself so as to break free from the onto-ideologico-
epistemic archive of past and present knowledges? To effectively look forward to
bringing about its own death in order to recreate itself anew by seeking to step
beyond and by doing so step/not beyond the ground of metaphysics and its institutions? Is philosophy without philosophy possible? Desirable? Can there be a
closure or/and an end of metaphysics? And would this constitute an ethical crisis
for philosophy and its archeo-logical institution that is disseminated and regulated culturally as/in a form of teaching and learning? And what of its pedagogy?
The right of its pedagogy both as form and content. Who would have the *right to
philosophy, to teaching and learning philosophy* (the *right* philosophy?) and its
"other heading," *the right of its other heading*?[20] These are no doubt difficult
questions. Impossible interrogations, *aporias* we could assuredly call them with
some confidence of the designation. In relating as they do to the history of philosophy and its institution, these questions I have posed *without precaution* attempt to reiterate and readdress what Derrida identifies—in the four scenarios
from "Violence and Metaphysics: An Essay on the Thought of Emmanuel Levinas" cited at the beginning of this chapter—to be the "problems put philosophy
as problems philosophy cannot resolve."[21] I must consequently disarm myself of
any claims to knowledge presumptuous of "final solutions" and its liberal affec-
tations of a teleological exodus of sorts. The force of the questioning cannot
subside, however, and be absorbed in the paralyzing desire for an end-thought, an
end to thought. Because it simply will not happen that I will solve the riddle of
finding a way out of philosophy. It would be wiser, and surely ethical enough,
to forgo any such analytico-idealistic aspirations from the start, so as to prepare
the path for the possibility of an affirmation arising from *within* or *through* the
aporia of a non-passage, to what may lie beyond the borders of metaphysics yet
remains ensconced in the haunt of logocentrism.[22] This disarmament, curiously
enough, therefore, also constitutes a necessary precaution, much needed *guardrails* to work against and, if possible, to exceed, Derrida would say, and thereby
re-marking the dangerous boundaries of the "limits of truth" where the solid
ground of reason gives way to the undecidability of the abyss, an *ur-ground* perhaps of an-other type, an impossible one, itself being grounded, like deconstruction, in an un-grounding of its groundedness (e.g., presence as absence or lack,
neither emptiness nor a void). If I were wholly bound by a finite sense of the
debt owed to the scholarly duty of attempting *at all costs* to reach terminal—
rather than provisional—conclusions that are intended to "wrap up" research and
halt discussion, I would not be predisposed to what may unexpectedly announce
itself out of my rereading of another of Derrida's "educational texts" that I have
temporarily suspended as I attempt to begin to engage these fundamental questions concerning the "right" of philosophy's birth and death, and the ethics of its
body of teaching, also of its teaching body *(corps enseignant).* Still, it is not a
matter of throwing all caution to the wind in order to make laudable pronouncements. So, I will proceed according to the caveat Derrida applies to his original

presuppositions and works around, as well as under: "It may even be that these questions are not *philosophical,* are not *philosophy's* questions."[23]

The thought is remarkable. Especially considering the fact that not so dissimilar questions regarding the future of metaphysics have been posed at different times during the recent history of philosophy—in a variety of registers, pitches, and tones, apocalyptic, idealist, and otherwise—by Immanuel Kant and Martin Heidegger, for example.[24] But with Derrida and the deconstruction of logocentrism, we are cognizant of the need to move to new ground now, after and out of the path of idealism and ontology, to proceed ethically with and beyond the debt and duty owed to the archeo-logical excavations of a past time. Only through a responsible questioning that rises out of what is said and left unsaid in the Western tradition of metaphysics can a reaffirmation of "philosophy" as the interpretational moment of a disciplinary line of inquiry, as the translation of an institutional framework, and as the enactment of a pedagogy potentially occur. Derrida—and I will have reiterated the following before—has consistently tried to make an epistemic shift from ontology and a classical thinking of difference to de-ontology and the affirmative ethics of *différance* happen, with the help of deconstruction, "an institutional practice for whom the concept of institution remains a problem."[25] The ethical moment of this opening of location and locality, the space and place, *khorismos* and *khora,* from which to engage and facilitate a return to questions of academic responsibility in hopes of transforming the ground of thinking and practice, is vital in its importance for what is at stake—that is, for the future of philosophy itself. Despite its wanting "to reach the point of a certain exteriority [non-closure, alterity or otherness] in relation to the totality of the age of logocentrism,"[26] deconstruction nevertheless must remain hopelessly and forever tied to the normative discourse of metaphysics. But it perseveres at taking an affirmative line of questioning with respect to the reductive formulizability of binaric thought and its hyper-simplistic, teleo-idiomatic construction of the ontological difference of identity in both conceptual and empirical terms. Deconstruction, whether it wants to or not, redefines the conditional determinacy of the axiological limits to thinking that it meets and will ultimately test, so as to converge upon uncharted destinations of thinking, teaching, and learning without the confines of a ready-made *(etymon),* contextualized map, an inalterable archive of "what knowledge is of most worth." Its duty to question what is held sacred, taken for granted as **TRUTH** (always in boldly capital letters), even venerated, risks both *all* and *nothing* because of its open responsibility to the Other whose effects on the formation of the subject and subjectivity are incalculable. This is what Derrida's careful resigning of deconstruction to a reconsideration of these problems of philosophy that I have cited at the start of this chapter entails, implies, signifies. And, of course, dare I say it, more! As we shall see.

Whither Deconstruction?
Of Philosophy from the Cosmopolitical Point of View

To address now the "where" of this ethical (re)ground of deconstruction and the question of the future of philosophy after the unclimactic *apocalypsis* of its multiple and infamous deaths. We must necessarily rebegin again. This time from a more *"appropriate"* and apoplectic location and locality, yet in a more polemically analytical tone adopted without apologies or a posture of consolation. We need to ask, like Derrida, in "Of the Humanities and the Philosophical Discipline: The Right to Philosophy from the Cosmopolitical Point of View (the Example of the International Institution)," "where?, in what place can a question [of the right to philosophy] take place?"[27] Is a location that still occupies the space of philosophy and is at the same time alterior to it possible? For, even though we have already started to engage this theme of the necessity of marking the interior and exterior limits of metaphysics without the self-conscious nostalgia of a postmodern pose of mourning the loss of the archive, my reading of Derrida's text will inevitably lead to some judgments about the certainty of "where ought it take place."[28] The ethical problem of who can, should be, or is capable of determining the propriety of the formal location of inquiry—the space and place of the culturo-institutional indexicality marking the public paths of its entrances and exits—is a flash point of conflict. It implicates deconstruction in the perennial question of democracy and discipline, of excessive delimitations and the archiving of knowledge, and brings us face-to-face, yet again, with the violent opening of the institution of pedagogy and the difference of Other.

It is in the body of the aforenamed lecture presented at an international colloqium on philosophy and education hosted by UNESCO that the qualitative essence of the problematic is translated by Derrida through the open-ended form of an interrogative modality focused (with only a little assistance provided from myself) as follows: "Where does ['the question of the right to philosophy'][29] find today its most appropriate place?"[30] The readily obvious and easy answer would be, "in the university." But it would be an understatement to say that this response in itself is not enough of a justification for restating the case to uphold what has been an institutional appropriation of the decision-making power and its obligation of accountability with respect to the curricular course of public education. Although, this tidy retort—"in the university"—may suffice (and it surely does!) for those who like and are adept at building walls around the right to philosophy as the private property of a select few, the "self-chosen ones," who have the discipline and training to *"think"* and *"do"* philosophy *"properly,"* it does not show a love of philosophy, a desire to embrace the asking of questions, as John D. Caputo explains, "always from a love of what philosophy loves—knowledge and truth (no capitals, please) and ethics and every other honorable and prestigious name in philosophy's intimidating repertoire."[31] The moment of axiomatic interrogation can be taken further to address the academic responsibility of educational institutions and by extension those who teach, work, and live *in* and, perhaps, *for* them, as this is how the teaching body *(le corps eneignant)* begins and where it ends.[32] What does this mean exactly? To say that a pedagogical institution, and those who are a part of it, are it, possess total and unabiding and hence *irresponsible and unaccountable* control of the intellectual domain they survey is to surmise a legacy of exclusion. There is no space left to welcome another. It is a question of affinity and openness toward embracing the difference of the Other without giving way to hesitance or reservation, empirical qualification and moral judgment, let alone indignation (the very thought of it! not to mention the very idea!). But what does this have to do with philosophy as an institutional discipline, the curricular organization of its knowledge and its learning, teaching?

Deconstruction, if it could, would probably answer, "Everything and nothing." But the question of a "proper domain" of the question of rights of institution—of propriety and domination, appropriation, expropriation, of property, participation, ownership and fairness, and therefore of law, ethics, and ultimately, of social justice—brings us back to the proliferative connections to be made between culture and philosophy, also among *democraticity,* governance and governmentality, of the responsibilities and principles relating to the formation and formativity of a system of public education on an international scale. It is a matter of locating the axiomatic difference of these terms, the difference of their axiomaticity, and their inter-relatability, within a hospitable space and place that only deconstruction can entreat them to via a hyper-genealogical route of concept excavation eventually leading to a productive recognition of alterity. That is, an ethical expansion of thought and thinking without limitations or borders. Derrida redefines the heterogeneous scope of this impossible territory wherein the struggle over the right to philosophy occurs, after Kant's "risky" envisioning of the cosmopolitical condition: a hypothetical situation of geoglobal interconnectivity or "mondialization" having an "inter-national or inter-state dimension"[33] and related to the question of the *emanation* and diaspora of the *polis* and *politeia as a way of life* by solidifying the problem of a universal history or "the link among the cities, the *poleis* of the world, as nations, as people, or as States."[34] Although, to make it very plain, the deconstructive constellations of this panoptic vision do not harbor the same omniscient hope of confirming the epistemologico-historical foundations of an "abstract universalism"[35] upon which a template for writing the blueprint of any and all institutions *to come* can be inscribed. The interrogative modality of this desire for a re-thinking of the future of thinking works toward illuminating and transforming rather than dismissing or deriding the historicity of "philosophical acts and archives."[36] Deconstruction, in questioning the ground of institutions and the reason of their institutionality, engages the real-world effects produced by the performative force of epistemological discourses and their responsibility as instances of founding and therefore of foundation. Its anti-utopian thrust, however contrary to the ideal of a natural universalism of thought and action uniting thinking and subjectivity in the image of the global citizen, nevertheless enables Derrida to conjoin the problem of the right to philosophy with the Kantian conception of a cosmopolitical point of view in a positive rather than a negative way. Here we must acknowledge something parenthetical, bracketed because it is more literally "literary" than prophetic, though not to be ignored. Derrida, in the subtitle of his lecture, alludes to *Idea (in View) of a Universal History from a Cosmopolitical Point of View (Idee zu einer allgemeinen Geschichte in weltbürgerlicher Absicht),* one of an "ensemble of Kant's writings that can be described as *announcing,* that is to say, predicting, prefiguring and prescribing a number of international institutions which only came into being in this century, for the most part after the Second World

War. These institutions are already philosophemes, as is the idea of international law or rights that they attempt to put into operation."[37] The intertextual association sets the tone for a rereading of the reading of the event and its surroundings Derrida performs, then and there. It reauthorizes the focus put on highlighting the importance of recognizing the legitimacy of UNESCO as "the privileged place"[38] for asking the question of the right to philosophy from a cosmopolitical point of view. And the contextual markers of the lecture, to whom it is addressed and why (for what purpose, effect, reason, and so on), compel us toward a consideration of what Derrida defines to be "two types of relation"[39] involving the university and the politico-cultural grounding of the human sciences:

1. The *international* relation among universities or research institutes on the one hand, and among international institutions of culture (governmental or non-governmental) on the other.

2. The particular *interdisciplinary* relation between philosophy and the "humanities." "Philosophy" names here both a discipline that belong to the "humanities" and that discipline which claims to think, elaborate, and criticize the axiomatic of the "humanities," particularly the problem of the humanism or the presumed universalism of the "humanities."[40]

Relative to the situational dynamics of the discursive presentation of the lecture itself, the reference is multiplied in its associations and disassociations by its applicability to the unique case of UNESCO. An institution of the postwar era "perhaps born from the positing of a right to philosophy from the cosmopolitical point of view,"[41] it imbibes in its constitutional commitments and formal configurations "an assignable philosophical history"[42] that "impl[ies] sharing a culture and a philosophical language."[43] Or, the exchange of a tradition of knowledge and knowing as articulated by the continual re-aggregation of the logic of the letter, the terms of its reading as production and reproduction, and domain of its archive. The problem of how to go about securing both private and public "access to this language and culture, first and foremost by means of education,"[44] involves, more or less, the working-out of the "two types of relation" Derrida identifies above as being central to answering the question of academic privilege (who has the right to philosophy?) and the power of location (how? and why?). The pedagogical onus on an affable (simple, crude, vulgar) modality of cultural production and reproduction without the complexity of resistance or complications fixes the parameters of an institutional ethic of response and responsibility. But this reduction of the frame of reference to categorical imperatives that willfully ignore the limitations and boundaries of a project of repeating the historicity of Western education occurs only if and when the cosmopolitical nature of UNESCO is not taken into account. For it would be wrong to ignore the diversity within its composition and to call this institution an academicized model of universalism without difference. Derrida explains the emanation of the cosmopolitical view—and its gathering of multiplicity—through the image of a charter (constitution, treaty, settlement, founding document, statement of rights and obligations, laws, etc.), so as to underscore the implications of the covenant of relation UNESCO enacts by involving a contractual obligation between philosophy and action that articulates the ethical terms of its responsibility:

> All the States that adhere to the charters of these international institutions [such as UNESCO, the United Nations also], commit themselves, in principle and philosophically, to recognize and put into practice in an effective way something like philosophy and a certain philosophy of rights and law, the rights of [wo]man, universal history, etc. The signature of these charters is a philosophical act which makes a commitment to philosophy in a philosophical way. From that moment on, whether they say so or not, know it or not, or conduct themselves consequently or not, these States and these peoples contract a philosophical commitment by dint of joining these charters or participating in these institutions. Therefore, these States contract at the very least a commitment to provide the philosophical culture or education that is required for understanding and putting into operation these commitments made to the international institutions, which are, I repeat, philosophical in essence.[45]

An organization of many parts and partners, nations, states, and peoples whose materiality comprises and cannot but exceed the conceptual totality of its essence, UNESCO "bears the response and responsibility for this question"[46] of the right to philosophy and for a reconsideration of the obligation to unite response with responsibility within the milieu of the international and interdisciplinary institution of the university and other places of research it represents by virtue of its associations. The "form of this question concerning a question—namely, 'where?, in what place can a question take place?'"[47]—implies both complementary and contradictory assumptions, also judgments. On the one hand can be found the need for an adjudication of the legitimacy of the opportunity given or taken to respond to the question of the right to philosophy and the determination of its "most appropriate place": the locality, we could and would have to say, of its most "proper" location. On the other, it goes directly to evaluating the quality of the response. But both aspects are not unrelated insofar as such ethico-qualitative judgments also deem necessary an identification of who would have the privilege and opportunity of participation regarding curricular decisions about the future of the philosophical discipline and why. We shall get on to this a little bit later. It is enough to say now that this will lead us toward the impossibility of the future of UNESCO and the global diaspora of philosophy education. That is, the institutional interconnections of a *democracy-to-come,* with a *pedagogy-to-come,* and the potentially diverging paths of its filiations, friendships, what is held close, in affinity, to the spirit and the heart, not the mind.

But going back once again to the image of UNESCO as the overriding reality and symbol (the objective correlative?) of what "would thus, perhaps fundamentally, be the privileged place"[48] for asking the question of the right to philosophy: The necessity of its very existence, certainly less than fate but more than chance, enjoins us to inquire after the historicity of the institution and its ideo-ground from the Kantian delineation of the cosmopolitical point of view. This is easily justified by Derrida:

one would say that there are places where *there are grounds for* asking this question. That is to say, that here [at the UNESCO conference] this question [of the right to philosophy] is legitimate and rightfully not only possible and authorized but also necessary, indeed prescribed. In such places, such a question, for example, that of the right to philosophy from the cosmopolitical point of view, can and should take place.[49]

By citing the grounds of a deconstructive propriety, Derrida prepares the way to radically modify the idealist presupposition of a "plan of nature that aims at the total, perfect political unification of the human species *(die vollkommene bürgerliche Vereinigung in der Menschengattung)*"[50] through the unfolding of the history of the transcendental unity of the Idea. Kant's ethical universalism, and its infamous Eurocentric bias, is used in a novel way by turning it toward the question of the right to philosophy to mobilize the cosmopolitical as a viewpoint *not only* for reconceptualizing the "eternal becoming"[51](Discussion Surfaces 3) of being-in-the-world, *but as a new approach to realizing the impossible futures of a "progressive institutionality" to come and the unforeseeability of its educational methods and apparatus.* This does not simply mean a securing of the opportunity for freedom in thinking and teaching; neither does it defer pedagogically, nor ethically, to the teaching of thinking without reference to the tradition of Western episteme, however it may be defined in curricular terms. I have emphasized this earlier. Derrida cites the Kantian notion of the cosmopolitical to reawaken and to resituate the Eurocentrism of the concept and its implications for reinscribing the "horizon of a new community"[52] of the question and the impossibility of the question that teaches the Other to question the sources of the Self and the Other. This may sound strange to those who envision and portray deconstruction as a *destruction* of Western metaphysics, its institutions and its teachings. We need to remember, however, the case of UNESCO as an institution that is *a priori* "Kantian in spirit."[53] Which is to say, it *predicts* a Western trajectory of thinking along a "teleological axis"[54] with respect to the epistemologico-cultural ideal of the "infinite progress" of Being and the temporal procession of beings toward perfectability, achievable or not. Anything else "would be nothing but a novel"[55] given the inseparability of the European history of philosophy from the notion of the universal, "a plan of nature that aims at the total, perfect political unification of the human species *(die vollkommen bürgerliche Vereinigung in der Menschengattung).*"[56] As Derrida explains,

> Whoever would have doubts about such a unification and, above all, about a plan of nature, would have no reason to subscribe even to the fact of sharing a philosophical problematic, of a supposedly universal or universalizable problematic of philosophy. For anybody having doubts about this plan of nature, the whole project of writing a universal—and therefore philosophical—history, and thus as well the project of creating institutions governed by an international—and therefore philosophical—law, would be nothing but a novel.[57]

An institution is founded on memory and the material conditions of its working-out as a dynamic tradition of theory and practice, philosophy and action. Derrida recognizes this and has never denied it. In fact, I would say his *work of decon-struction* is predicated *on taking memory into account*: accounting for the causal-ity of its effects, its bias, its exclusions, rendering an account of what makes memory, disrupts it, constructs its limits, openings, how and why it favors. To bring the analysis back to the text we are rereading, UNESCO as an international institution is founded on the principles of European philosophy, its charter and its concepts "are philosophical through and through,"[58] which does not make them universal in scope or essence, despite the reality that UNESCO does at-tempt to influence, "for the better," the educational landscape of the world-picture. This latter point is important in reading the dimensions of the first. That the aim of this organization is, in theory, altruistic cannot be denied, as the logic of its existence is predicated, in principle, on the presupposition of the idea of an infinite perfectability of human being. It mobilizes a thoroughly Western conceit and philosophical project directed toward the rectification of Being as presence and the sending of itself forward in time. For Derrida, it is not a matter of ques-tioning the existence of UNESCO outside of the scope of its mission statement and the theoretical grounds of the practical action laid-out by the logic of its charter. In ethical, philosophical, and real-world terms, we can easily justify the necessity of its "being-there" on an international, global scale, especially when considering that its charter upholds the point of view of a cosmopolitical model of membership, governance, and responsibility for decision making to sanction the development and sustenance of democratic means and conditions for securing public access to education. It would not make sense to dismiss or defame UNESCO either as an instrument of Western influence and cogitation or as an indicator of the extent of Western domination across the hemispheres with re-spect to propagating a "certain philosophy of rights and law, the rights of man [Derrida's word], universal history,"[59] and so on. A critique—coming down on one side or the other—of its efficacy is not at all useful, but a misleading en-deavor seeking an ethical refuge in the evaluative power of a binary form of metaphysical reasoning pitting "the good" against "the bad," "essentialism" against "anti-essentialism," "Eurocentrism" against "anti-Eurocentrism," and so on. The endwork of such a critical task that freely places blame or adjudicates value for the sake of a castigation or rejection of worth is performed too quickly and easily. Its decisions are rendered by and appeal to the dictates of a universalist conception of "reason" and its demotic (and not at all democratic) corollary of "common sense" to construct the ideologico-conceptual grounds of what is "good" and what is "bad." The judgmental edifice of its EITHER/OR rationale presumes a lack of interpretative complexity, a plainness of truth that is totally transparent and obvious to everyone, a clear-cut and unarguable judgment made with no fathomable case to be made for the possibility of opposition or exemp-tion to the rule of law. One life-world. One reality. One Truth. The metaphysical value of this ethic of perception and its monological model of representation determines the non-oppositional grounds of truth. Conditional and definitive limits thereby demarcate the freedom of what it is possible to know and to think and what it is possible to say without offending the much guarded sensibilities of "reason" and "good taste"—however their values might be constructed and articulated—as the ideals of commonly held responses to cultural institutions and practices. Difference is abdicated in favor of a community of shared interpretative responsibility and the unethical hegemony of its "majority rules" attitude that bids one to erect barriers against diversity, "to see and talk about things only as they are or could be." For the priority of clarity as an ethical prerequisite of a "responsible response" is, without a doubt, everything when the analytical imperative is NOTHING BUT an exercise of choosing sides. There is a more productive approach, nevertheless, that would open up the possibility of reaffirming the utility and necessity of UNESCO as a cosmopolitical institution by recontextualizing the conditions of its founding to the "new situation"[60] of the present day without having to tear down the conceptual frame of its material structures in order to set up something else that would reproduce and multiply the faults of the original. What would this involve? Deconstruction, of course!

Derrida provides a way to begin reassessing and reaffirming the responsibilities of UNESCO in relation to the demands and conditions of a "new international" by opening up the logic of its existence as a "world institution" concerned with the problem of global education to the question of the right to philosophy and its teaching:

> What are the concrete stakes of this [new] situation today? Why should the large questions of philosophical teaching and research, and the imperative of the right to philosophy, be more than ever developed in their international dimension? Why are the responsibilities to be assumed no longer simply national, less national today than ever, and even less tomorrow than ever, in the 21st century?
>
> What do "national," "international," "cosmopolitical," and "universal" signify here, for and with regard to philosophy, philosophical research, philosophical education or training, and indeed for a philosophical question or practice that would not be essentially linked to research or education?[61]

The questions are succinct and precise because in looking forward to a *future-to-come* they go right to the heart of the childhood age of philosophy and education—"specifically European, specifically Greek"[62] in its origins—that spawned the possibility and impossibility of UNESCO in the first place. Derrida does not call for an uncritical rejection of the memory of the institution, the conceptual history of the institution's memory, its *Begriffsgeschichte*, to avoid the consequences of what Kant feared most: the dangers of a non- or anti-philosophical development of human being and its institutions. A disturbing implication follows as it both inaugurates and repeats the classical divisions of Eurocentrism by distinguishing those who are perceived to have civilization and those who supposedly do not, essentially, by providing the ethico-logical and historico-epistemic basis for differentiating between the sources of a Western culture and the "errant traditions" of its Others. This "guiding thread of a pattern of nature"[63] Kant identifies, and the Occidentalism of its cosmopolitical trajectory, "first of all tak[es] this history in its Greek, and then Roman, beginnings—in opposition to the so-called barbaric nations."[64] A condemning statement. A "convenient instrument of representation *(Darstellung)*,"[65] Derrida calls it, this uncomplicated identification of a "guiding thread." The affective influence of its trace demarcates and legitimizes the general culture of a Western subjectivity as the only "authentic" mode of *being-in-the-world,* distinct from and *a priori* to its alien Others. "This is why," Derrida stresses, "this text [of Kant's] which is cosmopolitical in spirit, according to a law that could be verified well beyond Kant, is the most strongly Eurocentered text that can be, not only in its philosophical axiomatic but also in its retrospective reference to Greco-Roman history and its prospective reference to the future hegemony of Europe which, Kant says, is the continent that 'will probably legislate some day for all others.'"[66] Again, it would be too easy, perfunctory, and without forethought to leave the analysis there. And, as can be expected, Derrida does not. UNESCO cannot be viewed simply as a political *organon* that represents and wields the interests and power of a Western intellectual imperialism obsessed with promoting the archival essence of itself at the expense of an Other that it performatively inheres, and therefore *appropriates,* as part of the axiomatics and axiology of its governing charter. This negative aspect of its institutional history and historicity cannot be denied given its Eurocentric response and responsibility, the "rational ruse"[67] of its origins as a union of nations, states, and peoples of "equal partnership" but of unequal participation, voice, power, and representation. Derrida makes numerous references to Kant's text and copiously documents the implications it inheres and therefore exemplifies about the cultural domination of the cosmopolitical reality, viewpoint, or condition by Western Europe, a "continent *(in unserem Weltteile)* (which [I repeat] will probably legislate one day for all other continents [*der wahrscheinlicher Weise allen anderen dereinst Gesetz geben wird*])."[68]

This is familiar territory, though not because I have re-cited the quotation in order to reiterate and augment the force of its importance. The ethical impetus of the "post-colonial," "anti-colonial," or even the "neo-colonial" moment as it is called by Gayatri Chakravorty Spivak begins with a philosophical nod to what is, for Derrida, the legacy of the institutions and models of "Greco-European memory."[69] Addressing the textual composition of this epistemic and cultural genealogy of Western knowledge, Kant's discourse is only one example of a host of writings by philosophers who possess the temerity to have made such audacious and largely accurate statements about the dominance of "the guiding thread *(Leitfaden)* of Greek history *(griechische Geschichte)*"[70] with respect to explaining the unfolding of the Reason of Being across space and over time. The axiomaticity of this logic directed at excluding an "Other" from the fundamental (pure) archive of its heritage would be only natural from a philosophical perspective of human historicity that narcotizes the productive value of difference and thus denies the validity of allowing for the possibility of heterogeneous opening to a world community from a cosmopolitical point of view. As Derrida says, "One encounters [its Eurocentric axiology] again and again, intact and invariable throughout variations as serious as those that distinguish Hegel, Husserl, Heidegger, and Valéry."[71] But of course there is a difference in what Kant proposes by way of a vision of the world from a cosmopolitical point of view and its universal enactment in the form of a "Society of Nations" despite the emphasis he places upon Greek philosophy and history, because it attempts to *sublate,* to synthesize and at the same time keep, the tensions of the values of cultural difference in an amicable and moral unification of humanity worked out, more or less, along with the trajectory of the "teleological axis of this discourse [that] has become the tradition of European modernity."[72] The concept of nature, and specifically the "unsociability *(Ungeselligkeit, Unvertragsamkeit)*"[73] of human being *by nature*, is actually the means to a salvation "through culture, art and artifice *(Kunst)*, and reason, to make the seeds of nature grow."[74] And Kant truly believes in the potentially unifying power of this "natural or originary state of war among men"[75] (again Derrida's word, and it is quite appropriate here, for in Kant's time there could literally only be a state of war *among men*). Because of the propensity of subjective (cultural) differences to force antagonisms, territoriality, and conflict, there is only one possible solution that "resembles a novel-like story yet isn't one, that which in truth is but the very historicity of history, is the ruse of nature."[76] And here we may be amazed (or not) by what Derrida's citing of Kant's text embellishes and reveals about the philosophical historicity of UNESCO:

> Nature has thus again used the unsociability *(Ungeseloligkeit, Unvertragsamkeit)* of men, and even among the large societies and state bodies which human beings construct, as a means of arriving at a state of calm and security through their inevitable *antagonism*. Wars, tense and unremitting military preparations, and the resultant distress which every state must eventually feel within itself, even in the midst of peace—these are the means by which nature drives nations to make initially imperfect attempts, but finally, after many devastations, upheavals and even complete inner exhaustion of their powers, to take the step which reason could have suggested to them even without so many sad experiences—that of abandoning a lawless state of savagery and entering a Society of Nations of peoples in which every state, even the smallest, could expect to derive its security and rights not from its own power or its own legal judgment, but solely from this great Society of Nations (of peoples: *Völkerbunde*) *(Foedus Amphyctionum)*, from a united power and the law-governed decisions of a united will.[77]

Violence—and its threat to the security of human *Dasein*—is the catalyst that allows nature "to aid reason and thereby put philosophy into operation through the society of nations."[78] For Derrida, this is a troubling but understandable sublating *(relèver)* of the anti-theses holding together the diffuse logic of the cosmopolitical community of global proportions. On the one hand, peace achieved through the danger of violence is not really a peace made at all. It is a provisional state of human entropy with respect to the appeasement of the tensions of difference and the possible uprising of transgressions and aggressions against subjective alterity that depends on the ethico-philosophical essence of the cosmopolitical covenant of being. The condition of peace represents the satiating of a reaction to nullify the difference of difference. On the other, a peace compelled by the dark side of the human spirit is perhaps the only *possible and natural* peace that could be rendered effective or legislated under circumstances within which no other decision or action is acceptable, viable, or defensible given the alternative of violence. This of course begs the question of the constitutive force of community—whatever that IDEAL may entail as an affective identification of a subjective sense of belonging, a *being-at-home-in-the-world WITH OTHERS*—and the responsibility of its opening-up of the Self unto the difference of the Other. When these two states or conditions of existence, peace (community) and violence (war), are placed in direct opposition to each other, the ethical choice is clearly delineated by the power of a humanistic appeal that is made to a *universal* and hence *moral will* denying the propriety of any transgression of subjectivity at all costs, even if this means suppressing human rights and freedoms for "the greater good." Community, then, is a matter of instilling and practicing a homogeneous concept of culture, a *general* culture whose model of a collective intersubjectivity acts as a unified resistance to the threat of alterity. The promoting of common points of recognition and identification within the ideologico-philosophical consciousness of its constituents in order to defy or suppress the propensity for violence against the threat of difference—or at the very least to quell the performativity of the desire to do so—establishes the psychic and figural ground for the foundations of friendship and belonging. Playing by the determinative ethics of these rules of consensus in the name of community and commonality, and also of communication, reduces the Other to the Same and minimizes the potential of a subjective resistance to the inclusion of contrariety within the sphere of a closed system of shared associations. This illusion of unity masks the radical violence of alterity and softens the risk of its provisional acceptance by replacing the shock of its reality with the comforting image of a single, harmonious group, a majority without difference. *They is Us.* The correlation of subjectivity relieves the discord of diversity because one has to inhere and adhere to the fundamental agreements of a consensual state of abstract universalism to be part of the general yet specific culture of a community. *I am We.* An ethical and philosophical contrition of sorts must be achieved in this case by the subject to ensure the manifestation of a "responsible response" that is itself a coming to peace of the Self with the avowable laws of a community and its effacing of difference.

If we consider the Eurocentrism of the reasoning Kant puts forward for pursuing a universal alliance of humanity from the cosmopolitical view, and its prefiguring of new models of global gathering and world institutions like the United Nations and UNESCO, we cannot avoid addressing the ethico-philosophical focus of such an idea aimed at re-articulating the notion of community. The appeal made to the "higher value" and "intrinsic right" of "Greek historicity or historiographicity"[79] is an attempt to formalize the vision of the endless progression of being toward its positive ethical articulation in "the good life." To avoid the Hegelian nightmare of a "bad" or "poor infinity" *(schlechte Unendlichkeit)*[80] that does not realize the Reason of the History of itself in a dialectical resolution of identity, it becomes quite essential to provide the teleology of an *a priori* epistemic framework "to contradict this novel-like hypothesis [of an international community from a cosmopolitical point of view] and to think human history, beyond the novel, as a system and not as an aggregate without plan, program nor providence."[81] For Kant, the living memory of Greek philosophy and culture—whether it be *in and of itself* or appropriated as it eventually was by Roman thinking—is "the only one in which all other earlier or contemporary histories are preserved or at least authenticated."[82] Again, the subsumption of all humanity under the ideological framework of institutions that are the product of a West European historicity cannot be an innocent and happy coincidence. Surely, this summation could not be not the clever fabulation of a

novel *(Roman)*. To protect against the danger of "the becoming-literature of philosophy"[83] that Kant so desperately feared would lead human nature astray by
inhibiting Being's potential to actualize the intentional apperception of the idea
of transcendence and its ideal of infinite progress, there was only one direction
along the path of thinking that could lead beings toward the fulfillment of Reason—"the living thread of Greek history."[84] Derrida explains the "paradoxical
incitement"[85] of the judgment, e.g., the oppositional conclusions it ultimately
leads to regarding whom it excludes, what it privileges, why, where, and how:

> For, in this teleological ruse of nature, Greco-Roman Europe, philosophy
> and Western history, and I would even dare saying continental history, are
> the driving force, both capital and exemplary, as if nature, in its rational
> ruse, had assigned Europe this special mission: not only that of founding
> history as such, and first of all science, not only that of founding philoso-
> phy as such, and first of all as science, but also the mission of founding a ra-
> tional philosophical (non-novel-like) history and that of "legislating some
> da'" for all other continents.[86]

The Eurocentrism of the utopia that Kant champions also predicts the creation of
organizations such as UNESCO, for example, because the philosophical enactment of its promise for a state of lasting peace is what motivates the impossible
achievement of persuading its members to a non-violent surrendering of their
individual autonomy to the security of the collective, essentially by "contracting
artificial and institutional links, and into entering a Society of Nations."[87] Even
so the question cannot but remain: Why? What privileges Greek history—"history both in the sense of *Geschichte* and *histoire,* history in the sense
of event and of narrative, of the authenticated account, of historical science"[88]—to mediate and guide the future of a cosmopolitical unification of all
humanity? The argument comes back, full circle, to what is called "philosophy"
and "who" has a right to it, why, where, in what place; the question of the right
to philosophy is also a question of the *right* philosophy.

Impossible Horizons and Other Headings:
Of Democracy, Community, and the Right of Philosophy

Tempering what we already know, perhaps always have known, with what we
discovered or invented along the way to learn more about what we do not, cannot, know, we therefore must come back to the scenarios we started with to hy-
pothesize the impossible state of a future of thinking after metaphysics. Having
worked at avoiding an impatient reading to arrive at this destination, we are now
ready—in light of the cosmopolitical point of view and the case of UNESCO,
whose "mode of being is one that is *a priori* philosophical"[89]—to attempt an
answer to the irreconcilable nature of the original problems from the opening of
"Violence and Metaphysics" that I have used as an epigraph to get this chapter
under way. We will have to remind ourselves why Derrida insists "these should
be the only questions today capable of founding the community, within the

world, of those who are still called philosophers,"[90] which is of course, everyone and not everyone. Three points are worth further elaboration. All pertain to the critical issue of *how deconstruction can help us to untangle, demystify, transgress the limits and limitations of the aporia of the death of philosophy and resolve the question of its question, and of its right, it institution, as well as who has the right and responsibility to respond to it. And why.*

1. The first concerns the post-metaphysical horizons of community, both public and academic. For Derrida, it is not a simple matter of *fighting against the pronouncement of the death of philosophy, even though it may be a premature burial.* Or so we would like to, and have to, think. To try to resist what is posed as the end of metaphysics by mounting arguments against the finality of this perspective in the tradition of a "critique" or "negative determination"[91] that seeks its own affirmation through the violence of opposition is a wasted effort. "A philosopher is always someone for whom philosophy is not given, someone who in essence must question him or herself about the essence and destination of philosophy."[92] Which is to say, that the alterity of metaphysics as well as the power of its teleology is always close at hand, whether or not a transcendence of its logic *ever takes place* or *can even happen*, essentially, whether or not it *is possible*. Questions about the end of philosophy, and thus of the end of the historicity of history, still abound. Some pose more productive challenges to the thinking of "what, if anything, comes next?" than do others. Nevertheless, a sense of community is (oddly enough, some may say) formed around the asking of the question of the end or the death of philosophy. And this is to be expected, when the point is just to a Heideggerian *overcoming (Überwindung)* of metaphysics. It is the responsibility of each individual to interrogate the limits of "a sort of axiomatic, a system of values, norms and regulating principles"[93] that justify "the existence then of a properly philosophical space like UNESCO."[94] "For," Derrida warns, "such a situation and such a duty are more particular than it seems. And this can lead to fearsome practical consequences."[95] Such as the temptation to take a stance on one side or the other of philosophy, *with* or *against* those who desire to remember and keep alive its memory or those who choose to forget the historicity of metaphysics and forswear the finality of its death. "A community of the question about the possibility of the question"[96] is what Derrida calls the publicly academic space of a more productive ground of inquiry into the right to philosophy than one of either support or diffidence. It would neither reject nor embrace the Eurocentric historicity of Western thinking and its epistemico-cultural specificity that is articulated via humanism as the infinite perfectability of subjective being: the finding of the NATURE OF THE SELF and its center at the cost of losing affinity with the Other. It could not, because it is a "community of the question"—a community wrought of dissensus and not of consensus. Its potential lies in the openness of its capacity to honor and respect the value of difference, to welcome the impossibility of alterity, but not to dismiss or celebrate the ground of *au courant* memory for its own sake, over the unfamiliar archive of another. So, rather than dismantling the arguments of those who would like to see the demise of the right to philosophy and its Eurocentric historicity, Derrida has attempted to answer and is continuing to address the larger question of the death of metaphysics, its future, both directly

and obliquely, because none of the answers posited are as yet satisfying enough to do justice to the persistent problem of *finding a way out of philosophy.* Certainly, there is an *aporia* at work here that seeks refuge in its displacement. And Derrida construes its difficulty in the following way:

> This Eurocentric discourse forces us to ask ourselves . . . whether today [referring both to the context of the lecture and to the epochal dimension of empirical time] our reflection concerning the unlimited extension and the reaffirmation of a right to philosophy should not both *take into account and de-limit* the assignation of philosophy to its Greco-European origin or memory. At stake is neither contenting oneself with reaffirming a certain history, a certain memory of origins or of the Western history (Mediterranean or Central European, Greco-Roman-Arab or Germanic) of philosophy, nor contenting oneself with being opposed to, or opposing denial to, this memory and to these languages, but rather trying to displace the fundamental schema of this problematic by going beyond the old, tiresome, worn-out and wearisome opposition between Eurocentrism and anti-Eurocentrism. One of the conditions for getting there—and one won't get there all of a sudden in one try, it will be the effect of a long and slow historical labor that is under way—is the active becoming-aware that philosophy is no longer determined by a program, an originary language or tongue whose memory it would suffice to recover so as to discover its destination, that philosophy is no more assigned to its origin or by its origin, than it is simply, spontaneously or abstractly cosmopolitical or universal. What we have lived and what we are more and more aiming for are modes of appropriation and transformation of the philosophical in non-European languages and cultures. Such modes of appropriation and transformation amount neither to the classical mode of appropriation that consists in making one's own what belongs to the other (here, in interiorizing the Western memory of philosophy and assimilating it in one's own language) nor to the invention of new modes of thought which, as alien to all appropriation, would no longer have any relation to what one believes one recognizes under the name of philosophy.[97]

No discourse "disciplined" body of knowledge claiming epistemic status, such as philosophy is and does, *self-consciously* undermines its grounding conceits in both methodology and content. The principle of non-contradiction forbids it. What governs the institutional legitimacy of philosophy as a *scientific endeavor* is its ability to render the logic of its conclusions accountable *to* and *for* the provisions of episteme laid out by the historicity of its own doctrines of self-evident truth and the generalizability of conclusions regarding the study of empirical phenomena: what its discourse says and reveals, confirms and proves by way of an experiential facticity, about *being-in-the-world.* In this respect, an ethical moment attends the academic pursuit of knowledge. It occurs when thinking becomes *like a science,* becomes "philosophy," is conceived as a universal project, inaugurates a discipline replete with models of practice to be guarded, and is not defined idiosyncratically as the general process of thought. This distinction, besides giving credence to the institutional and pedagogical formalization and formulizability of the human intellect for and within the structures of the modern university, remains highly problematic. The division between "philosophy and *Denken*, thinking,"[98] re-enforces the ethico-epistemic specificity of academic responsibility in this manner by setting down the template for marking out the limits of the paragon of a community (to be) instituted, whereby the laws it creates ultimately support and mobilize a divining line that distinguishes those "who belong" to it from those "who do not" and, in all probability, never will. The partisanship of discipline and disciplinarity plays upon the need for philosophy to be affiliated with the historicity of a "culture." Here we must give way to caution, though, not to presume to know too much. "There are cultural aspects of philosophy," Derrida maintains, "but philosophy is not a cultural phenomenon." What does this mean, exactly, in both the narrow and broader sense of a community of shared and differing interests?

2. This brings us to the second point. To say that philosophy is a cultural phenomenon would be to universalize it, to deny "the relationship between philosophy and natural languages, European languages,"[99] living and breathing languages, that are proper to and establish the propriety of philosophy as a Western invention of the consciousness of the West and the articulation of its archive. And Derrida is sufficiently clear about this undeniable linguistic historicity, while attempting "to avoid the opposition between two symmetrical temptations, one being to say that philosophy is universal":[100]

> Today it's a well-known phenomenon—there is a Chinese philosophy, a Japanese philosophy, and so on and so forth. That's a contention I would resist. I think there is something specifically European, specifically Greek in philosophy to say that philosophy is something universal. . . . Philosophy is a way of thinking. It's not science. It's not thinking in general. So when I say, well, philosophy has some privileged relationship with Europe, I don't say this European-centrically but to take seriously history. That's one temptation, to say philosophy is universal.[101]

The closure of philosophy does not mean a gathering together of the Greco-European reality of its roots and forcefully bringing them to an end that would, for all intents and purposes, lack any semblance of historicity and is then without a future. The breakthrough of *what-is-to-come* must always arise out of the resources of a past thinking that cannot be effectively renounced. The trace of Greco-European cultural memory in philosophy will neither allow itself to be eradicated nor to be abandoned at the limit of the archive of knowledge it *is* and *represents* in method, form, and content. The first "temptation" leads to the second, both contrary and complementary, one Derrida warns us about—the desire to say:

> well philosophy has only one origin, a single pure origin that is its foundation, its institution, through a number of grounding concepts which are linked to Greek language, and we have to keep this in memory and constantly go back to Greece and back to this Greek origin, European, through anamnesis, through memory, to what philosophy is. This is a symmetrical temptation which I would like to avoid.[102]

The Eurocentric myopia of this monocultural view of the archive of Western episteme is another peril of taking sides without actualizing sufficient precautions against the irresponsibility of academic solipsism. Magnifying the question of the historicity of philosophy and of the purity of its Greek origins, the example foreshadows the necessity of moving beyond the concept of a universal thought and recognizing the rise of the cosmopolitical condition that Kant predicted as a moment in the infinite process of eternal becoming, or the point in history where a giant step in the progress of humanity can be seen resulting from an outgrowth of the global self-awareness and situatedness of human being. Derrida stresses the virtues of "another model"[103] whose approach to truth cannot be distilled quite so easily into a program of "Eurocentrism and a simple-minded anti-Eurocentrism.":[104]

> that is, while keeping in memory this European, Greek origin of philosophy, and the European history of philosophy, take into account that there are events, philosophical events, which cannot be reduced to this single origin, and which meant that the origin itself was not simple, that the phenomena of hybridization, of graft, or translation, was there from the beginning, so we have to analyze the different philosophical events today, in Europe and outside of Europe.[105]

In essence, the attempt to make philosophy live out its future after the historicity of its Greco-European past, requires the space of an *aporia* "that cannot be locked into this fundamentally cultural, colonial, or neo-colonial dialect of appropriation and alienation."[106] There must be more. "There are other ways for philosophy than those of appropriation as expropriation (to lose one's memory by assimilating the memory of the other, the one being opposed to the other, as if an *ex-appropriation* was not possible, indeed the only possible chance)."[107] Derrida is right. The testimony of memory and its reaffirming of an ethical response and responsibility to the historicity of the past is important for inscribing and building the "horizon of a new community."[108] It is not a matter of reasonable speculation: as the "speculative moment within the academy"[109] will not do justice to re-thinking the new situation of nations and states, of peoples, that must "transform their assumptions"[110] (Discussion 3) in relation to what we now know is the urgent necessity of "displacing some concepts which are absolutely essential to th[e] constitutions"[111] of international institutions like the United Nations and UNESCO. The cosmopolitical hybridization of empirical and epistemic identity Derrida speaks of does not involve trying to erase the history of one's own memory by working (in vain) to appropriate the effects and affectivity of another archive—the archive of an "Other"—whose expropriation would be causally determined via the need for a political maneuvering or strategically motivated as the willful adoption of its tenets would just happen to jibe with the dominant ideology of the day. Nor does it imply making an attempt to start over without history by pursuing misguided efforts to efface the contextual and institutional specificity of subjectivity through a haphazard rejection of the philosophical grounding of one's sense of *being-in-the-world*. On the one hand, a rethinking of "Eurocentrism and anti-colonialism"[112] as "symptoms of a colonial and missionary culture"[113] would facilitate other beginnings and other directions for the infinite progress of human being. On the other, "a concept of the cosmopolitical that would still be determined by such opposition would not only still concretely limit the development of the right to philosophy but also would not even account for what happens in philosophy."[114] Do we have any chance of surpassing the hindrances and obstacles of respecting a desire to promote and protect the call for either the appropriation (expropriation) or ex-appropriation of Western metaphysics on a global and international scale?

If philosophy could ever hope to overcome the impossible dream of achieving its own end, it would be precisely from a curious rupturing of the idea of its historicity, the memory of its *being-past*, which, of course, could and would never happen. And we should not want an expunging of the history of philosophy to occur, if it were even possible. Metaphysics does not have to be forcefully sedated, sanitized, and subdued. Also, we do not have to issue a proclamation that would render it alive or sentence it to death. Derrida explains, "Not only are there other ways for philosophy, but philosophy, if there is any such thing, is the *other way*. And it has always been the *other way*."[115] To be unequivocal, philosophy "has always been bastard, hybrid, grafted, multilinear, and polyglot."[116] The teaching body of the discipline has always known this fact to be true.[117] Pedagogical systems highlighting methods of recitation and repetition in the delivery of its curriculum were designed as a defense against a mnemonic underdetermination of the totality and authenticity of philosophical archive. By this I mean the competing models and systems of the reason of Western episteme that explicate the ontico-ontological sources of human consciousness and being. What signals the "crisis of philosophy" and leads to a questioning of the value of its teaching and learning—thereby feeding the naive illusion of its untimely demise—are the meta-conditional links of possibility, to be more specific, the *conditions of impossibility* within its complex lineage that work to destabilize the history of philosophy and, consequently, open up the concept of philosophy to what is not "philosophy proper" or "proper to philosophy." It is this realization of an originary difference always already present within the writing of its archive that displaces and dislocates the authority of its power to signify and *speak for* the truth of itself. The violence of alterity as the immutable trace of the difference of an Other thoroughly permeates the historicity of Western knowledge. For "philosophy has never been the unfolding responsible for a unique, originary assignation linked to a unique language or to the place of a sole people. *Philosophy does not have a sole memory.*"[118]

3. We will now consider the third point. The working within and against a tradition of canonical associations wrought by the instauration of memory and the limitations of its capacity exemplified in the act of forgetting *(lethe)* brings out the tensions of disassociation and dissonance that redefine the path of metaphysics. To achieve a spatial and temporal closure of "first philosophy" involves a segue to something *other than philosophy, a thinking of philosophy lacking philosophy*, where "we must adjust our practice of the history of philosophy, our practice of history and of philosophy, to this reality which was also a chance and which more than ever remains a chance"[119] for the impossibility of realizing the headings of a philosophy yet to come. Derrida anticipates the future after

metaphysics taking place along these lines of a debt and duty to the tradition of the past traced out by the limitations of memory and its openness to an expansion of the difference of itself as the *khora* of the Other. It is not only a matter of affirming the existence of philosophy, but of recognizing and acknowledging its natural right to determine the grounds for asking the questions about its sources, its limits (*peras*, *linea*) and its future, if only to establish the boundaries of debt and duty that would serve to prepare us for a thinking of what comes next from what came before. Derrida is quite clear on this: "Philosophy has always insisted upon this: thinking its other. Its other: that which limits it, and from which it derives its essence, its definition, its production."[120] One cannot beat the antimetaphysical drum *(tympan)* too loudly and still expect to hear the echoes of a timelessness reserved the task of thinking. Indeed, it would be unwise to "philosophize with a hammer,"[121] like Friedrich Nietzsche's Zarathustra, and ponder on how best to go about the mobilization of a "noisy pedagogy" that would displace the internal sound of seeming truth in the ears of those who enjoin a claim to knowledge with the light of a sagacity drawn from the premises of what is a risky (re)visioning of epistemology poised "to transform what one decries"[122] in metaphysics. The danger is that, as Derrida has warned, "in taking this risk, one risks nothing at all."[123] For what is *unthought* and therefore *untaught* always already opens the future of a history of thinking and directions of teaching that are "yet to come" *(à-venir, Zu-kunft).*

If an institution—and this word *takes in* philosophy, *imbibes* and *performs* it—is true to its constitution and its name, it must allow for the opportunity to inaugurate something "new" out of its ground, the undying memory of "the old," to repeat the ethico-political performance of its founding contract and its obligations to the legitimacy of the Other in an affirmative way, "to criticize, to transform, to open the institution to its own future."[124] Derrida explains,

> The paradox in the instituting moment of an institution is that, at the same time that it starts something new, it also continues something, is true to the memory of the past, to a heritage, to something we receive from the past, from our predecessors, from the culture. If an institution is to be an institution, it must to some extent break with the past, keep the memory of the past while inaugurating something absolutely new. . . . So the paradox is that the instituting moment in an institution is violent in a way, violent because it has no guarantee. Although it follows the premises of the past, it starts something absolutely new, and this newness, this novelty, is a risk, is something that has to be risky, and it is violent because it is guaranteed by no previous rules. So, at the same time, you have to follow the rule and to invent a new rule, a new norm, a new criterion, a new law. That's why the moment of institution is so dangerous at the same time. One should not have an absolute guarantee, an absolute norm; we have to invent the rules.[125]

Deconstruction welcomes the risk to participate fully in the awkward tensions between the conservation and violence of this moment of institution and the originality or newness that it produces. It embraces the opportunity to go where it cannot go and to usher in the impossibility of experiencing an other heading by pushing the limits of what is beyond the predictability of the possible. "That is what deconstruction is made of: not the mixture but the tension between memory, fidelity, the preservation of something that has been given to us, and, at the same time, heterogeneity, something new, and a break. The condition of this performative success, which is never guaranteed, is the alliance of these to newness."[126] This may help to explain the reason why Derrida has been empirically and philosophically present—in the role of instigator or invited guest, or both—at the founding of so many programs and institutions. Deconstruction enacts, in itself and for itself, *in the name of being responsible, just, to the alterity of the Other,* an affirmation of the difference of the wholly other *(tout autre),* by mobilizing and navigating the tensions between (1) what is undeconstructible, unforeseeable, *à venir,* to come, and (2) what is deconstructible, the rule of law, its structural security and the foundation itself, so as to create the conditions for initiating something new. And this leads us back to the question of space and place, of disciplinarity and democracy, and the problem of determining *who has the right to philosophy.* Not an easy task, as we will see.

So, is the question *"of the right to philosophy"* also a question of democracy and of the right of all to participate in the curricular orientation of a public education, e.g., who should study philosophy, how should it be taught, what should be taught, and why? And what does this imply for academic responsibility, for the future of philosophy, and for the educational institution, *for the academic responsibility of the institution of philosophy education?*

The question of the right to philosophy is *precisely a question of democracy* and of the validity of its systems of governance, of which the institution of pedagogy is a vital element of its inner and outer workings. For, we well know, and I will have discussed this earlier, that public education initially began as a way to educate the subject into citizenhood by legislating the ways of the State and its interpretative judicature into the experience of schooling. Leaving the unlettered innocence of childhood behind has historically meant becoming a "responsible member of society," defined via a liberal utilitarian concept of functional literacy as the ability one has to read and thus adhere to the letter of the law. To be more specific, then, the idea of willfully exercising the right one possesses to teach and learn philosophy, in moving from the study of law to that of philosophy *(du droit à la philosophie),* constitutes the initial step taken toward realizing the historico-conceptual groundwork for the immanent reality of the institution of education in a "democracy to come." What would it look like? What would it imply for the right to philosophy? for pedagogy? for the university?

Its instauration would be empowering. That is, its ethic of practice would take into account the right to philosophy from a cosmopolitical point of view by addressing "the competition among several philosophical models, styles and traditions that are linked to national or linguistic histories, even if they can never be reduced to effects of a nation or a language."[127] Here, Derrida gives a specific example of the directions of a possible heading that can be explored further:

> To take the most canonical example, which is far from being the only one and which itself includes numerous sub-varieties, the opposition between the so-called continental tradition of philosophy and the so-called analytic

or Anglo-Saxon philosophy is not reducible to national limits or linguistic givens. This is not only an immense problem and an enigma for European or Anglo-American philosophers who have been trained in these such traditions. A certain history, notable but not only a colonial history, constituted these two models as hegemonic references in the entire world. The right to philosophy requires not only an appropriation of these two competing models and of almost every other model by all, men and women (*par tous et par toutes,* and when I say *toutes,* it is not so as to be prudent regarding grammatical categories—I'll come back to this in a moment), the right of all (men and women) to philosophy also requires the reflection, the displacement and the deconstruction of these hegemonies, the access to places and philosophical events which are exhausted neither in these two dominant traditions nor in these languages. The stakes are already intra-European.[128]

Exercising the right to philosophy from the cosmopolitical point of view would not be the result of any politicized determination of a revolutionary movement or populist gathering intended to reclaim control of subjective agency, of the freedom over thought and thinking, back from the *modus organum* of the intellectual apparatus of "the State"—the educational system including the model of the university—in order to render it unto a nameless, faceless, sexless, and ultimately indistinguishable mass of humanity so endearingly called "the people." This is no route to a contemporary rethinking of the "concepts of state, of sovereignty"[129] in relation to the struggles of actualizing the differences of a new global community as we are experiencing them today. For the efforts undertaken to install the hegemony of an empirico-philosophical ground for "rationalizing" a new structurality of governance, no matter how "egalitarian" or "democratic" in principle, would be haunted by the living ghosts of resentful memories that would no doubt shape the future of a "democracy to come" in a highly reactionary way by limiting its conditional possibility to a negative determination of the moment of institution.

The simple (thoughtless) act of reinstitution unwittingly repeats the appropriatary logic of the hierarchy and re-enacts a litany of exclusionary injunctions, both consciously and unconsciously, whether it wants to or not, across the cultural and academic border wars of what constitutes a welcoming of the right to philosophy from the cosmopolitical point of view. It would make absolutely no sense to attempt to level an institution such as the university, to want to (if indeed one ever could) bring its efficacy to a standstill and make its existence superfluous or an anachronism. Even though, on the surface at least, the material formation of its regulative idea and operative ideal may seem to be a system quite closed unto the reality of itself, and devoid of any space through which to achieve a productive opening to alterity. Deconstruction is not Destruction *(Abbau),* however. A counterresistance to the conditions and effects of institutionality must maintain and occupy the discursive form of an intractable questioning that always already takes place from within the language practices of the institution but at the outer periphery of its limits, as Derrida explains, with respect to the discipline of philosophy:

Even before one speaks of visible or overriding structures (primary and secondary education, the university, authority, legitimacy), there is the very experience of discourse and language: the interest of philosophy already finds itself involved there in institutions. Everywhere and always, institutions articulate teaching and research, they attempt to dictate our rhetoric, the procedures of demonstration, our manner of speaking, writing and addressing the other. Those who think they stand outside institutions are sometimes those who interiorize its norms and programs in the most docile manner. Whether it is done in a critical or deconstructive way, the questioning of philosophy's relation to itself is a trial of the institution, of its paradoxes as well, for I try to show nonetheless what is unique and finally untenable in the philosophical institution: it is there that this institution [of the university and/as of philosophy] must be a counter-institution, one which may go so far as to break, in an asymmetrical fashion, all contracts and cast suspicion on the very concept of institution.[130]

A question *of the right to philosophy (du droit à la philosophie)* and of *the right philosophy* is one that must interrogate the "how" and the "why" of justifying the assignation of privilege over a domain of knowledge and its institution within the university to a governing body that is thereby given power to instruct and dictate a judgment claiming, more or less, the force of law regarding the future destination of a discipline and who may or may not have access to it. The intermingling of language with power to augment or repress voice is nothing new. It has always existed to reinforce the act of institution by fusing the constative and performative functions of speech to legitimize the seriousness of the scene of founding and all that it signifies as the reproduction of the reconstitution of a body of knowledge into a material form of *praxis*. The illusion of newness enters the world in this familiar way via the difference of the repetition of what is old. And here "the appropriation but also the *surpassing of languages*"[131] brings back the element of cultural memory in philosophy as that which foresees, on the one hand, "the phenomena of dogmatism and authority"[132] established by the linking of the past to the construction of a universal public knowledge and, on the other, "paths that are not simply anamnesic, in language which are without filiational relation to these roots."[133] The right of institution accentuates the imperative to control the lines of communication. To make reasons make sense without recourse to the contrariety and complementarity of the arguments of an "other side." The "trick" of a deconstructive defiance to this effect of etiologizing, however, is to insert oneself within the openings of the system, at the periphery, its margins, where its center breaks down, fissures and cracks, welcomes heterogeneity and difference. "With a sole language [the global extension of English as an international language is the example Derrida uses], it is always a philosophy, an axiomatic of philosophical discourse and communication, which imposes itself without any possible discussion."[134] By not preserving, at the very least, the "due process" of an open and public discussion on matters "educational," and for our purposes "philosophical" also, then justice is not served, is not accounted for, and is thus *not seen as being served* with respect to reinforcing the socio-historical preconditions of an affirmative reconciliation of the Self with the Other in the discursive arena of the civic sphere. Something that is a necessary and integral feature of the legal and ethical outworkings of a participatory democracy. To be more precise. When one individual or group *has*, *is given*, or *takes* all but total control of the constructible field of public knowledge (e.g., the institution of pedagogy) and has discreet power over the conditions of its material/cultural dissemination (e.g., a curriculum defines and models its method of teaching and learning, establishes evaluative criteria), then this self-limiting structure of closed governance reinforces the divisive criteria of inclusion and exclusion that make any decisions regarding public education void of any sense of responsibility and respectful response to the alterity of another. Such is the power of right, and the sense of its law, for it is forcefully bestowed and exercised freely and autonomously without the necessity of providing a reason, justification or explanation.

Deconstruction counters the hegemony of a universal language and the monodimensional references of its teaching and learning by stressing the ties between philosophy and the idiomatic. The right to a free thinking and its expression without fear of punishment or reprisal characterizes the democratic imperative. For Derrida, this not so obvious relationship between the everyday utility of philosophy and what it enables one to achieve in the unique contexts of an infinitely perfectable life-world is what concretizes the value of knowledge and liberates the utterance and circulation of ideas in the public sphere. It is a matter, then, of difference and of democracy, of "putting into operation each time in an original way and in a non-finite multiplicity of idioms, producing philosophical events which are neither particularistic and intranslatable nor transparently abstract and univocal in the element of an abstract universality."[135] A sovereign monolingualism, Derrida will contend, obliges the responsibility of a response by way of a questioning of the question, the legitimacy of its space and place:

> suppos[ing] that between the question and the place, between the question of the question and the question of the place, there be a sort of implicit contract, a supposed affinity, as if a question should always be first authorized by a place, legitimated in advance by a determined space that makes it both rightful and meaningful, thus making it possible and by the same token necessary, both legitimate and inevitable.[136]

Would we not expect as much of "imposing and legitimating appelations"?[137] Well, yes and no. Deconstruction would not have it any other way. Derrida poses the problem of the propriety of the question of the right to philosophy, *where and how it should be asked and by whom*, because he knows we cannot refuse an affirmative response to the implications of the scenario—e.g., UNESCO is "the privileged place"[138] for inquiring into the right of philosophy. It is a matter of reaching a "proper destination"[139] by navigating the journey of the mission the institution "has assigned to itself."[140] Could we refuse the possibility of arriving at a cosmopolitical utopia? Could we do such a thing, reasonably support its resistance, and still be responsible to the democratic rights and principles that sanction the appearance of an institution such as UNESCO in the first place? The deconstructive "stunt" of offering impossible alternatives for the reader to choose from is one Derrida often indulges in. This one is highly rhetorical and dramatic, but not overdetermined in its effects. It defies us to simultaneously agree and disagree, by putting our assumptions temporarily under erasure so as to question the premises both of the context of the lecture and of the constitution of UNESCO, whose preamble is laced with the following words and concepts: "peace," "dignity," "democratic principles," "humanity," "justice," "liberty," "sacred duty," "mutual assistance," "perfect knowledge," "mutual understanding," "education," "culture," "war, "differences," "ignorance," "prejudice," "mutual respect," "doctrine," "inequality," "moral solidarity," "communication," and so on. Nowhere is philosophy and the right to philosophy mentioned. The constitution of UNESCO is suspiciously silent in this regard. Even though, philosophy, in every respect, structures the semantic field of the list of the words I have compiled by providing the basis for a conceptual historicity of denotations and associations relating these lexemes to ideas and the types of practices they point to. We still have free will and an open conscience however. We can disagree at any moment with what Derrida suggests and dismiss UNESCO and its constitution as being "both too naturalist and too teleologically European."[141] This criticism is true enough. And UNESCO does eschew acknowledging its debt and duty to philosophy, preferring as a reactionary and "new" institution to concentrate instead on the securing of educational rights and the profusion of a scientific knowledge that champions forms of research whose intentionality is guided by and directed toward the predetermined ends its constitution spells-out. A pedagogy of technological advancement becomes the chosen way to achieving economic success as a precursor to democracy and "cosmopolitical communication."[142] Relating to the effects of this curricular intention, Derrida has an unfulfilled "wish" about sustaining and expanding an exploration of the extent to which philosophy is "in solidarity with the movement of science in different modes"[143] that he expresses in the form of a deconstructive "hypothesis":

> that, while taking into account or taking charge of this progress of the sciences in the spirit of a new era of Enlightenment for the coming millennium (and in this respect I remain Kantian), a politics of the right to philosophy for all (men and women) not be only a politics of science and of technology but also a politics of thought which would yield neither to positivism nor to scientism nor to epistemology, and which would discover again, on the scale of new stakes, in its relation to science but also to religions, and also to law and to ethics, an experience which would be at once provocation or reciprocal respect but also irreducible autonomy. In this respect, the problems are always traditional and always new, whether they concern ecology, bio-ethics, artificial insemination, organ transplantation, international law, etc. They thus touch upon the concept of the proper, of property, of the relation to self and to the other within the values of subject and object, of subjectivity, of identity, of the person, i.e., all the fundamental concepts of the charters that govern international relations and institutions, such as the international law that is, in principle, supposed to regulate them.[144]

Derrida is acutely aware of the fact that "philosophy is everywhere suffering, in Europe and elsewhere, both in its teaching and in its research."[145] This is the motivation for the lecture. To address the reason of "a limit which, even though it does not always take the explicit form of prohibition or censure, nonetheless amounts to that, for the simple reason that the means for supporting teaching and research in philosophy are limited."[146] The turn to "end-oriented sciences, and to techno-economic, indeed, scientifico-military imperatives"[147] is cultivated, sometimes rightly and sometimes wrongly, by the desire for outcomes "labelled useful, profitable, urgent."[148] As Derrida correctly comments, "it is not a matter of indiscriminately contesting all of these imperatives."[149] There is more to it, however, than a cool detachment and acceptance of this narrowed distinction between what teaching and research is needed and what is necessary "be they in the service of economy or even of military strategy."[150] Derrida explains:

> the more these imperatives impose themselves—and sometimes for the best reasons in the world—the more also the right to philosophy becomes increasingly urgent, irreducible, as does the call to philosophy in order to precisely think and discern, evaluate and criticize, philosophies. For they, too, are philosophies, they that, in the name of techno-economico-military positivism and according to diverse modalities, tend to reduce the field and the chances of an open and unlimited philosophy, both in its teaching and in its research, as well as in the effectiveness of its international exchanges.[151]

So, why shouldn't we reject the example of UNESCO and choose to re-examine the nature of its propriety to ask the question of the right to philosophy? As we enter the uncertainty of a new millennium, what does it have to offer the future of thinking beyond the economic potential and promise of a scientific and technological cosmopolitanism?

To say that UNESCO is not a legitimate institution, a "good" institution, would be to deny the good it has done or can do by ignoring its potential for an effective improvement of what—among other things—it does do well: it fights for a limitation in the reduction of access to education on a global scale. Which is to say, it has the capacity and is "duty bound,"[152] in principle, to protect the right to philosophy from a cosmopolitical point of view, even if its constitution does not explicitly say so. And this responsibility is what foreshadows the possibility of enacting the progressive movement of joining together nations, states, and peoples in a transformational enterprise aimed at negotiating the effectivity of a *democracy to come*. It involves taking the risk of affirming that in "today's world the stakes have never been as serious, and they are new stakes,"[153] whose formations call into question the very concepts defining human organizations and relations embodied in the constitution of UNESCO, what we in the West automatically accept as self-evident truths about the universal plan of nature, and its cosmopolitical democracy Kant made so much of. The violence of authority is not determinate, however. It is subtle, stratified, and discontinuous in its effects, and therefore it must be approached with a respectful skepticism, like that of deconstruction, which lies "between a certain erasure and a certain reaffirmation of debt—and sometimes a certain erasure in the name of reaffirmation."[154] That is, if we really want to make our way toward a philosophical reconciliation of difference and autonomy in light of the colonialist historicity of the West. For "what one calls, in Greek, democracy"[155] can neither stand nor do without the presence of real dissensus in its community. So, we must be careful not put philosophy "off limits." Not at all! We must mobilize the right to philosophy in a way that would address the violence of authority in democracy by situating its ethical efficacy and validity according to "what today may constitute the limit or the crisis most shared by all the societies, be they Western or not,"[156] as to the internal and inter-national negotiation of their future from a cosmopolitical point of view. Again the reason for Derrida's lecture is not to safeguard the boundaries of a discipline that is always already its other. It voices the "call for a new philosophical reflection upon what democracy, and [he insists] the democracy to come, may mean and be."[157] The violence of authority has power to induce silences, but it does not totally restrict the interpretative engagement of consciousness. Interestingly enough, it can produce a heightening of thinking, sharpening its philosophical intensity by expanding rather than reducing the human capacity to "respond responsibly," to question the absolute right and legitimacy of knowledge, its privilege, in an ethical way by opening up the self-validating aspect of the institution to the voice of what is "Other." This is the underlying theme of the lecture. It details the importance of not abandoning the right to philosophy, its teaching and learning. For what Derrida maintains will and can happen, and what he hopes for, is a reconfiguring of democracy according to a post-Kantian view of cosmopolitanism. Through a fundamental interrogation of the ground of the reason of UNESCO, its mission in practice and in principle, deconstruction locates the transformative field of its hermeneutic constellation "among several registers of debt, between a finite debt and an infinite debt"[158] that articulate the space between the place of the question of philosophy, the question of the place of philosophy, and the question of the question of philosophy. That would, hence, situate the ethical impetus of its interpretative domain of the institution within the structural locality of its right to question the question of the right to philosophy as well as the nature of institution and institutionality in its relation to the cosmopolitical. Deconstruction, we must recall, is above all affirmation. Its *"yes, yes," "come, come,"* is a confirmation of its unconditional acceptance of the Other rooted in an infinite responsibility *for* and *to* the Other, whose deferral and difference, its *différance,* it faithfully protects at all costs. Without reservation or doubt. Safeguarding the possibility of the question of the right to philosophy, deconstruction heralds the impossibility of a (re)teaching of the Self to be open to a learning from the alterity of the Other. That is, its integrity is tied to its original and originary aim at raising the spirit of human perfectability through its vigilance of the ethical terms of what constitutes a just response to difference and otherness and the infinite responsibility that comes with this unprovoked and selfless affirmation.

Last Words:
Questions and Prayers

To return to the question of the right to philosophy and to renew the framing of its articulation within the question of the question. I am referring also to its institutional place of asking, that may also be a space of meditation. For a question is like a prayer: its hope needs to be answered. Though not always. For a question that in the form of its expression authorizes and is authorized by the law of its origins is always a "prosthesis of the origin."[159] The clash between the interdiction of a line of inquiry and the heteronomy of its language are obvious dissonances that push at the internal limits of the institution. But what of the legitimacy of the "unauthorized question"? In going counter to the authority of "the right to question" by exercising the freedom of its own right to counter-question the legitimated code of a dutiful response and responsivity, the terms of the "responsible response," does it not also arise from the same ground that it questions, of which it is an *other* part? I should think so. At least, this is what Derrida alludes to, leaves out, yet allows us to fill in regarding the question of the future of philosophy and who can and should be able to, indeed *have the right to*, respond to it. The ethical dimension interposes itself here again—given it did not really leave us—with respect to what I previously called the problem of the "death of metaphysics" conceived as either closure or end. For the incipit of "the question of philosophy," we must not forget, also involves the task of how to go about negotiating the "question of the right to philosophy,"[160] and by exten-sion, "who should do it?" and "where, in what space?" And here we arrive back at the beginning, where we first started, in the difference of that space between us, me and you.

Notes

1. Jacques Derrida, "Violence and Metaphysics: An Essay on the Thought of Emmanuel Levinas," trans. Alan Bass, in *Writing and Difference* (Chicago: Univer-sity of Chicago Press, 1978), 80.

2. Derrida, "Violence and Metaphysics," 79.

3. See Jacques Derrida, *Archive Fever: A Freudian Impression*, trans. Eric Pre-nowitz (Chicago: University of Chicago Press, 1996).

4. See Jacques Derrida, *Aporias*, trans. Thomas Dutoit (Stanford: Stanford Uni-versity Press, 1993); and Jacques Derrida, *The Gift of Death*, trans. David Wills (Chi-cago: University of Chicago Press, 1995).

5. Jacques Derrida, "Tympan," trans. Alan Bass, in *Margins of Philosophy* (Chicago: University of Chicago Press, 1982), xxiii.

6. Derrida, "Tympan," xxiv.

7. See Derrida, *Aporias*.

8. Derrida, *Archive Fever*, 3.

9. See Jacques Derrida, "Of the Humanities and the Philosophical Discipline: The Right to Philosophy from the Cosmopolitical Point of View (the Example of an In-ternational Institution)," trans. Thomas Dutoit, *Surfaces* Vol. IV. 310 Folio I (1994), 5-21. All page references to this text are from the Web site version of the journal: http://tornade.ere.umontreal.ca/-guendon/Surfaces/vol4/derrida.html.

10. See Derrida, *Archive Fever*.

11. Jacques Derrida, "Between Brackets I," trans. Peggy Kamuf, in *POINTS. . . Interviews, 1974-1994*, ed. Elizabeth Weber (Stanford: Stanford University Press, 1995), 5-29.

12. See Martin Heidegger, "The End of Philosophy and the Task of Thinking," trans. David Farrell Krell, in *Martin Heiddeger: Basic Writings*, ed. David Farrell Krell (San Francisco: HarperCollins Publishers, 1977), 373-392.

13. On the relationship between death, memory, mourning, and the archive of metaphysics as the cinders of fire and fever marking an opening to the trace of the Other, see Derrida, *Archive Fever*, and Jacques Derrida, *Cinders*, trans. Ned Lukacher (Lincoln & London: University of Nebraska Press, 1987).

14 See Martin Heidegger, "The End of Philosophy."

15. Derrida, *Archive Fever*, 29.

16. See Jacques Derrida, *Cinders*; Jacques Derrida, *The Post Card: From Socrates to Freud and Beyond*, trans. Alan Bass (Chicago: University of Chicago Press, 1987); and most recently Jacques Derrida, *Resistances of Psychoanalysis*, trans. Peggy Kamuf, Pascale-Anne Brault, and Michael Naas (Stanford: Stanford University Press, 1998) for a discussion of the relationship between the death drive and the pleasure principle and how deconstruction interacts with psychoanalysis.

17. See Jacques Derrida, *Of Spirit: Heidegger and the Question*, trans. Geoffrey Bennington and Rachel Bowlby (Chicago: University of Chicago Press, 1989).

18. See Derrida, *Aporias* and Derrida, *The Post Card*.

19. An interesting discussion of this aspect of deconstruction can be found in (among other places) Derrida, *Aporias*, Derrida, "Violence and Metaphysics," and the farewell and final tribute Derrida expressed to Emmanuel Levinas. An English version of that testimonial and oration was published as Jacques Derrida, "Adieu," *Philosophy Today* 40, no. 3 (1996): 33-340.

20. Regarding the question of the right to philosophy see Derrida, "Of the Humanities and the Philosophical Discipline" and Jacques Derrida, *Du du droit à la philosophie* (Paris: Galilée, 1990).

21. Derrida, "Violence and Metaphysics," 79.

22. Refer to Derrida, *Aporias*.

23. Derrida, "Violence and Metaphysics," 79.

24. Peter Fenves, ed., *Raising the Tone of Philosophy: Late Essays from Immanuel Kant, Transformative Critique by Jacques Derrida* (Baltimore: Johns Hopkins University Press, 1993) contains a fine overview of the "topicality of tone" in the history of philosophy that is the cause and the precursor to the call for an end to metaphysics since Heidegger.

25. Derrida, *Du droit à la philosophie*, 88. (All translations from this text are my own.)

26. Jacques Derrida, *Of Grammatology*, trans. Gayatri Chakravorty Spivak (Baltimore: Johns Hopkins University Press, 1974), 161-162.

27. Derrida, "Of the Humanities and the Philosophical Discipline," 1.

28. Derrida, "Of the Humanities and the Philosophical Discipline," 1.

29. Derrida, "Of the Humanities and the Philosophical Discipline," 1.

30. Derrida, "Of the Humanities and the Philosophical Discipline," 1.

31. John D. Caputo, ed., *Deconstruction in a Nutshell: A Conversation with Jacques Derrida* (New York: Fordham University Press, 1997), 55.

32. See Jacques Derrida, "Où commence et comment finit un corps enseignant," in *Du droit à la philosophie,* 111-153.

33. Derrida, "Of the Humanities and the Philosophical Discipline," 2.

34. Derrida, "Of the Humanities and the Philosophical Discipline," 2.

35. Derrida, "Of the Humanities and the Philosophical Discipline," 2.

36. Derrida, "Of the Humanities and the Philosophical Discipline," 2.

37. Derrida, "Of the Humanities and the Philosophical Discipline," 2.
38. Derrida, "Of the Humanities and the Philosophical Discipline," 2.
39. Derrida, "Of the Humanities and the Philosophical Discipline," 1.
40. Derrida, "Of the Humanities and the Philosophical Discipline," 1.
41. Derrida, "Of the Humanities and the Philosophical Discipline," 2.
42. Derrida, "Of the Humanities and the Philosophical Discipline," 2.
43. Derrida, "Of the Humanities and the Philosophical Discipline," 2.
44. Derrida, "Of the Humanities and the Philosophical Discipline," 2.
45. Derrida, "Of the Humanities and the Philosophical Discipline," 2.
46. Derrida, "Of the Humanities and the Philosophical Discipline," 2.
47. Derrida, "Of the Humanities and the Philosophical Discipline," 1.
48. Derrida, "Of the Humanities and the Philosophical Discipline," 2.
49. Derrida, "Of the Humanities and the Philosophical Discipline," 1-2.
50. Cited in Derrida, "Of the Humanities and the Philosophical Discipline," 2.
51. The "Roundtable Discussion" on Jacques Derrida's "Des humanités et de la discipline philosophiques"/"Of the Humanities and Philosophical Disciplines" in *Surfaces* Vol. VI.108 (v.1.0A-16/08/1996), 5-40 involved Hazard Adams, Ernst Behler, Hendrick Birus, Jacques Derrida, Wolfgang Iser, Ludwig Pfeiffer, Bill Readings, Ching-hsien Wang, and Pauline Yu. All further quotations from this text are comments made by Derrida. The page references are from the Web site version of the text to found at http://tornade.ere.umontreal.ca/guedon/Surfaces/vol6/derrida.html. This endnote refers to a quotation from page 3.
52. Derrida, "Des humanités" 3.
53. Derrida, "Des humanités," 3.
54. Derrida, "Des humanités," 3.
55. Derrida, "Of the Humanities and the Philosophical Discipline," 2.
56. Derrida, "Of the Humanities and the Philosophical Discipline," 2.
57. Derrida, "Of the Humanities and the Philosophical Discipline," 2.
58. Derrida, "Des humanités," 2.
59. Derrida, "Of the Humanities and the Philosophical Discipline," 2.
60. Derrida, "Des humanités," 3.
61. Derrida, "Of the Humanities and the Philosophical Discipline," 2.
62. Derrida, "Des humanités," 3.
63. Derrida, "Of the Humanities and the Philosophical Discipline," 3.
64. Derrida, "Of the Humanities and the Philosophical Discipline," 3.
65. Derrida, "Of the Humanities and the Philosophical Discipline," 3.
66. Derrida, "Of the Humanities and the Philosophical Discipline," 3.
67. Derrida, "Of the Humanities and the Philosophical Discipline," 3.
68. Immanuel Kant cited in Derrida, "Of the Humanities and the Philosophical Discipline," 3.
69. Derrida, "Of the Humanities and the Philosophical Discipline," 4.
70. Derrida, "Of the Humanities and the Philosophical Discipline," 3.
71. Derrida, "Of the Humanities and the Philosophical Discipline," 3.
72. Derrida, "Of the Humanities and the Philosophical Discipline," 3.
73. Immanuel Kant cited in Derrida, "Of the Humanities and the Philosophical Discipline," 3.
74. Derrida, "Of the Humanities and the Philosophical Discipline," 3.
75. Derrida, "Of the Humanities and the Philosophical Discipline," 3.
76. Derrida, "Of the Humanities and the Philosophical Discipline," 3.

77. Immanuel Kant cited in Derrida, "Of the Humanities and the Philosophical Discipline," 3.

78. Derrida, "Of the Humanities and the Philosophical Discipline," 3.

79. Derrida, "Of the Humanities and the Philosophical Discipline," 3.

80. See the comments of Ernst Behler in the "Round Table" on Derrida's "Des humanités," 3.

81. Derrida, "Of the Humanities and the Philosophical Discipline," 3.

82. Immanuel Kant cited in Derrida, "Of the Humanities and the Philosophical Discipline," 3.

83. Derrida, "Of the Humanities and the Philosophical Discipline," 3.

84. Immanuel Kant cited in the "Round Table on Derrida's "Des humanités," 2.

85. Derrida, "Of the Humanities and the Philosophical Discipline," 3.

86. Derrida, "Of the Humanities and the Philosophical Discipline," 3.

87. Derrida, "Of the Humanities and the Philosophical Discipline," 3.

88. Derrida, "Of the Humanities and the Philosophical Discipline," 3.

89. Derrida, "Of the Humanities and the Philosophical Discipline," 2.

90. Derrida, "Violence and Metaphysics," 79.

91. Derrida, "Violence and Metaphysics," 80.

92. Derrida, "Of the Humanities and the Philosophical Discipline," 2.

93. Derrida, "Of the Humanities and the Philosophical Discipline," 2.

94. Derrida, "Of the Humanities and the Philosophical Discipline," 2.

95. Derrida, "Of the Humanities and the Philosophical Discipline," 3.

96. Derrida, "Violence and Metaphysics," 80.

97. Derrida, "Of the Humanities and the Philosophical Discipline," 3.

98. Derrida, "Des humanités," 2.

99. Derrida, "Des humanités," 2.

100. Derrida, "Des humanités," 2.

101. Derrida, "Des humanités," 2.

102. Derrida, "Des humanités," 2.

103. Derrida, "Des humanités," 2.

104. Derrida, "Des humanités," 2.

105. Derrida, "Des humanités," 2.

106. Derrida, "Of the Humanities and the Philosophical Discipline," 4.

107. Derrida, "Of the Humanities and the Philosophical Discipline," 3.

108. Derrida, "Des humanités," 3.

109. Derrida, "Des humanités," 3.

110. Derrida, "Des humanités," 3.

111. Derrida, "Des humanités," 3.

112. Derrida, "Of the Humanities and the Philosophical Discipline," 4.

113. Derrida, "Of the Humanities and the Philosophical Discipline," 4.

114. Derrida, "Of the Humanities and the Philosophical Discipline," 4.

115. Derrida, "Of the Humanities and the Philosophical Discipline," 4.

116. Derrida, "Of the Humanities and the Philosophical Discipline," 4.

117. See Derrida, "Où commence et comment finit un corps enseignant."

118. Derrida, "Of the Humanities and the Philosophical Discipline," 4.

119. Derrida, "Of the Humanities and the Philosophical Discipline," 4.

120. Derrida, "Tympan," x.

121. Derrida, "Tympan," xiii.

122. Derrida, "Tympan, xii.

123. Derrida, "Tympan," xiii.

124. Caputo, "Deconstruction in a Nutshell," 6.
125. Jacques Derrida cited in Caputo, "Deconstruction in a Nutshell," 6.
126. Jacques Derrida cited in Caputo, "Deconstruction in a Nutshell," 6.
127. Derrida, "Of the Humanities and the Philosophical Discipline," 4.
128. Derrida, "Of the Humanities and the Philosophical Discipline," 4.
129. Derrida, "Des humanités," 3.
130. Derrida, "Once Again from the Top: Of the Right to Philosophy" in *Points . . . Interviews, 1974-1994*, 327-328.
131. Derrida, "Of the Humanities and the Philosophical Discipline," 4.
132. Derrida, "Of the Humanities and the Philosophical Discipline," 4.
133. Derrida, "Of the Humanities and the Philosophical Discipline," 4.
134. Derrida, "Of the Humanities and the Philosophical Discipline," 4.
135. Derrida, "Of the Humanities and the Philosophical Discipline," 4.
136. Derrida, "Of the Humanities and the Philosophical Discipline," 1.
137. See Jacques Derrida, *Monolingualism of the Other; or, The Prosthesis of Origin*, trans. Patrick Mensah (Stanford: Stanford University Press, 1998), 39.
138. Derrida, "Of the Humanities and the Philosophical Discipline," 2.
139. Derrida, "Of the Humanities and the Philosophical Discipline," 2.
140. Derrida, "Of the Humanities and the Philosophical Discipline," 2.
141. Derrida, "Of the Humanities and the Philosophical Discipline," 5.
142. Derrida, "Of the Humanities and the Philosophical Discipline," 4.
143. Derrida, "Of the Humanities and the Philosophical Discipline," 4.
144. Derrida, "Of the Humanities and the Philosophical Discipline," 4.
145. Derrida, "Of the Humanities and the Philosophical Discipline," 5.
146. Derrida, "Of the Humanities and the Philosophical Discipline," 5.
147. Derrida, "Of the Humanities and the Philosophical Discipline," 5.
148. Derrida, "Of the Humanities and the Philosophical Discipline," 5.
149. Derrida, "Of the Humanities and the Philosophical Discipline," 5.
150. Derrida, "Of the Humanities and the Philosophical Discipline," 5.
151. Derrida, "Of the Humanities and the Philosophical Discipline," 5.
152. Derrida, "Of the Humanities and the Philosophical Discipline," 4.
153. Derrida, "Of the Humanities and the Philosophical Discipline," 4.
154. Derrida, "Of the Humanities and the Philosophical Discipline," 5.
155. Derrida, "Of the Humanities and the Philosophical Discipline," 4.
156. Derrida, "Of the Humanities and the Philosophical Discipline," 5.
157. Derrida, "Of the Humanities and the Philosophical Discipline," 4.
158. Derrida, "Of the Humanities and the Philosophical Discipline," 5.
159. See Derrida, *Monolingualism of the Other.*
160. Derrida, "Of the Humanities and the Philosophical Discipline," 1.

Chapter Five

An Opening Toward a Praxis of the Future
The Ethics of Deconstruction and the Politics of Pedagogy

> Philosophy consists of offering reassurance to children. That is, if one pre-
> fers, of taking them out of childhood, of forgetting about the child, or, in-
> versely, but by the same token, of speaking first and foremost *for* that little
> boy within us, of teaching him to speak—to dialogue—by displacing his
> fear or his desire.
> —Jacques Derrida, *Dissemination*[1]

Jacques Derrida is indeed a most profound thinker on matters educational, addressing in highly provocative and original ways through more or less "unconven-
tional" readings of the history of Western metaphysics some of the most basic
philosophical questions of teaching and of learning. Michel Foucault and Edward
Said have suggested—albeit in derisive ways—that *deconstruction is perhaps
nothing else but the elaborate expression of a new didactics, a poststructural
pedagogy of the text.*[2] And yet, on the one hand, to say Derrida presents the
means to a *"method" of teaching,* and *this only,* would be wrong, for there are no
directives to educational practice prescribed, no rules imposed upon the right to a
"freedom-of-thinking" or responsivity, and no *apriority* of absolute truths to be
found as could suffice to constitute the operational basis of an *ideal model or
mode of instruction.* But, on the other hand, the *"philosophemes of deconstruction"* carry on the "contradictory and conflictual" *polemos* of a theoretical backdrop that looks forward to the real necessity of informed action transcribed across
the post-structural, post-phenomenological passage from "thetic" to "a-thetic"
rationality, the movement away from an obstinate stance of single-minded opposition ready to tear down the existing "System" and toward an economy of reflective matriculation within the structurality of the institution to a *working-out of
the essential trials of its undecidability at the expense of the metaphysical*

grounding of its architectonics. Due to the awareness of the stretched parameters
of the dilemma of this "double-sided" stratagem—the tensions of its *aporias*—that I have endeavored to develop and expand upon in the previous chapters, to try to bring closure to a writing about the *ethics of deconstruction* with
respect to the *politics of education* by attempting to enact the finality of *the last
word* on the subject, especially in the form of a statement, "of positional or oppositional logic, [overdetermined in] the idea of position, of *Setzung* or *Stel-
lung*,"[3] would be both problematic and irresponsible given the non-adequation of
the "critical demonstrativity" of the interpretations of these texts of Derrida
"worked-through" here, with an undisputable and self-revealing truth. The meta-
physico-theoretical fidelity of such a standard closing of argumentation seeking
to culminate in a full stop of studied silence would most surely contravene the
unpredictable inter-spaces of the *risk of writing* that opens signification up to an
in-sertion of the alterity of the Other and invites the creation of the *difference of
meaning* as the disseminative interruption of a stable conditionality of the sign.
It thereby cancels out, in advance, the possibility of any *coming-to-resistance* an
examination of the ethico-political exigencies of thought and expression deconstruction could run against with respect to a "thinking-of-the-end" as the *telos* of
philosophy by its being contrapuntal to the *curricularization of pedagogy* oriented from the "historico-topologico-socio-cultural" regulation of its implemen-
tational styles. Still, we must proffer reasons and bestow "sound reasons" in
good faith for the sake of the debt that is owed the institution of reason and its
academic duty of upholding the rule of closing off the opening of a thesis according to THE RULE OF ARGUMENT. I must justify, in principle and by practice, the tendency of a hesitation to *simply conclude,* thus accepting responsibility for the lack of *clôture* to the readings presented of these *unread* or *underread*
texts of Derrida, as I have described them, *writings that will always already be
open before us.* And yet, to follow the path of a certain *non-repetition of form
and formality* does not mean it is necessary to abdicate rigor or the demands of a
scholarly obligation, "to substitute for what exist[s] some type of non-thesis,
non-legitimacy or incompetence,"[4] but rather requires the assumption that an
even greater accountability be demanded of the critical invention of the transformative gesture to explain itself. For a path-breaking cannot take place without a
careful knowledge and an immense respect or keen observance for the most ever
subtle nuances of *"academic tradition."* And in this way of uncompromising
justness surpassing the minimal responsibility of the protocol of "good conscience," this trailblazing is what I have tried to show deconstruction *does above
all else or makes possible regarding the most fundamental of educational themes,
"what it means to know."* Derrida has articulated as much through a prolific body
of texts sometimes taken to be anathema to the history of knowledge and knowing after the legacy of the ancient Greeks. *Deconstruction traverses the ethics and
the politics of the logic of the Same to introduce from beyond the horizon of its
impossibility the transcendence of a teaching/writing of the Other.* It upsets the
surety of the "phenomeno-semio-logical" foundation of the institutional history
of Western epistemology at the level of its theorizing about the value of the
sign, reproducibility and representation, or what is the heart of the educational
future of all philosophy and science as indicative of the empirical foundation of

the certainty of truth. *For nothing can be taught or learned other than what is believed to be known and understood.*

From the above premise follows Chapter 1, and how—through the "theoretical matrix" of deconstruction Derrida has supplied most conspicuously in *Of Grammatology*—it is indeed feasible to intervene at the base of the institutional monolith amid the play of the forces of the particular implications and effects *leading to* and *resulting from* the exclusion of writing by metaphysics. Through the imperious dismissal of exteriority, the ethnocentric terms of the limits of signification and meaning creation are posited in the immediate (tonal) substantiality of the voice or speech for the reduction of difference within the ideal determination of the self-presence of the *logos*. In this sense, it is the non-ethical beginnings of the "ethicity" of the teachings of metaphysics and the "living reason" of the spoken word that warrants, because it underwrites, the closing-off of the trace of otherness. The unique importance of the "grammatological" focus I have cross-cultivated with the anteriority of its semiological influences is remarkably suitable here to an expansion of its consequences for education tendering, as it does, through a confrontation with the Derridean conception of a "poststructural" version of "understanding" or "meaning-making" surpassing the nomothetics of speech, a re-interpretation of the *cultural politics of the sign.* An analytical "breaking-down" of the constituent features of the reason of its prejudiciality concerning consciousness and language delegitimizes the ontotheological groundedness of the voice feeding a *pedagogy of mimesis,* an imitativeness of the example or a clarifying of explainability required for the sake of perpetuating the *illusion of truth* from the demands of an altogether *"natural"* or *"good usage."* The problem of negotiating the arbitrary objectification of the semantic values of the cognitive and affective results comprising the interpretative bandwidth of the epistemic framework that constructs the institutionalization of *theory as praxis,* I have contended, brings to the fore the importance of the question of ethics for deconstruction relative to the theme of education, teaching and learning. And this is where we will already have begun to examine and articulate the pedagogical ramifications so prominent in the radical specificity of the scope of Derrida's engagement with the genealogy of philosophical concepts. As I have argued in Chapter 1, enabling an investigation of the semio-logicality of the metaphysical model of cognition crucial to the scene of a "classical pedagogy" that posits the flawless transmission of signs between the relational formulizability of a "sender-receiver" dyad and, hence, the possibility of the interexchanging of well-received meanings, deconstruction reveals how the privileging of speech over writing is the ethnocentric outcome of comprehending the representationality of language formations or their potential for expressivity solely as an "economy of signification" involving the immediate and autoaffective substantiality of the spirit of the voice. This skepticism of the teleology of the predication of the desire to communicate can lead to a *pushing-beyond* the "vulgar" notion of a teaching and learning directed, without doubt, as the transference and implantation of the truth of knowledge from "above" and "outside" the psychico-experiential realm of an intersubjective violence. For example, it permits a renouncing of the *tabula rasa* theory of the inscriptibility of a malleable consciousness of unblemished wax existing only to be shaped or *given image* by the artful engraving of a master teacher operating at the critical points of a "weakness-to-know" where the clean slate of subjective being is at the mercy of the probing intentionality of the deep etching of signs. Derrida, we have noted, characterizes the conventional or classical act of teaching and learning to be the pragmatic reproduction of the "metaphysics of presence" as cultivated from the premises of the interchangeable chain-linking of its orienting function at the fabulaic center of the syntagm of the Western *mythos* of "pure origins," uncorrupted beginnings. As the *arche-thememe* of logocentrism defining the effluence of the voice, it stands in symbolic difference and non-difference to itself, a *mise en abîme* of an arche-typal thinking of the plenitude of the sign that guides the conceptual immanence of an archive of cultural knowledge, be it scientific, aesthetic, philosophical, or religious, and so on, to render it replicable without a hint of doubt. The initiative we have taken to reread Derrida's reading of Jean-Jacques Rousseau regarding the origins of language *"before the letter"* concentrates on the foundational and corollary arguments detailing the elements of a pedagogical method relying on the phonocentrism of an image of the natural piety of humanity to bring out the extent of the incoherence of the utopianism of an idyllic vision of a "community of speech." Deconstruction exposes the blindness of the figural identification of innocence prior to the exteriority of the voice as the mark of writing—e.g., the worldliness of delimited contextuality and the predictable consequence of sign-meaning correlations—through which a resistance to the difference of supplementation is operationalized by and within the romantic appeal of the rhetoric used to secure the nostalgic call for the elimination of the violence of culture from the organismic whole of a society capable of pure spirited, unaffected relations of genuinely filial obligation. With respect to the effects of education, we have addressed not only why, but how, Derrida "turns back" upon Rousseau the question of the social construction of concepts such as "immediacy," "propriety," "nature," and so on, the interest being to show, thereby, the ways in which the applicability of deconstruction for the *general problem of education* extends from its ability to liberate the repressed contradictions always already present within the constitution of the texts on the subject referred to, using the selected terms of their expressions and expressivity to interrogate the deeper facets of a lamenting of the catastrophic passing of naive simplicity to learned experience. The non-ethical post-script of the irreversible transformation of the child is represented by the inculcated ability for the apprehension of the metaphysics of the sign, the debility of representation, (de)contextualization, removedness, supplementarity honing the displacement of the *truth of the Being of being* in the moment of the reversal of self-identity through teaching and learning. Deconstruction, however, if we are to believe Derrida as I think we should, *does not, cannot, nor does it wish to exact the death of logocentrism,* to eliminate it, despite troubling the epistemic validity of a phonological prototype of signification that linearizes the relation of *signans* and *signatum. It inhibits the reduction of the play of difference in an effort to counter-act and counter-balance for the mitigation or repression of the presence of the Other within the expression of the Same.* Behind the improbable terms of the educational connection of semiology as an "old science of signs" and deconstruction as a "new way of reading" lies the presupposition that "there has never been anything but writing,"[5] a circumspection bringing to fruition the contextual over-drift or grafting-on of the grammatological to the pragmatico-theoretical field of (philosophical) anthropology. To keep within the "age" of Rousseau and a certain "auto-bio-graphical temporality" of a self-present *écriture* is not difficult for Derrida, when considering the structural ethnology of Claude Lévi-Strauss. For it is through the teaching of one, the former, who excludes the supplementarity of writing but, nevertheless, wants to add to a supposedly ideal state of human nature and provides an educational manual to do so, that another, the latter, transforms the discipline of anthropology as a *science of difference* that desires "to decipher, dreams of deciphering a truth or an origin that transcends play and the order of the sign, and for it the necessity of interpretation is lived as a kind of exile."[6] We have reread the ethical aspects of the deconstruction of the ethnocentrism of the description of the Nambikwara in "The Writing Lesson" of *Tristes Tropiques* to illustrate the ramifications of the intersubjective violence Lévi-Strauss exacts upon this group of people in light of the cultural politics of a structuralist agenda dismissive of script, but still using the distinction of the *graphie* to hierarchize, categorize, and exoticize the Other by Western criteria of belief, knowledge, or education. The logocentrism of semiology encompasses a theory of language and representation that reduces the elements of teaching and learning to the preserving of (self-)presence; in fact, it precludes, on a more significantly ethical plane, the possibility of the recognition of difference outside of a closed system of an authenticating set of limits, the opposite extremes for inclusion and exclusion. The cultural politics of the sign works through these opposite extremes reinforcing the objectification of value toward the "practical" purpose of the inclusion and exclusion of entities. To say, and Lévi-Strauss does, that the Nambikwara lack the mark of "writing" and are therefore closer to nature than to culture is not only wrong, but also unethical, because the judgment recuperates the steroetypical image of the "primitive mind" as diachronically untaught and technologically undernourished, in other words, as the animate presence of "Being-lacking." It is an ethnocentric caricature of "prescientific genius" supporting the mytheme of the *bricoleur* and not a depiction of the empirical reality or the truth of the situation. With the deconstruction of the phonocentric normativity of the laws governing the intersubjective violence of the unspeakable trace of the writing of the Other, the possibility, *the hope,* through which we can and must learn to reflect upon the ethicity of our own thinking and practices of representation is situated in the in(de)terminable unfolding of *différance.* Derrida elaborates a grammatological overhauling of semiology to re-think the differential and deferred relations of the iterativity of the sign, its spatio-temporal *im-print,* the excesses of which manifest themselves in an alterity that the teleological perspective of an "ego-logical" philosophizing cannot comprehend or care to admit. The irreducibility of *différance* "shows up" the infinite exteriority of the *arche-trace of the Other* through the *symploke,* or a weaving together of the diverse strands, of deconstruction, e.g., the yoking of undecidability with the heterology of its transcendental preconditions. Upon the "unthought" difference between identity and difference, that which is the exteriority of writing, hinges the turning point of the reversal and then displacement of the nature/culture dichotomy of metaphysics, the primary pragmatico-epistemic focus of its teaching we have been concerned with. Exposing how the teleo-*phone* of the *logos* is postponed in the self-irradiating trace of the fullness of presence, *différance* complicates the desire of the archive madness of the ancient thinking of the West that does not grant standing to the idea of the Other, *its infusing in the idea of perpetuity, stasis, and fixed order the semblance of an outside, exteriority, to a pedagogy of the Same.* Deconstruction contends, Derrida says,

> as always, [with] the institution of limits *declared* to be insurmountable, whether they involve family or state law, the relations between the secret and the non-secret, or, and this is not the same thing, between the private and the public, whether they involve property or access rights, publication or reproduction rights, whether they involve classification and putting *into order*. What comes under theory or under private correspondence, for example? What comes under system? under biography or autobiography? under personal or intellectual anamnesis? In works said to be *theoretical*, what is worthy of this name and what is not?[7]

We would include with this proliferation of questions the need to address the consequences of theory for the "topo-nomological" archive of the educational institution and the classification of knowledge in accordance with the historicity of the sign and the means of *con*signation, *the construction of a gathering place of domiciliation before and after the letter.*[8] As I have stressed in Chapter 1, a deconstruction of the normative rendering of what it means *to think, to learn, to teach, to know* begins to take root in the earliest of Derrida's "texts" before *Of Grammatology*, where the non-natural ethics of speech informing the socio-theologico-philosophical violence of metaphysics are put into doubt. It would not be *hyperbole* to suggest that from the start this post-structural, post-phenomenological mode of intervention plays upon the thematic variability of the most fundamental and essential versions of the educational problematic of supplementarity discerning the continual transitivity of the human subject: for example, the heterogeneity of origins, the paradoxes of mimetology, childhood, reason, subjectivity, and so on as problems of mediacy and mediation. In short, it is the non-ground between presence and absence deconstruction *breaks into,* slowly making it possible to imaginatively empathize or "fill up" the openness of the abyss of this excluded space, *the space of the writing/teaching of the Other,* to re-approach the responsibility of the horizon of intersubjective violence and the ethnocentric teleologicality of the cultural politics of the sign.

Chapter 2, in taking the pedagogical impetus of the grammatological re-evaluation of the ethnocentrism of the sign further afield to the Hegelian era of speculative dialectics and the Absolute Idea, ponders the birth and death of the philosopher and, thus, the thinking and teaching of the child through life that Derrida considers to be associated with the themes of writing and memory.[9] In *Glas,* we read a quite startling answer to a familiar but difficult question: "What is education? The death of the parents, the formation of the child's consciousness, the *Aufhebung* of its consciousness in(to) the form of ideality."[10] Using this quotation as a heuristic tool to approach some final comments on the question of the contradiction Derrida finds in the proposal for a speculative didactics of infinitizing and hyperstatic memory that G. W. F. Hegel lays out for a solicited "report" on philosophy curricula would seem to be appropriate and somewhat precarious at the same time. Nevertheless, for us, it will have already been necessary, if not essential, given its direct relation to any consideration of the topic of deconstruction and pedagogy at hand. The ideological symmetry between the text and the context of the report Derrida puts into question re-inforces the need for the *auto-bio-graphical* projection of the image of the child, before the end of philosophy and after the beginning of schooling, that Hegel submits to an eager state ministry ready to support an "instruction of memory." For a questioning and critical consciousness does not a good citizen always make from the perspective of *the-powers-that-be*. And yet, the symbolic death here is not only of the parents, the decrease of their ability to have influence over the thinking of their dependent and powerless offspring. It is also the passing away of "the child" as such, a being of "non-knowledge" whose re-birth is achieved by the Hegelian propaedeutic through the retranslation or return of the essence of subjective formativity to a safekeeping of the "mobility" of consciousness within the bounds of the dialectical sublation of the idealizing moment of absolute insight or the Idea of Reason, the faculty represented most by the eternal logic and "Right" of the State. For Derrida, the fundamental problem is that of the acceptability of such provocatively generalizing recollections put forward as the result of a self-fulfilling prophecy of a vision of the truth of a past connected to a present future that is all too removed from a time of reflection far gone and well lost. Because the auto-affective nature of the image of the pre-philosophical "child-Hegel" cannot but re-gather the presence of the sign of the Self toward an inwardly reflecting point of imaginative centration reconciling elements of fact with those of fiction to comprise the temporal bridge between the "then" and the "now," to resurrect in the annals of memory the gathering power of an ideal re-creativity is to more or less pursue the path to the teaching of false example, an exemplary teaching of falsehood coveting a *prosopopoeia* of the wishful apostrophe. So, the difference of consciousness and self-consciousness builds the symptomatic tensions of a hidden economy of loss that becomes evident in the rewriting of anamnesis after the deconstructive rereading of the report Hegel signs. We have analyzed the problematic synthesis of these antinomies of the *relève* of subjective identity in Chapter 2 to comment on the theoretical validity of the example of the unsupplemented age of childhood, where the speculative schematism connecting empirical being to its "past being"—a Being-past *(Gewesenheit)*—is framed according to the productive representation of a dialectical modality of circularly coherent reflexivity closed unto the reason of itself. The exteriorization of memory, its removal from the interiority of self-absorbing thought, "stays with traces, in order to 'preserve' them, but traces of a past that has never been present, traces which themselves never occupy the form of presence and always remain, as it were, to come—come from the future, from the *to come*."[11] And the signature of the proper name of Hegel as a life-writing of "the Self," in this sense of the auto-genetic reproduction of the metaphorical singularity of subjective identity, is an attempt to secure control over the hermeneutic effects of the aftermath of the ends of inscription by concretizing in the otherwise plain and customary mark of referential authority the pedagogical truth of the figure of the child prior to the experience of philosophy and the difficulty of thinking. Its be-latedly teleologizing function of identifying difference that serves to "fill-in-the-spaces" of the socio-cultural puzzle of the categorical status of beings is a sym-bolic sanctioning of the logic to institute and implement a speculative curricu-lum of rote memorization for the teaching and learning of philosophy. The Hegelian model of pedagogy so defined within the possibility of the repeatability of the proper name, as such, is a progression of delay and derivation following the semantic aftereffect of the originating source of the truth of the sign. And the time lag of its *already-not-yet (déjà-pas-encore)* structure authenticates the prag-matic working-out of the educational configuration of speculative dialectics by sustaining, in its formal processes of dictation and memorization, the means to a looking-back toward the generation of a "first" and "correct" meaning of a signi-fier to confirm its accuracy through the unmediated transmissibility of its proof. It should be clear considering what we have stated about the ethics of deconstruc-tion up to now that Derrida could not support a mnemotechnical pedagogy favor-ing the passing of knowledge from the "expert teacher" to the "obedient student" or an institution that encourages the (re)playing and perpetuation of these mono-dimensional roles. Having become important as the interactive site of competing interests and differential forces, the scene of teaching is the territorial mainstay of the political struggle its participants wage for the right of opportunity to inter-vene in the planning or actualization of curricular possibilities. Derrida, it would seem from reflections made about the commitment of his involvement with the GREPH (since 1974),[12] has taken this activist role very seriously for the sake of saving the discipline of philosophy from those elected powers that have consid-ered it an esoteric and dangerous subject, a part of the French educational system not worth the trouble of dealing with or keeping at bay. He decided not to write a "thesis"—a dissertation would most certainly have been a chance to secure an eminent position suitable for a scholar of such international stature[13]—because

> it was neither consistent nor desirable to be a candidate for any new aca-demic title or responsibility. Not consistent given the work of political criticism in which [he] was participating, not desirable with regard to a lit-tle forum that was more internal, more private and upon which, through a whole endless scenography of symbols, representations, phantasies, traps and strategies, a self-image recounts all sorts of interminable and incredible stories to itself.[14]

But as regards the type of interference deconstruction can provide to alter the onto-encyclopaedic reason of the educational institution, to make its charity more equitable to acknowledging and accepting the logic of the Other, Derrida has never promoted the general dismantling of the architectonics of the pedagogi-cal system. Rather, the focus of attention has been on finding a more "neutral" and less contentious site from which to interrogate the axiomatics of the appara-tus of teaching and learning, one that effaces the tensions of the historico-political codification of the academic/bureaucratic dualism tranquilizing the coop-erative processes of reflective transformation. Derrida explains,

It is this complementarity, this configuration ["often scarcely readable, but solid, between the most immobilized, contracted academicism and all that, outside the school and the university, in the mode of representation and spectacle, taps almost immediately into the channels of the greatest receivability"][15]—everywhere that it appears—that we must, it seems to me, combat. Combat simultaneously, and joyously, without accusation, without trial, without nostalgia, with an intractable gaiety. Without nostalgia for more discreet forms, sometimes (sometimes only) more distinguished, less noisy, that in large part will yesterday have prepared the way for what we inherit today.[16]

As I have endeavored to show throughout the text, deconstruction has been misrepresented by many critics, theorists, and philosophers unable or unwilling to take an *account of* and provide an *accounting for* its ethical and political implications, preferring instead to eschew or disregard both its effectivity in responsibilizing the principles of action or its informing and questioning of the reason of pragmatic utility. Attenuating the thematic scope of the analysis on the Derridean call to rethink the grounds of academic responsibility, e.g., the motivational imperative to respond according to a principle of "Right," Chapter 3 attends to the *aporia* of what is beyond the rationality of the institution of the university. It attempts to build a bridge between the double-sided precipice of deconstruction, on the one hand, and the self-effacing void of metaphysics, on the other. This, of course, involves the question of responsibility and what is "proper" and "right," of "the law" and "the political": not to raise fears about the unjustifiable eradication of the university, an institution old and dear, as ancient as philosophy itself, *a traditional knowledge structure that is the structure of knowledge,* very much in need of painstaking reconstitution, but to allay them in the well-meaning desire to rejuvenate serious exchange on the reason for its being. What Derrida does through deconstruction is to set up the positive parameters within which we can discourse on the subject ethically without barriers or boundaries, though not without obligation and the danger of failure. The rereading of "The Principle of Reason: The University in the Eyes of Its Pupils" I have attended to shows how the discourse works on the figural play of the tropic framework circumscribing the living and metaphorical dimensions of these negative perimeters to broach the educational question of foundation and of ground, of principle and of law, of departure and destination. Essentially, by relating the foci of these complementary pairings Derrida introduces—that are very different and yet also thematical the same—to the topological formativity of the structure of the institution itself, it has been possible to reread the ethico-political undertext of this instance of deconstruction through the metaphorical register of the text on the theme of the historicity of reason. We cannot dismiss, in this case, the use of the example of Cornell University, with its bridges stretching the campus across an abyss, as the living symbol or animate example of the parable being retold while its speaker is taking the first steps through the ordeal of this inaugural lecture toward the expressing of gratitude, re-turning its gift-countergift for the honor of being selected to a prestigious appointment. The specific conditions of the discourse—demanding a specific type of rhetorical demeanor appealing to an axiology of symbolic exchanges—generate the opportunity taken to comment on the interstices of text-context relations that construct the epistemic and empirical values of the constative and performative aspects of the academic responsibility Derrida culls after the "double science" of deconstruction. And this, *more than less,* translates the emphatic urgency of the topic or theme and the timeliness of its message for a sustained re-appraisal of the ethics of academic responsibility patterned after the principle of reason. What I have tried to show is that there is no overcoming *(Überwindung)* of the techno-philosophical grounding of intellectual freedom or action within the speculum of an all-seeing, all-knowing university, *the oto-scopic-bio-graphic sensibility of an instrumental and poietic landscape of the idea of the modern mind.* And deconstruction does not—it cannot—claim to "come down" upon the reason of the institution with a full-forced vengeance in search of justice, for it has no grudge to vindicate, no end to finagle, *it is not outside the law.* But this is not altogether true. *It is outside the law.* Rather, Derrida would say, and he has,

> Deconstruction is justice. It is perhaps because law *(droit)* (which I will consistently try to distinguish from justice) is constructible, in a sense that goes beyond the opposition between convention and nature, it is perhaps insofar as it goes beyond this opposition that it is constructible and so deconstructible and, what's more, that it makes deconstruction possible, or at least the practice of a deconstruction that, fundamentally, always proceeds to questions of *droit* and to the subject of *droit*. (1) The deconstructibility of law *(droit),* of legality, legitimacy or legitimation (for example) makes deconstruction possible. (2) The undeconstructibility of justice also makes deconstruction possible, indeed inseparable from it. (3) The result: deconstruction takes place in the interval that separates the undeconstructibility of justice from the deconstructibility of *droit* (authority, legitimacy, and so on). It is possible as an experience of the impossible, there where, even if it does not exist (or does not yet exist, or never does exist), *there is* justice.[17]

The "real-as-absent" ground deconstruction covers, on both sides, as it were, of *how one should not speak of the university* is the situation of its re-positioning of ethics toward the possibility and impossibility of justice, that is, the undecidable responsibility symptomatic of the irreducible difference of an academic community *in extensio.* This "double-edged" pragmaticogrammatology Derrida endorses, a metacontextual metadiscursivity critical of the sign of reason embedded within and exemplified by the regulatory principles of the institution, does not refer to a pre-destined plan of action, demands no disciples or followers, concedes to the direction of no political program. Instead, it invites interpretation and invention that will produce a performative intelligibility or an inkling of purpose "yet-to-come" *(avenir)* out of the non-projection of a justification. The notion is terrifying for some and self-mockingly illogical for others, especially concerning issues of institutionalized practice, pedagogical or techno-scientific, for example, and other research areas we have delineated pertaining to the disciplinary system of the university. But considering the outcome of reason once rendered for a future action is a moment of insurance or assurance already finite and past, there is no immanence of aspirations left other than a feigning of presence suffered as a remote-controlling of *praxis* toward the unconditionality of what is the certainty of a non-end, the non-end of certainty. As Derrida has admitted of his own journey of deconstruction, a curiously convoluted and ardous path away from the thesis, eventually leading him to his present post of *Directeur d'Études: Institutions de Philosophie*, "If I clearly saw ahead of time where I was going, I really don't believe that I should take another step to get there."[18]

Chapter 4 takes up the subject of the postmodern retreat from metaphysics. That deconstruction calls for the death of philosophy has been perhaps the most controversial and misrepresented aspect of Derrida's work on the archive of Western episteme. The poststructural radicalization of phenomenology after Martin Heidegger shifts the terrain from speech and voice to writing and textuality, thus, breaking the historicity of metaphysics by wearing away the logocentric foundations of the source of reason in the power of the sign to reference a reality outside of itself. After deconstruction, we cannot have faith in philosophy to provide us with a picture of the world that corresponds to its actual states and conditions of being. The contingency between particularity and universality is made explicit by the fact that the History of Reason is already over, has always already been over, even before it began, and certainly before deconstruction, because no thinking can ever be separated from the ideological investments of its governing concepts and the language used to express them to Others. After more than two millennia, even though we have only begun to understand the effects of this realizations—and Derrida most definitely helped us to get to this point—it does not mean that we therefore reject philosophy and the opposition between truth and non-truth upon which it is founded. This would be a *right* of death. And ill deserved too! Philosophy, however, will not and cannot die so easily after a proclamation of its end articulated not from the love of reason and truth, but as the expression of a desire to embrace an Other way at all costs—even if it means rejecting the historicity and tradition of a body of thought, an archive, without thinking about the difficulties and consequences of an attempt to start over. Some judgements are indeed more correct than others. We cannot deny this fact and the reality that philosophy as an expression of the Greco-European origins of Western episteme and science has been responsible for unethical and exclusionary practices in the name of sustaining the hegemonic dominance of some cultures over others so as to pursue colonial and missionary imperatives. But this is only one side of the argument, and it justifies the overcoming of metaphysics for the sake of enacting a freedom of choice by heading in another direction supposedly bereft and unburdened of memories of a past. For Derrida, this desire to break with history can be nothing besides an illusion that will end-up unwittingly repeating the hierarchical structures and institutions of what was rejected in the first place. A bad repetition of infinity (à la Hegel) could only take place precisely because the efforts made to re-institute codes of ethics and of practice would be an attempt to alter the direction of historicity without a responsibility to memory, and therefore without the possibility of a reflective questioning of exiting structures.

As I have argued, in the spirit of Derrida's lecture at UNESCO, there is no need to mourn philosophy or to blame it for what are the natural excesses and limitations of the mechanics of human perception. The teleological axis of metaphysics is a defining characteristic of the rise of a Western consciousness. It had to be there because there was no other choice or chance. It happened. We must recognize this idea and embrace the seriousness of its implications, but the ideal of Western consciousness is by no means the end route of a pure body of reflection, of "philosophy," a single body of thought belonging to the Greeks or other European cultures. Its epistemico-conceptual archive was always already permeated with the trace of difference, heterogeneity and alterity, from the start. We must remember and acknowledge this serious fact. The right to philosophy, to what we have called "philosophy" by one name, its "own" name and that given to it by other cultures, is what Derrida wants to protect in order to secure a future (for) thinking. The "natural plan" of a universalization of humanity that Kant wants to bring back to the origins of Greek culture provides the model with which to enact a cosmopolitical reconfiguration of the global condition enjoining nations, states, and peoples in a joint peace. And Derrida is not against the principle of it. How could he or anyone be against a peaceful reunion? A consideration of the right to philosophy from a deconstructive point of view joins together a reflection upon the legitimacy of the cosmopolitical and the ethics of its practice with other questions of space and place that relate to the founding of community and to the future of a *democracy-to-come*. Which is also a matter of pedagogy and education with respect to the perfectability of humanity and the becoming of human being. This is what UNESCO stands for and represents as an institution that puts philosophy and the right to philosophy into practice from the cosmopolitical point of view. It fulfills the impossible promise of the future and of a *democracy-yet-to-come*. To transform the responsibility of the individual beyond the obligations of the "global citizenship" and the complex demands of living in a shrinking world, we need to redefine our view of community according to the debt and duty of what we owe to our histories and to ourselves via a serious and sustained reflection on the historicity of our pasts and the obligation we have to the memory and testimony of what came before us. This would involve neither a simple rejection (exappropriation) of philosophy nor an uncritical acceptance (appropriation, expropriation, assimilation) of something else to replace it. The cosmopolitical point of view after deconstruction would perhaps be the opportunity for inaugurating a new enlightenment out of the transformation of what we believe to be true about the ways in which we relate to Others and to the life-world we construct. In this sense, philosophy is indispensable for re-evaluating the responsibility we in the West have to the memory of the past. To metaphysics and what has been done and achieved, both "good" and "bad," by institutions such as UNESCO who have been guided and guide others according to a Eurocentric model of community and democracy. That is why Derrida does not seek to denounce philosophy, to mourn and celebrate its death. One cannot proceed to an affirmation of a thinking of the Other by destroying the differences that bind each of them together and creates the eternal possibility of articulating a new ethical ground for knowledge and for practice. To interrogate the historicity of Western institutions like UNESCO in order to improve them, to make them more responsive and responsible to alterity, therefore ethical and "better" suited to the constitution of their original intentions and purposes, the right to philosophy must be safeguarded. This involves making the commitment to realizing a community of the question that puts what we think we know always under erasure. Moving toward the impossibility of the future from a cosmopolitical point of view requires looking backwards to the memory of the past and rearticulating the terms of our responsibility to what happened before. To do this, Derrida explains, "the right to philosophy may require from now on a distinction among several registers of debt, between a finite debt and an infinite debt, between debt and duty, between a certain erasure and a certain affirmation of debt—and sometimes a certain erasure in the name of affirmation."[19]

We could and will end quite comfortably here, and in so doing leave this writing at the peril of its own non-end and, of course, the beginning of the praxis of its future.

Notes

1. Jacques Derrida, *Dissemination*, trans. Barbara Johnson (Chicago: University of Chicago Press, 1981), 122.

2. See Edward Said, "The Problem of Textuality: Two Exemplary Positions," *Critical Inquiry* 4 (1978): 673-714; and Michel Foucault, *Madness and Civilization: A History of Insanity in the Age of Reason,* trans. Richard Howard (New York: Random House, 1965). In an appendix to the 1972 edition (the original was published in the form of a *Thèse d'Etat* in 1961), Foucault responds to what he perceived to be an "attack" on his work by Derrida in the "lecture" "Cogito and the History of Madness," trans. Alan Bass, in *Writing and Difference* (Chicago: Chicago University Press, 1978), 31-63, by describing deconstruction as nothing more than a conservative and well-entrenched "pedagogy of the text."

3. Jacques Derrida, "The Time of a Thesis: Punctuations," trans. Kathleen McLaughlin, in *Philosophy in France Today,* ed. Alan Montefiore (Cambridge: Cambridge University Press, 1983), 42.

4. Derrida, "The Time of a Thesis," 42.

5. Jacques Derrida, *Of Grammatology,* trans. Gayatri Chakravorty Spivak (Baltimore: Johns Hopkins University Press, 1974), 158.

6. Jacques Derrida, "Structure, Sign, and Play in the Discourse of the Human Sciences," trans. Alan Bass, in *Writing and Difference,* 427.

7. Jacques Derrida, *Archive Fever: A Freudian Impression,* trans. Eric Prenowitz (Chicago: University of Chicago Press, 1996), 4-5.

8. See Derrida, *Archive Fever.*

9. This is evident in Derrida, *Dissemination.*

10. Jacques Derrida, *Glas,* trans. John P. Leavey Jr. and Richard Rand (Lincoln: University of Nebraska Press, 1986), 132

11. Jacques Derrida, *Memoires for Paul de Man,* trans. Cecilia Lindsay, Jonathan Culler, and Eduardo Cavava (New York: Columbia University Press, 1986), 58.

12. See Derrida, "The Time of a Thesis."

13. And, indeed, it was the reason Derrida was persuaded to submit his candidacy for a doctorate based on published texts, as he was encouraged to do so in order to be elected to the Collège de France, in succession of Paul Ricoeur. The chair was eventually suppressed by the Ministry of Education. And those colleagues who had extended to Derrida the "invitation" to apply for the post eventually voted against him, and he was given another position, the one he currently holds, on certain conditions.

14. Derrida, "The Time of a Thesis," 48.

15. Jacques Derrida, "Philosophie des états généraux," in *États généraux de la philosophie (16 et 17 juin 1979)* (Paris: Flammarion, 1979), 43. Editor(s) not specified. (All translations from this text are my own.).

16. Derrida, "Philosophie des états généraux, 43. Derrida here explains what deconstruction ought to inspire in remarks made to the États Généraux de la Philosophie, a meeting of approximately twelve hundred participants who congregated at the Sorbonne on June 16-17, 1979 to find common ground through which to combat the deteriorating situation of the discipline of philosophy.

17. Jacques Derrida, "Force of Law: The 'Mystical Foundation of Authority,'" trans. Mary Quaintance, in *Deconstruction and the Possibility of Justice,* ed. Drucilla Cornell, Michel Rosenfeld, and David Gray Carlson (New York: Routledge, 1992), 15.

18. Derrida, "The Time of a Thesis," 36.

19. Jacques Derrida, "Of the Humanities and the Philosophical Discipline: The Right to Philosophy from the Cosmopolitical Point of View (the Example of an International Institution)," trans. Thomas Dutoit, *Surfaces* Vol. IV. 310 Folio I (1994), 5. All page references to this text are from Web site version of the journal: http://tornade.ere.umontreal.ca/-guendon/Surfaces/vol4/derrida.html.

Index

About the Author

Peter Pericles Trifonas is assistant professor at the Center for Social Justice and Cultural Studies in Education at the Ontario Institute for Studies in Education of the University of Toronto. He has taught at schools and universities in North America and Europe. His work has been published internationally in many journals. Among them are: *Social Semiotics, Interchange, International Journal of Applied Semiotics, Educational Researcher, Discourse: Studies in the Cultural Politics of Education, JCT: Journal of Curriculum Theorizing, Postmodern Culture, Educational Theory,* and *Semiotica.* Some of his forthcoming books are *The Future of Postcolonialism, Revolutionary Pedagogies: Cultural Politics, Instituting Education, and the Discourse of Theory,* and *Coloring In the Sign: Narration, Semiosis and the Picture Book.*